Chekhov

Anton Chekhov offers a critical introduction to the plays and productions of this major canonical playwright. A century after his death, the genius of Chekhov's writing, the innovatory nature of his approach to theatrical representation, and the profundity of his philosophy are beginning to be re-examined.

Emphasising his continued relevance, humour and mastery of the tragicomic, the author provides an insightful assessment of Chekhov's life and work. The text analyses many Chekhov favourites including *The Seagull, Uncle Vanya* and *The Cherry Orchard* in addition to Chekhov's vaudevilles and one-act plays, making reference to Chekhov's stories and using both traditional criticism and more recent theoretical and cultural standpoints including cultural materialism, philosophy and gender studies.

Anton Chekhov provides the reader with a comprehensive and comparative study of the relationship between Chekhov's life, career, ideological thought and view of art and analyses, with reference to historical and recent productions, his continued appeal.

Rose Whyman is Lecturer in Drama and Theatre Arts at the University of Birmingham. Her book, *The Stanislavsky System of Acting, Legacy and Influence in Modern Performance*, was published by CUP in 2008. She reads Russian fluently.

ROUTLEDGE MODERN AND CONTEMPORARY DRAMATISTS

Series editors: Maggie B. Gale and Mary Luckhurst

Routledge Modern and Contemporary Dramatists is a new series of innovative and exciting critical introductions to the work of internationally pioneering playwrights. The series includes recent *and* well-established playwrights and offers primary materials on contemporary dramatists who are under-represented in secondary criticism. Each volume provides detailed cultural, historical and political material, examines selected plays in production, and theorizes the playwright's artistic agenda and working methods, as well as their contribution to the development of playwriting and theatre.

Volumes currently available in the series are:

J. B. Priestley by Maggie B. Gale
Federico Garcia Lorca by Maria M. Delgado
Susan Gaspell and Sophie Treadwell by Barbara Ozieblo
    and Jerry Dickey
August Strindberg by Eszter Szalczer
Anton Chekhov by Rose Whyman

Future volumes will include:

Mark Ravenhill by John F. Deeney
Jean Genet by David Bradby and Claire Finburgh
Caryl Churchill by Mary Luckhurst
Maria Irene Fornes by Scott T. Cummings
Brian Friel by Anna McMullan
Sarah Kane by Chris Megson

Anton Chekhov

Routledge Modern and
Contemporary Dramatists

Rose Whyman

 Routledge
Taylor & Francis Group

LONDON AND NEW YORK

First published 2011
by Routledge
2 Park Square, Milton Park, Abingdon, Oxon OX14 4RN

Simultaneously published in the USA and Canada
by Routledge
270 Madison Ave, New York, NY 10016

*Routledge is an imprint of the Taylor & Francis Group, an
informa business*

© 2011 Rose Whyman

Typeset in Sabon by Taylor & Francis Books
Printed and bound in Great Britain by
TJ International Ltd, Padstow, Cornwall

British Library Cataloguing in Publication Data
A catalogue record for this book is available from the British
Library

Library of Congress Cataloging in Publication Data
Whyman, Rose.
Anton Chekhov / Rose Whyman.
   p. cm. – (Routledge modern and contemporary dramatists)
Includes bibliographical references and index.
1. Chekhov, Anton Pavlovich, 1860–1904—Criticism and
interpretation. I. Title.
   PG3458.Z8W49 2010
   891.72'3 – dc22
                    2010009720

ISBN13: 978-0-415-41143-1 (hbk)
ISBN13: 978-0-415-41144-8 (pbk)
ISBN13: 978-0-203-84355-0 (ebk)

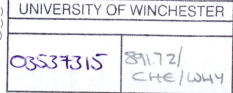

For Brian Door with all my love and thanks

Contents

Illustrations

Acknowledgements

I would like to thank the University of Birmingham and the Arts and Humanities Research Council for their support of this project. Many thanks also to the series editors, Maggie B. Gale, and Mary Luckhurst, for all their help. The opportunity to discuss Chekhov with directors of his theatre work has been invaluable; my thanks go to Philip Holyman, Rachel Kavanagh, Ian Rickson, Declan Donnellan, Katie Mitchell, Yuri Lyubimov. In addition, I have had much support and help from colleagues and friends, including Mike Berry, Mike Pushkin, Nina Ischuk-Fadeeva, Alevtina Kuzicheva, Olga Kuptsova, Andrei Kirillov, Anna Seymour, George Taylor, Brian Crow, Russell Jackson, Kate Newey, Bella Merlin, Bill Marshall, Victoria Door, Diane Willetts, Liz Tunnicliffe, Martin Leach, Roy Thompson, Valerie Finegan, Janyce Hawliczek and colleagues in the Professional Association of Alexander Teachers. I would also like to thank my family, Rose Lilian, John, Lynne, Laurie and Georgia Whyman. A special acknowledgement goes to students in the Department of Drama and Theatre Arts at the University of Birmingham, whose enthusiasm and ideas in studying and working on Chekhov have been invaluable.

Figure 1.1 Portrait of Chekhov (1902)

Part I

Life and context

OVERVIEW

Over a hundred years after they were written, Anton Chekhov's plays fill theatres throughout the world, his stories are continually reprinted and retranslated and critical material on Chekhov is produced in abundance. However, Chekhov's personality and his work apparently continue to mystify critics, audiences and readers. Narratives about his life persistently refer to the 'elusiveness of Chekhov' (Turkov 1995: x), the 'enigma' of Chekhov (Llewellyn Smith 1973: x) and present descriptions of him that are full of paradoxes and contradictions. For example, Gillès states 'this gentle face of a young Christ ... masked a strange resolution' (1968: 44), Karlinsky refers to 'the gentle subversive' (Chekhov 1973: 1) and Troyat to 'the agnostic' with 'ardent faith in the future' (1987: 50). Rayfield portrays a Don Juan who could be vindictive, writing 'cruel parody' of people he knew (1998: 376, 352). Kelly describes him as 'deeply subversive ... a figure whose originality is as yet poorly understood' (1999: 171). Chekhov's expression of own persona was ambiguous: he was deliberately self-abnegating, he wrote little about himself, admitting to, as he styled it, 'autobiographophobia' (Chekhov 1973: 366). He presented himself in different ways to different correspondents, as analyses of his letters demonstrate (see O'Connor 1987). 'His "sociability" particularly as expressed in his enormous correspondence, was one of his most successful disguises' (Miles 1993: 187). He was very hospitable, filling his family homes with guests, while complaining in letters that his visitors gave him no peace to write; those who knew him well spoke of his friendliness, his sense of humour and his deep reserve (Gorky *et al.* 2004: 49).

The problems for biographers and critics, both western and East European, have been compounded in the past by a lack of access to all the material and information on the context in which Chekhov wrote. Karlinsky has described layers of censorship, including both state censorship and editorial choices made to protect privacy by Chekhov's sister, in the publication of papers after his death (Chekhov 1973: xii). Previous restrictions have now been lifted and the emergence of new material from archives in Russia that have opened since *perestroika* in the 1990s has resulted in new translations, and in new biographical studies such as those by Donald Rayfield, Rosamund Bartlett and Alevtina Kuzicheva. This has facilitated new approaches to the work, such as A. A. Chepurov's re-examination of the first performance of *The Seagull* at the Alexandrinsky Theatre in St Petersburg, and Galina Brodskaya's account of the cultural background to Stanislavsky's and Chekhov's lives and work. Critiques of Chekhov's work from feminist and other theoretical standpoints, such as Peta Tait's analysis, combining studies of gender theory, emotion and phenomenology, John Tulloch's analysis of the work as theatrical event and Michael C. Finke's psychoanalytic approach, have supplemented biographical approaches to Chekhov scholarship, such as that of Ronald Hingley or David Magarshack. The main subjects for critical material on Chekhov remain the multiplicity of possible interpretations of his work, its autobiographical significance, its relationship to literary movements such as naturalism and symbolism, his worldview and his use of language. In general, the extent of the intertextual allusions and literary references, and the subtlety of Chekhov's use of language have only relatively recently begun to be fully analysed (see de Sherbinin 1997: 3, Senderovich and Sendich 1987, Stepanov 2005) and much work continues to present a Chekhovian persona that is informed by the bias of the writer (McVay 2002: 64, 77).

Topical references have not been fully understood, especially in the west, and it is important in any consideration of Chekhov to have an understanding of the historical context in which he was writing. He was born in 1860, in a Russia under the autocratic rule of Tsardom, essentially a feudal system before reforms in 1861. He came from a family of serfs, peasants who were owned by the state or by the upper classes, but his grandfather had managed to buy his family's freedom and Chekhov's father subsequently became a merchant. Chekhov gained an education, training and working as a doctor as he also began to be known as a writer. His fame began to spread through *fin-de-siècle* Europe and he died in 1904, just before the first Russian revolution of 1905. Political currents after this eventually led to the overthrow of the Tsars in the revolution of 1917 and the establishment of communist rule in Russia. Chekhov's formative years and working life, therefore, were in a Russia undergoing a period of political and cultural turmoil, which is examined in Chekhov's work.

The complexity of interpretation is demonstrated by the wide variety of readings in the production history of the plays since their first chequered reception in Russia and the west (see Senelick 1997a). Labelled 'The Voice of Twilight Russia' (Toumanova 1937), Chekhov was considered by many in Russia and the west to be the poet of the decline of the nobility and the gentry in pre-revolutionary Russia. He was known first in the west as a short story writer, and was compared with French realist writers such as Guy de Maupassant; critics viewed his work as expressive of pessimistic philosophies (Emeljanow 1997: 2). Interestingly, in the Russia of his own time, the plays, though controversial, were hugely acclaimed, but thereafter for some time seen as examples of historical pessimism, presenting the past nostalgically in an idealized way (Simonov 1969: 23). After the 1917 revolution, there was an ideological imperative in Soviet times for the work to be interpreted as an exposition of the state of a dying class, a class that was the enemy of the proletariat or workers and had been vanquished by the revolution, out of keeping with the new Soviet age. New interpretations began from the 1940s in Russia (see Shakh-Azizova 2000) and in the west from the 1950s, but in the late 1970s, Trevor Griffiths asserted that the dominant western interpretation of Chekhov's plays remained 'plangent and sorrowing evocations of an "ordered" past no longer with "us", its passing greatly to be mourned ... ' (2007: 266). Arguing that Chekhov's was a coded revolutionary agenda, Griffiths and others have re-examined the political aspects of Chekhov's work.

Class politics are very important; the presence of servants, of landowners and merchants, literati and artists, is central to Chekhov's playwriting. The turmoil brought about by shifts in the class system as a result of the emergence of new ideologies and economies in Chekhov's lifetime has echoes in many other contexts and has resulted in the adaptation, in recent years, of Chekhov's plays to settings such as South Africa after apartheid, as in Suzman's *The Free State* (2000), or Mustapha Matura's *Three Sisters, after Chekhov* (2006), a reworking set in colonial Trinidad in 1941. Similarities between the situation in Ireland and that of Chekhov's Russia have been drawn in many adaptations and the work of writer Brian Friel (see Pine 2006: 104–16, Kilroy 2000: 80–90).

Arguably, some of the appropriation of Chekhov – whether the lyrical English Chekhov, or the Soviet politicized Chekhov – results from a narrow view of the context in which he was writing. An understanding of context is important not so that the cultural context can be reproduced authentically in production – the work is open to a variety of performance styles – but to acknowledge that Chekhov's work occupied a specific historical position and provided a perspective on the ideological thought of the time. Many stories and the full-length plays are a locus for the discussion of current philosophical and political ideas in the debates and attitudes of the characters, reflecting the ferment of the times. His work surveys the inheritance of nineteenth century romanticism and idealism and the nihilisms and pessimistic philosophies that characterized a strong strand of thought in his epoch, while also examining optimistic philosophies ranging from that of Tolstoy to Marx. Chekhov provides no answers, as he famously said, seeking rather to formulate questions correctly (Chekhov 1973: 117). Drawing on his own experience and observation of others, he questions the basis for people's ideas of how to live life, and his writing, though discussing the cultural and political currents of a particular epoch, has resonances today.

This book seeks to survey the historical context, to position Chekhov in relationship to political ideologies and to contribute to the reappraisal of his work facilitated by new biographies and translations. In looking at selected productions, I will consider whether directors of widely differing interpretations of Chekhov are working from a socially and historically contextualized reading of Chekhov and how necessary this is to a production's success.

1 Life, context and ideas

Art, politics and philosophy were entwined in the intellectual landscape for Chekhov's work, as artists, critics and social agitators attempted to engage with political superstructures in the hope of bringing about reform in Russia. Chekhov's own experience of life gave him a unique perspective on the problems of his society.

Chekhov's life: serf's son to *intelligent* in nineteenth century Russia

Chekhov was the first famous writer in Russia to emerge from his class. His Russia was a vast empire with extremes of wealth and poverty, diverse cultures and a predominantly rural economy. Three tsars of the Romanov dynasty ruled in his lifetime: Alexander II (1855–81), Alexander III (1881–94) and his son Nicholas II (1894–1917). It was, until the year after Chekhov's birth, a feudal system, where the basis for the economy was the enslavement of the peasantry; the serfs (four-fifths of the population) paid 'quit-rent' in cash or labour services, whereas the gentry did not pay income tax. By the nineteenth century, there was a rigid, inefficient, and in some ways corrupt, centralized bureaucracy.

In the eighteenth century, a Table of Ranks for the civil and military services was established, ascent through which conferred hereditary nobility, an opportunity for commoners to become noble and rich. This established a hierarchical and careerist society, which Chekhov was to satirize in plays like *The Wedding*. He drew attention to the effects of living in such a status-ridden environment in stories such as *The Death of a Government Official* (1883), *Anna*

on the Neck (1895) and characters such as Kulygin, a school teacher
in *Three Sisters*.

In the 1860s, later than in western countries where more progressive economies were developing, a new intelligentsia, *razno-
chintsy* or 'persons of other ranks', who came from social classes
other than the nobility began to emerge. (A member of the intelligentsia was called an *intelligent*.) Chekhov's life typified the changes
in Russia's social strata. He was born in Taganrog, a bustling cos-
mopolitan port in southern Russia on the Azov Sea, an inlet of the
Black Sea. His paternal grandfather had been a serf in the Voronezh
region and became a foreman in his master's sugar beet factory,
saving to buy his freedom and that of his family. Yegor Mikhailo-
vich then took a post as steward of an estate in Taganrog. His son,
Pavel Yegorovich, Chekhov's father, in turn had aspirations for his
own family of six (one daughter died in infancy) to improve on
their lowly beginnings, and Chekhov was sent to the Taganrog
school for boys in 1868, which prepared him for university education. Pavel Yegorovich kept a grocery shop, in which Chekhov
worked and bought himself into the 'Second Guild of Merchants'.
Pavel Yegorovich was an orthodox churchman and Chekhov had a
religious education, was compelled to sing in the choir and under-
take other church duties. His father often punished his children
harshly. Brutality against women and children within the family
was sanctioned in this patriarchal society.

In 1875, the older brothers left Taganrog to pursue their studies
in Moscow, avoiding conscription. In the same year disaster fell.
Pavel Yegorovich was having a house built, but was cheated and
had to borrow to complete the project. The business was failing as
railways were being extended through the steppe to Taganrog,
ruining local tradesmen who had supplied farmers and waggoners
(Miles 2008: 11), and in 1876, Pavel Yegorovich had to declare
himself bankrupt. He left for Moscow, followed soon by other
family members and at the age of sixteen, Chekhov was left alone in
Taganrog in order to finish school, supporting himself by tutoring.

In 1879, Chekhov began his studies in the Faculty of Medicine at
Moscow University with the aid of a scholarship. He saved his
family from poverty; he began writing, solely to earn money at
first – humorous stories, articles and sketches under pseudonyms
such as 'Antosha Chekhonte' and 'Brother of my brother' – and

recognition of his prose work increased through the 1880s. He began to write more for the theatre, and in 1896 (the year he was diagnosed with tuberculosis), by then a writer for seventeen years, he completed *The Seagull*. It was initially produced in St Petersburg, then by the Moscow Art Theatre (MAT). This was the beginning of Chekhov's connection with the theatre and Konstantin Stanislavsky and Vladimir Nemirovich-Danchenko. Despite his illness, Chekhov's dramatic writing reached its apogee towards the end of his life. *On the Harmfulness of Tobacco* first appeared in 1886, went through rewritings until the final one appeared in 1903, a demonstration of his mastery of the tragicomic. *Uncle Vanya* opened at the MAT in 1899 and *Three Sisters* in 1901. He married MAT actress Olga Knipper in May 1901. *The Cherry Orchard* was written slowly by the dying Chekhov from 1902 and was premiered in January 1904. He died in July that year in Badenweiler, Germany.

Views of Chekhov's life

Chekhov emerged from the inheritance of serfdom, from poverty, violence and domination to become a famous artist and thinker in a repressed and troubled society. His work is a reflection on the complexity and problems of such a life. Biographical accounts have often simplified this reflection and present a variety of Chekhovs. The first Russian biographies such as Yermilov (1957) have a tendentious aspect: the myth of the great Russian artist in Soviet times promoted Chekhov as a sort of higher being, devoted to his family, always gentle and compassionate, emphasized his commitment to social change, and in keeping with Soviet puritanism, censored references to his sexual life in letters. Family memoirs such as *About Chekhov* by younger brother Mikhail aimed to protect the family, leaving out much personal detail. Some western biographers (Simmons 1963, Gillès 1968, Troyat 1987) largely inherited the view of Chekhov's 'saintliness', some sentimentalizing it further, though Simmons provides a valuable account and commentary on the development of the writing. As a reaction against this image, Magarshack connected Chekhov's biographical self with images in writing (1980) and Hingley (1976) attempted to present a more rounded view. Some studies, making use of material in letters that was initially censored, have focused on Chekhov's relationships with women, and have identified misogynistic tendencies in the quest to debunk the myth of his saintliness and find flaws in his character (Llewellyn Smith 1973), echoed in Rayfield (1998: 347–48), in a comprehensive account of the writer's life and work. Rayfield finds the final import of Chekhov's work essentially elusive (1975: 226) whereas others, such as Karlinsky (Chekhov 1973), by linking the writer's life and the historical context with the work, seek to find ways into an understanding of Chekhov's thought.

Contemporary analyses seek to extend knowledge of the context for Chekhov's work in a variety of ways. Kuzicheva (2004) throws new light on Chekhov 'the family man' by her depiction, using extensive documentary evidence of the lives of his parents and siblings, and their relationship as a family that had emerged from serfdom with a son or brother who became viewed as a literary genius. Bartlett (2004) depicts Chekhov's life through the places where he lived and visited, indicating the profound influence environments had on his art and the depth of his ecological insight. Finke (2005) takes a psychoanalytic approach, linking the biography with the intellectual milieu and providing new insights into how Chekhov's medical training influenced his art. Marsh (2000) and Tait (2002) offer feminist analyses. Other aspects of Chekhov are seen in his correspondence. Pitcher (1979) and Benedetti (1995) use letters to depict Chekhov's complex relationship with his wife Olga Knipper, and also their writer–actress relationship; this has now been supplemented by new material (Chekhov 2004a).

Chekhov on his life

Critical response to Chekhov's work in his own time is documented in two recent anthologies (Sukhikh 2002, Le Fleming 2006). Chekhov's work was viewed as lacking commitment to the social issues of the day. Part of what has been perceived as his 'elusiveness' was a conscious refusal to suggest answers to social problems, in the way that was expected of an artist in his society. In discussions of Chekhov's outlook on life as expressed in his work, Chekhov's brief autobiographical note of 1889 is important:

> What upper class writers have always taken for granted, those from humbler origins must sacrifice their youth to acquire.

Try writing a story about a young man, the son of a serf, a former shop boy and chorister, school boy and student, brought up to be respectful of his betters, and to kiss the priest's hand, to submit to the ideas of others, to be grateful for every crust of bread, who is constantly thrashed, who goes out without galoshes to tutor other people's children, who gets into fights, torments animals, savours the taste of good dinners with rich relations, unnecessarily plays the hypocrite before God and his fellows purely from a realization of his own insignificance – then go on to tell the story of how this young man drop by drop wrings the slave out of himself until, one fine morning, he awakes to feel that flowing in his veins is no longer the blood of a slave but that of a complete human being ...

(Chekhov 2004b: 175)

Chekhov's personal struggle for intellectual and financial independence and to determine the course of his own life – to become 'a complete human being' – meant casting off the religious indoctrination and the brutal inheritance and poverty of serfdom, which instilled a sense of inferiority in generation after generation. His older brothers were not able to achieve this; Alexander also wrote and Nikolai became an artist, but neither was able to fulfil their potential, and both struggled with alcoholism and other personal problems. Pavel Yegorovich 'broke' them (Brodskaya 2000: 103). Chekhov's own experience of 'wringing the slave out of himself' and his understanding of those who struggled to do so informed a major theme of his work: how people 'submit to the ideas of others', enslaving themselves to falsehood.

He wrote in 1888, asserting the importance of independence of thought:

I would like to be a free artist and nothing else ... My holy of holies is the human body, health, intelligence, talent, inspiration, love and the most absolute freedom imaginable, freedom from violence and lies, no matter what form the latter two take. Such is the program I would adhere to if I were a major artist.

(Chekhov 1973: 109)

In seeking to expose the 'violence and lies' of his society and the preconceptions on which people based their behaviour, he took an oblique stance regarding politics and art, partly because of censorship, mostly from a reticence to impose a didactic view. This was much misunderstood by the intelligentsia of his day.

The Russian intelligentsia: politics and art

The nineteenth century Russian intelligentsia 'defined itself by agitating for social reform. Its members, *intelligenty,* were critical thinkers who regretted the primitive political state of their country under tsarism' (Chamberlain 2004 3). They raised awareness of Russia's economic and political backwardness, under-development and the plight of its rural population throughout the century; Chekhov participated in this work.

In 1825, during the reign of Alexander I, members of the Imperial Guard, who became known as the Decembrists, revolted. They aimed to abolish serfdom, fired by ideas of German idealist philosophy (whose main proponents were Friedrich Johann von Schelling, Johann Gottlieb Fichte and Georg Hegel), romanticism and the Enlightenment politics that inspired the French Revolution. The brutal suppression of the revolt meant that the intelligentsia throughout the century feared direct action; the next generation, the 'beautiful souls' of 1838–48,[1] notably leading thinkers Alexander Herzen and Vissarion Belinsky, had to contend with the continued repression of Nicholas I, who established the secret police, which was to become a long-term feature of Russian life. The 'new men' of the next couple of decades in Russia envisaged a society on western models, as new ideological currents, bourgeois democracy and humanitarian ideals spread from western Europe. Nikolai Dobrolyubov, Nikolai Chernyshevsky and Dmitry Pisarev, who translated the work of Charles Darwin, were three of the figureheads for the 1860s revolutionary movement, which was significantly influenced by literature.

The Decembrists had determined that literature had a civic mission to help develop a national consciousness for Russia, leading to the establishment of a more equal society. Therefore, Belinsky and other critics commented on all newly published literature. Open political discussion was impossible because of censorship (though Russian literature of the early nineteenth century, the work of writers like Alexander Pushkin and Nikolai Gogol, had flourished despite it), so writers often wrote in a coded way. A particular kind of literary criticism had been developed, in which works of fiction were discussed as a pretext for a critique of Russian society. Belinsky published 'A Survey of Russian Literature in 1847', in which, referring to Herzen's *Who is to Blame?* and I. A. Goncharov's *An Ordinary Story,* he argued for a utilitarian view of the function of art, that its value was in its contribution to social and political change. Pisarev and Dobrolyubov also promoted this view. The continued dominance of this view resulted in much criticism of Chekhov's writing. Arguably, it helped him to define his own thinking, taking an anti-didactic stance. Chekhov discussed these attitudes to art by means of a debate on avant-garde art and utilitarian art between his characters in *Three Years* (1895). Chekhov saw dogmatism as in the long term unlikely to achieve its purpose and contrary to his own aesthetic, where the role of art is not to supply answers but ask questions.

The reforms of Tsar Alexander II

All the tsars in some way attempted reform, while still believing that autocracy was the only way to govern Russia, so periods of some liberalization were often followed by repression. By the mid-nineteenth century slavery was being abolished everywhere else in Europe and so, with reservations, after his accession to the throne in 1855, Alexander II set about abolishing serfdom. His reforms also included building new schools and hospitals, the reform of the judicial system and establishment of a representative (to some extent) system of local government (*zemstvo*[2]). The emancipation of the serfs took place in 1861. However, the lot of the peasants was in some ways little improved, as Firs, the aged former serf, in *The Cherry Orchard* often points out. The freedoms gained were limited and freed serfs had to compensate the landowners financially for the land now theoretically theirs. They were tied to the *mir* or peasant commune and had to buy themselves out to leave. *Zemstva* made a difference immediately to primary education, peasant illiteracy and the provision of healthcare but they were primarily fundraising bodies. Chekhov supported *zemstva* and various characters in the plays and stories are involved in some way in the liberal movement for self-government – characters in *Ivanov*, for example, and Dr Astrov in *Uncle Vanya* – but the work was difficult because of the isolated nature of these movements and the fact that there was little actual government support.

Significantly for Chekhov, who went to Moscow University in 1881, educational opportunities for people from the lower classes, and for women, began to increase throughout the century. Educational institutions also became important forums for debate, and students in Russian universities increased by 67 per cent between 1869 and 1882 (Saunders 1992: 318). In 1872, the Ge're Higher Women's courses started at Moscow University, with the object of training women to teach in secondary schools. Official university-level courses for women, the first of their kind in Europe, opened in Russia in 1878, though they were closed again for a while, in a wave of repression in the 1880s (Saunders 1992: 314, 162). Chekhov returns often to the theme of women and education, for example, in *Three Sisters, The Cherry Orchard* and stories such as *The Marriageable Girl* (1904).

In the 1860s and early 1870s, before Karl Marx's socialism began to be known in Russia, various books, which could not previously have been published, examined the utilitarian question of how Russia could become a socialist society by taking 'a materialistic view of man, and to get rid of weakness of will, pessimism, guilt, tragic inevitability, by changing the social and economic conditions which might make him irrational' (Chamberlain 2004: 50). These included Chernyshevsky's novel *What is to be done?*, Nikolai Mikhailovsky's essay 'What is progress?', Peter Lavrov's *Historical Letters*, and Mikhail Bakunin's *Statism and Anarchy*. Chernyshevsky's novel (Chekhov drew on its portrayal of revolutionary ideas in *The Cherry Orchard*) was about a co-operative of seamstresses, who have left their dominating menfolk to support themselves by working together. Inspired by the emancipation of the serfs, its message was that ordinary people and even more remarkably, women, could take charge of their own lives. The other influential books discussed, in various ways, how ordinary people could and should bring about social change, to the point of preparing for revolution.

Alexander II allowed reform to go only so far and was determined to maintain autocracy, as he demonstrated in his persistent refusal to grant Russia a constitution. This meant the continuation of *proizvol*, arbitrary rule, a lack of legal rights or processes of justice for citizens. The task confronting the Russian leader was an immense one:

> to abolish an age-old order founded on slavery, replace it with civic decency and freedom ... to redesign the entire adminis- tration, freedom of the press, put a repressed and humiliated society on its feet ...

> (Saunders 1992: 213)

Alexander was not equal to this; therefore there was widespread disillusionment among the intelligentsia after the 1860s. By the time Chekhov was writing, there were a variety of responses to the ensuing stagnant political situation in the country and the margin- alization of the intelligentsia.

Nihilism and Ivan Turgenev

Ivan Turgenev's novels and plays were an important influence on Chekhov in various ways. (See Rayfield 1985, Briggs 1994.) Tur- genev was born in 1818 and from 1837 was at university in Berlin, where he was inspired by Hegelian idealism. His writing explored pessimistic and fatalistic philosophies; his novel *Fathers and Sons*, published in 1862 in the period of liberalism, satirized Russia's revolutionary youth. Bazarov, a revolutionary (based on Dobrolyu- bov), casts himself as an individual at war with society. Bazarov's system of belief is based on negation, or nihilism, an extreme scep- ticism and a kind of empiricism: a refusal to accept any authority except that of experience.

Ultimately, Bazarov concludes that Russia has no more need of him than of the 1840s liberal idealists; he is a 'superfluous' or 'use- less' person (*lishnii chelovek*). Turgenev invented this term, writing *The Diary of a Superfluous Man* in 1850. Other writers, including Pushkin, Herzen, Goncharov and Mikhail Lermontov, dealt with the theme. Turgenev's variation became a master image of the epoch for a person who tended to introspection and therefore lacked the will to fight for social change, a theme Chekhov was to deal with in his own way, particularly in *Ivanov*.

Other nihilist positions existed, the central thread being the exposure and rejection of social injustices. It was a materialist philosophy, anti-romantic, philosophically anti-idealist, and many nihilists also subscribed to 'scientism', a belief that all philosophical problems not already resolved through the researches of natural science would eventually be solved (Moser 1964: 29). Russian nihilism, whose chief proponent was Pisarev, was oriented towards the future: in anarchist Nikolai Bakunin's slogan – 'the negation of what exists … for the benefit of the future which does not yet exist'. Many characters in Chekhov's plays discuss the future and their discussions reflect these philosophical ideas.

The philosopher Arthur Schopenhauer (1788–1860) also had a profound influence in nineteenth century Russia, one of his main proponents being Ivan Turgenev (see Kelly 1998: 91). Schopenhauer's particular nihilism provided a new way of thinking about life in a post-Darwinistic world. His metaphysics, which drew from Buddhism and Hinduism, were explained in *The World as Will and Representation*, published in Germany in 1818. He viewed the human will as creating an idealized and egotistical representation of life from an individual perspective that must always be in conflict with the wills of others, and therefore must bring about universal suffering. The intellect can override the will but ultimately the only good thing is death, understanding that the 'world as representation', as the individual perceives it, is nothing and death, which cannot destroy our essential being, is the only cure for the sickness of life. Schopenhauer's work had great influence in nineteenth century Europe and Russia and also provoked a wave of suicides, especially among the young. Suicide is a major theme in Chekhov's work particularly in the plays; *Ivanov* and *The Seagull* both end with a suicide.

The intellectual nihilism defined in literary terms by Turgenev and others inspired the assassination of Alexander II in 1881. Bakunin, a Hegelian who was the first to articulate a Russian view of socialist revolution, famously said 'the urge to destroy is a creative urge!' (Hosking 2001: 306). The terrorist organization *Narodnaya Volya* (the People's Will) was responsible for the assassination of the Tsar. The organization dispersed in the mid-1880s but its ideology lived on to compete with Marxism, which became important in Russia after 1900, initially as one of several socialist movements as a whole. In *The Story of an Anonymous Man* (1893), Chekhov depicts an anarchist who plots to kill a government minister.

Leo Tolstoy and populism

By the time Chekhov began writing in the 1880s, there was fear and pessimism in the wake of the Tsar's assassination, further repression and a rejection of the philosophical materialism and positivism that had guided the intelligentsia in the 1860s and 1870s. The intelligentsia, including Chekhov, then found a new inspirational force in Leo Tolstoy. Schopenhauer's conviction that the material world is evil had influenced Tolstoy, who sought a new spirituality, rejecting the Orthodox Church as not truly Christian. He founded a sectarian movement, the principles of which were to seek moral self-perfection, oppose violence in any form and live in community with others. He was a vegetarian, and preached sexual abstention. Tolstoy also inspired a 'back to the people' movement, teaching the peasants on his estate, wearing peasant dress and living simply, teaching acceptance of God's will. Tolstoy joined the debate about work, or labour (*trud*), which had been an important aspect of democratic ideologies since the 1860s. For everyone, including the nobility, to join the workforce was seen as the key to equality in society, an idea that many of Chekhov's characters discuss in the plays and stories. Tolstoy's ideas were popular through the last decades of the century and his opposition to the instruments of the state – tsarism, the army, the government and the church – even chimed in some ways with the impact of Marxism in Russia as more active oppositions emerged.

Tolstoy re-inspired a populist movement, which had its roots in the 1840s, in a sense of injustice among the intelligentsia about the fact that the state took so little responsibility for the situation of the peasantry. Both those who looked to the west and the Slavophiles, who wanted to preserve aspects of Russian culture, saw in the peasant commune a chance to develop socialism from what had formerly been a feudal structure. In mid-nineteenth century England half the population lived in cities and in Russia only 7.8 per cent did (Saunders 1992: 143). Under Tolstoy's influence, the populist movement became more radical in the 1870s. In the context of famine in part of the empire a movement called 'To the People!' existed from 1872 to 1874, where many young people from the gentry went to live among the peasants with the aim of educating them. Mostly they and their efforts were greeted with curiosity rather than support; the fundamental concern of the peasantry in many areas remained survival amidst poverty and disease.

Tolstoy was very influential on Chekhov for the first half of his career as a writer (see Speirs 1992). Some stories written in 1886–87 express a Tolstoyan philosophy, such as *The Beggar, An Encounter, The Cossack* and *The Letter*. Later stories such as *My Life* (1896) explore populist ideas and *Ward No. 6* (1892) considers Tolstoyanism as well as other philosophies.

Chekhov: life and careers as doctor and writer

The reign of Alexander III from 1881 meant retrenching in educational opportunities and curbing of the powers of the *zemstva*. Chekhov's response to this oppressive political situation as a doctor was to work actively for social change; in his other career, as a writer, he refused to comment directly. Utilitarian critics condemned him for 'wrecking his talent'; Peter Lavrov called him an 'unprincipled' writer. However, Chekhov himself saw no contradiction between his approach to medicine and his approach to writing, noting that his medical studies had profoundly influenced his literary activity (Chekhov 1973: 367), envisioning science and art as a unity. He saw the goal of both as increasing understanding of life and freeing people from delusions. He wrote:

> When a person doesn't understand something, he feels discord within him. Instead of looking for the causes of this discord within himself, as he should, he looks outside. Hence the war with what he does not understand.
>
> (Chekhov 1973: 146)

Gaining insight into life was important in freeing oneself from inner conflict and unhappiness.

Chekhov the doctor

At university, Chekhov encountered the views of progressive doctors who believed in the importance of the doctor's social role, such as Grigory Zakharin, who promoted the idea of preventive medicine, Alexei Ostroumov and Nikolai Sklifosovsky. Russia was one of the first countries to offer free medical and dental care. Chekhov also encountered new scientific ideas permeating his epoch with the work of evolutionists Charles Darwin and Herbert Spencer, and that of Claude Bernard, who developed thinking on scientific method (see Tulloch 1980 and Coope 1997). Chekhov was also interested in the work on mental illness and psychiatry pioneered in Russia by I. P. Merzheyevsky. Like many of his scientific peers, he adopted (most of the time) a materialist viewpoint, noting in 1889, 'Outside of matter there is no experience or knowledge and consequently no truth' (Chekhov 1973: 144), and emphasized the intrinsic value of life itself, with all its imperfections.

His studies embraced the paradigm shift in science that had occurred with the advancement of the theory of evolution and he was deeply interested in Darwin's work. He rejected scientism, and also Social Darwinism, which selected aspects of Darwin's theory to promote the idea that the human race should progress according to the rule of the survival of the fittest. Chekhov preferred Darwin's ideas of chance in the development of human life rather than the idea that the human race was progressing through evolution towards a predetermined goal. He argued against Social Darwinism in 1891 that willpower and wisely directed education could overcome inherited evil traits (Hingley 1976: 152), a theme he explored in *The Duel* (1891), and demonstrated in the plays how the lives of the characters are subject to the vagaries of chance rather than predetermination. As such, he took a stance in opposition to prevailing ideas of his time.

After finishing his studies in 1884, Chekhov took locum work near Moscow at Zvenigorod, continuing to practise on and off as a doctor throughout his life. Over the next few years, writing occupied much of his time and in 1890, he undertook an arduous journey to Sakhalin, an island penal colony off the east coast of northern Siberia. He planned to write a doctoral thesis on conditions there, writing to Suvorin, 'I want to write at least one or two hundred pages and to pay a little of my debt to medicine, toward which, as you know, I've behaved like a pig'. Conditions in the penal colony were appalling. He added:

we have let *millions* of people rot in jails, we have let them rot to no purpose, unthinkingly and barbarously. We have driven people through the cold, in chains, across tens of thousands of versts, we have infected them with syphilis, debauched them, bred criminals and blamed it all on red-nosed prison wardens.

(Chekhov 1973: 159–60)

He conducted extensive research on the life of prisoners and their families. On his return to Russia, he collected money and books for schools and to set up an orphanage on Sakhalin. His work was rejected as a doctoral thesis in view of the implicit criticism of the government's treatment of prisoners, so he serialized his findings as *Sakhalin Island* in *Russian Thought* between 1893 and 1895, after battles with the censorship bodies. His efforts brought about further projects for the improvement of conditions on the island.

The winter of 1891–92 was a period of widespread famine in Russia, and Chekhov threw himself into famine relief work, and also, in 1892, purchased an estate in Melikhovo, fifty miles from Moscow, moving there with his family and developing a new interest in farming and gardening, There, he took on an active role in medical work for local *zemstva*, treating vast numbers of peasants for free, working to prevent the spread of cholera and improve sanitation. Over the next few years he raised funds for the building of three schools and the construction of new roads. He worked to develop libraries, was involved in running a mental hospital and promoted many other projects throughout the rest of his life.

Notably, there is a doctor in many of the stories and each of Chekhov's major plays except *The Cherry Orchard*, though not all are presented as positive figures. With Dr Astrov in *Uncle Vanya*, Chekhov demonstrates the plight of the socially enlightened doctor, under the *zemstvo* system in the provinces, working single-handedly, as so few doctors were available, in a vast area of deprivation.

Chekhov the writer

As a writer, Chekhov struggled at first to find a coherent response to his environment. Though his first pieces were purely comic, his powers of observation were apparent in them. He published thirty-two stories and sketches in *The Spectator* in 1882, then his output increased after he met the editor of *Fragments*, Nikolai Leikin, who was to publish much of Chekhov's work. From 1883, his writing began to reflect more serious aspects of life. A critical dialogue began with an intelligentsia, many of whom clung to fixed views of the social purpose of art through the repression of the 1880s. Chekhov had read the radical writers of the 1860s – Herzen, Nekrasov, Dobrolyubov, Pisemsky – during his time in Taganrog but disliked any tendentiousness, noting in 1892 of Pisarev's critique of Pushkin, that 'his criticism reeks of the malicious, captious public prosecutor' (Chekhov 1973: 220). D. Grigorevich, the author of the first published work in Russia on an anti-nihilist theme, whose fame had peaked in the 1850s, was one of the first to recognize Chekhov's talent and urged him to find a 'moral position' in his work. Chekhov began to take his writing more seriously and to contribute to *New Time*, a journal edited by Alexei Suvorin, friend and adviser to Chekhov for many years. The writing showed significant development, and a collection *Motley Tales* was published in 1886, but not the development of a 'moral position', as Grigorevich envisaged. Rather, the development was stylistic and in terms of content; *Dreams* was widely acclaimed and *On the Road* (1886) demonstrated how Chekhov had begun to engage more deeply with the *zeitgeist* in his work. The character Likharev confesses to a young woman that first he believed in scientism. He was a slave to it, studying day and night, but found that science 'has a beginning but no end, just like a recurring decimal' (Chekhov 1976a 5: 470). He then became consumed with 'faith in nihilism', next joined a Slavophile populist organization and 'went to the people'. He dedicated himself to manual work, embraced Tolstoyan ideology and so on. His new devotion is to his ideal of femininity, of woman's self-sacrifice through her loyalty to a man. Likharev has squandered his family life and wealth in the pursuit of his ideals. From the late 1880s, Chekhov's work focused on the currents of the times, reflecting philosophical and political ideas in popular thought.

In 1887, the collections *In the Twilight* and *Innocent Talk* were published and he became known also for writing drama, though his writing was attacked all that year for 'lack of ideas'. Chekhov perceived his work differently, writing in this period that he was learning how to convey people's ideas, stating 'I'm no longer afraid to write about things intellectual … ' (Chekhov 1973: 63). The one act play *Swan Song* was first published in 1887, and the drama *Ivanov* was performed at Korsh Theatre, Moscow, to a mixed response. In 1888, the story *The Steppe* was hugely successful and moreover was published by a prestigious journal, *The Northern Courier*. In the same year, short plays *The Bear* and *The Proposal* were performed. The collection *Tales* was published, and Chekhov won the Pushkin prize for *In the Twilight,* receiving however only half the monetary award with a reproach for writing too quickly and for cheap journals. The poet and editor A. N. Pleshcheyev referred to him as the greatest artistic force in Russian literature.

Despite the acclaim, attacks continued; Nikolai Mikhailovsky and Alexander Skabichevsky, well-known critics, denounced Chekhov's writing as subversive to the utilitarian cause. In his letter to Pleshcheyev in 1888, Chekhov professed that he feared those who sought tendentiousness in his work and were determined to categorize him politically. He stated that he was neither liberal nor conservative, and wished as 'a free artist' to oppose 'lies and violence in all of their forms'. He was against philistinism (*poshlost'*), stupidity and tyranny, wherever it occurred. He saw these attitudes in individuals from every class and social group and therefore refused to write in a way that made heroes of the younger generation, scientists or writers, or stereotyped other sectors of society such as the police as villains, as other Russian writers did. Chekhov had in mind writers such as N. Uspensky, A. Levitov, V. Sleptsov in the 1860s and P. Zasodimsky and N. Zlatovratsky in the 1870s, who wrote novels which presented the peasantry as good, honest folk and had 'positive heroes', often professional men who worked tirelessly for social change (see Offord 2001). 'I look upon tags and labels as prejudices' (Chekhov 1973: 109). As a mature writer, he aimed to expose prejudice, narrow-mindedness and authoritarianism in all sectors of society in his art.

Chekhov: life and ideas

The context for Chekhov's dramatic writing in Russia of the 1890s and the turn of the century was a Russia where change was beginning to occur. Chekhov's plays and stories of 1890–1904 and his letters from the later 1880s to his death reflect his views as an artist and thinker on the evolving situation in Russia.

Industrialism and modernization

Russia was far from being an industrial or bourgeois society in the way that many European countries were as the twentieth century approached. During the rule of Nicholas II from 1894, the desire among the intelligentsia for civil rights to be established by a constitution increased, nihilist movements continued in various forms, while reactionaries clung to autocracy as the only way to maintain the empire. There was continued suppression of any opposition. It took until this period for the sections of society previously under serfdom to become sufficiently empowered to begin to support transformation of the autocratic regime. Until 1905, however, there were few and relatively small-scale protests within the under-classes. The peasants' main complaint remained lack of land. Some regions had developed effective agricultural methods and trade links, but in many major regions farming conditions were depressed. Emancipation had meant that peasants farmed smaller plots, payments for land carried on for many years and productivity was low, while the rural population was increasing. The peasants, approximately 90 per cent of the population, still had no voting rights, and 80 per cent of the land was owned by 3 per cent of the population.

The average estate was in decline economically. Writer Mikhail Saltykov-Shchedrin had written towards the end of the 1870s of

> minor gentry scattered all over Russia, with nothing to do with themselves, divorced from the stream of life and without a position of leadership. Under serfdom they could subsist, but now they simply sit in their ramshackle estates, waiting to disappear.
>
> (Rogger 1983: 90)

This situation had changed little by the 1890s. A drought and crop failure in several regions in 1891 caused a famine that lasted into the next year, with cholera and typhus outbreaks claiming thousands of lives. Criticism of the regime became increasingly vocal. Large sums were paid out for relief, so that the government was in essence facing bankruptcy at a time of famine.

At the same time, industrialization was taking place, though this was later than in western European countries; it was more than fifty years after Britain that Russia began to experience industrial expansion and the development of towns. Most economic advisers in the 1860s considered the only way to break through from stagnation to higher levels of prosperity to be by building railways (Hosking 2001: 355), as in the mid-nineteenth century, only Italy and Spain in Europe had fewer miles of track than Russia. Railway building progressed slowly until the energetic Sergei Witte became the finance minister in 1892, accelerating industrialization, working to create a stable rouble and to export goods, so that the government could borrow abroad. However, in 1899, under attack from reactionaries, Witte was dismissed. Under his jurisdiction, migration to the towns increased, and the factory worker class began to grow. Conditions and wages were largely bad, and unions illegal until 1906 (Rogger 1993: 114–23). The factory class were not revolutionaries but some were aware of the protests by workers in other countries and wanted better wages, conditions, education and rights.

This was the Russia of Chekhov's plays – many of the gentry lived on declining estates in the provinces, owning less and less land. Russia's social and economic change altered the Russian landscape; the deserted houses on the lakeshore in *The Seagull* indicate the increasing rural depopulation. Industrial deforestation and the plundering of the rural landscape by peasants trying to survive result in Astrov's passionate pleas to preserve the forests in *Uncle Vanya*. The setting for *Three Sisters* is a city, with a rising bourgeoisie, but in rural surroundings, a far remove from metropolitan culture. With the symbolism of the trains in *The Cherry Orchard*, the character of the self-made millionaire Lopakhin, who has risen from serfdom, and the revolutionary politics of Trofimov, Chekhov presciently depicts a society on the brink of political and cultural change.

Chekhov the mature writer

Chekhov welcomed the modernization of Russian and with this, by the mid-1890s, abandoned his adherence to Tolstoyan philosophy, writing 'But now something in me protests. Prudence and justice tell me that there is more love for mankind in electricity and steam than in chastity and in abstention from meat.' He understood Tolstoy's anti-war stance and condemnation of state institutions in Russia, but rejected populism and Tolstoy's idealization of the peasants, stating, 'I have peasant blood flowing in my veins and I'm not the one to be impressed with peasant virtues'. Modernization was not a panacea: he rejected the myth of progress, the idea that any one economic system, form of government, artistic approach, religious or philosophical system, could lead towards a utopian future, discussing the issue by means of the polarized attitudes of characters in *Three Years*. Chekhov summarized his view of progress in a characteristic way: 'I acquired my belief in progress when still a child; I couldn't help believing in it, because the difference between the period when they flogged me and the period when they stopped flogging me was enormous' (1973: 261–62). More important than predicting or idealizing the future for Chekhov was how people respond in the present to their inevitably changing environment.

His writing continued to explore issues of the day without propounding solutions. He wrote *The Duel* (1891), *Ward Number 6* (1892) and *The Black Monk* (1894), the latter two both treating insanity. *Three Years* and *Ariadne* followed in 1895. All of these explore evolution. *Three Years* and *In the Ravine* (1900) feature factory owners and workers. The examination of pessimistic philosophies was a major theme, as in *The House with the Mezzanine* (1896). This story and *My Life* also examine the situation of the peasants, one of the most important topics in Chekhov's late stories. The incisive exposition of the peasants' plight in *Murder* (1895) and *Peasants* (1897) gained critical approval from Marxist critics such as Petr Bernardovich Struve, who referred to Chekhov as the outstanding literary figure of his generation, and saw the story as deeply revelatory of the divide between social classes in Russia and the dehumanizing effect of this on the peasants (le Fleming 2006: 563–65).

As his illness progressed, Chekhov spent time in warmer climates, taking several trips to Europe. In 1898, he moved to Yalta in the Crimea, remaining keenly interested in events throughout the empire. In 1899, there were widespread student disturbances. The universities had long been centres of opposition to the autocracy. In his time at Moscow University he had observed but did not participate in the radical student movements, and had written a rather sardonic letter to Suvorin about the student disturbances in 1890, which were about admission of women and Jews to university

(Chekhov 1973: 160). By 1899, he had changed his point of view, complaining to Suvorin about the coverage of the events in *New Time*. Suvorin had written in favour of the government's suppression of the disturbances and Chekhov pointed out the injustice of a system of arbitrary rule where those who had been beaten, whose rights had been violated, had no recourse to the law. Furthermore, though he had to write in hints, inexplicitly, because of censorship, he drew attention to the plight of student protesters in the plays: Konstantin in *The Seagull* has been sent down from university for political activities, and Trofimov in *The Cherry Orchard* is debarred from completing his course and has been imprisoned for his views.

After the Russian response to the Dreyfus affair – a scandal in France in the 1890s exposing anti-semitism – Chekhov protested vehemently about Suvorin's anti-Dreyfus, prejudiced stance, though he found the attitude of others far too condemnatory. When Suvorin was summoned to a trial of honour for the position adopted by *New Time* on the student disturbances by the Alliance of Russian Writers for Mutual Assistance, Chekhov was appalled by this summons.

> In a backward country where there is no freedom of the press or of conscience, where the government and nine-tenths of society considers journalists their enemies, where life is so oppressive and foul and there is so little hope for better days ahead, pastimes like slinging mud at one another, courts of honour etc. put writers in the ludicrous and pitiful position of helpless little animals biting off one another's tails when locked together in a cage.
>
> (Chekhov 1973: 353–54)

All in all, Chekhov thought that the Russian intelligentsia were unlikely to succeed in bringing about change, writing

> I have no faith in our intelligentsia; it is hypocritical, dishonest, hysterical, ill bred and lazy. I have no faith in it even when it suffers and complains, for its oppressors emerge from its own midst.
>
> (Chekhov 1973: 341)

Instead, he saw the work and vision of individuals, whether intellectuals or peasants, scattered throughout Russia, as hope for the future; because of individual efforts he saw science as moving forward, social consciousness increasing and moral debate becoming more challenging. He again defended the rights of the individual when Gorky – who associated openly with members of the Marxist social-democratic movement including V. I. Lenin – was elected an honorary Academician of Literature in 1902, though Nicholas II annulled this appointment. Chekhov and fellow writer and activist Vladimir Korolenko both resigned from the Academy in protest at this repressive act.

Conclusion

Chekhov was a progressive and democratic thinker, committed to equality and human rights. In his stories and plays, he exposes the problems of an authoritarian society and considers how people react within it, surveying the dominant ideas and ideals of the Russian intelligentsia – utilitarianism, utopianism, nihilism and, also, scepticism and pessimism resulting from disillusionment when ideals fail to become reality. Chekhov saw living life on the basis of false beliefs as a kind of enslavement. The ideological solutions to the problems propounded by political thinkers and artists in his time have, as he predicted, to some extent been superseded; however, his outlook on life, his deep insight into human beings, together with his humorous and compassionate approach as expressed in his art, continue to prompt audiences and readers into new considerations of the questions he asked about life.

2 Chekhov's art and worldview

Chekhov's worldview

Chekhov's examination of the problem of 'wringing the slave out of oneself' within a society like that of nineteenth century Russia is based on a philosophical approach that has its antecedents in philosophies of inner freedom. These include Stoic, Christian and Eastern philosophies. Chekhov studied Ancient Greek philosophy and also knew the work of European thinkers, including Schopenhauer, Spinoza, Kant, Proudhon, Lessing and Nietzsche (Eekman 1960: 30).

He wrote in a letter to Pleshcheyev in 1889:

> I'll keep to the framework which is nearer to the heart and which has already been tested by people stronger and more intelligent than I – this framework is man's absolute freedom – freedom from coercion, from prejudices, ignorance, the devil; freedom from passions and so forth.
>
> (Chekhov 1974: 113)

The letter proposes the framework for Chekhov's writing, a presentation of life as potentially a process of testing out principles that form the basis of actions and of ridding oneself of preconceived ideas as a way to achieve 'freedom'. The preconceptions he examines in his plays include romantic ideals: such as the belief that romantic love is essential to fulfilment in life, a belief held by many characters in his stories and plays, which often results in disappointment. There is the romantic idea of the artist as spiritual leader common among the Russian intelligentsia in the early part of the nineteenth century, which is scrutinized in *The Seagull*.

Characters in the stories and plays adopt a variety of religious, philosophical or political belief systems. Sonya asserts her Russian Orthodox faith in *Uncle Vanya*; characters in *Three Sisters* and *The Cherry Orchard* discuss work, referencing Tolstoy's philosophy that self-sacrificing work is the only way to live life. False ideas about life include submission to coercion instead of thinking for one's self. Consequences for characters who resist change, which is an inevitable part of life, such as the estate owners in *The Cherry Orchard*, are presented; the folly of living in the past is seen as a form of escapism, as is living for an idealized future. Characters self-dramatize and 'philosophize' in expressing their views and in this way Chekhov raises questions about their convictions, indicating that the 'philosophizing' may be badly thought through or that a character's assertions are more a dramatic pose than a deeply held conviction.

Pessimistic and destructive attitudes adopted when ideals are found unattainable, and the inheritance of nihilistic philosophies, are also examined, particularly in *Three Sisters* and also in *Ivanov*. There, Lebedev refers to challenging his uncle, who was a Hegelian, to a duel, 'all on account of Francis Bacon' (Chekhov 2005: 48). Bacon (1561–1626) represented empiricism and scientific method as opposed to Hegelian idealism. Lebedev has found his former philosophical beliefs of no help in dealing with day-to-day life and has given up the struggle to make sense of life, using alcohol as a way to get by. As Konstantin says in *The Seagull*, 'How easy, Doctor, to be a philosopher on paper and how hard it is in fact!' (Chekhov 2005: 175).

Chekhov shows that circumstances are often not conducive to the individual's search for meaning in life. He depicts the triviality of everyday life (*byt*) in the Russian provinces, where people have little artistic or intellectual stimulation. He noted: 'to live one must have something to hang on to … In the country only the body works, not the spirit' (Chekhov 1967: 87). Some of Chekhov's characters settle for superficial lives or find ways to escape the monotony of their lives through gambling, drunkenness, overeating, sex, self-seeking or obsession with money. In this way, Chekhov explores *poshlost'*, a Russian concept of narrow-minded philistinism, defined by writer Vladimir Nabokov as ' … not only the obviously trashy but mainly the falsely important, the falsely beautiful, the falsely clever, the falsely attractive'.[1] Giving way to *poshlost'* is to become hardened, or 'encased'.[2] Natasha in *Three Sisters* is consumed by the desire to assert her power and cruelly uses people around her to do so. Kramer notes that this hardening (*futlyarnost'*) is

> encasing oneself physically, psychologically, morally and spiritually in order to reduce the points of contact between oneself and the rest of the world.
>
> (1970: 62)

Therefore, in Chekhov's work 'the main events take place in the characters' consciousness; a discovery or a clinging to habitual stereotypes, an understanding or a failure to understand' (Kataev 2002: 271). There are no final answers; rather, life is a process of adapting to circumstances, finding a way to live a life of some meaning or resisting this. The characters who engage in the struggle to work out what life is all about gain a degree of inner freedom; some have some success in 'wringing the slave out of themselves', those who do not remain 'encased' in trivial lives.

The process of searching is of value in itself because for Chekhov, there are no absolute values that could prescribe the right way to live life. Chekhov appeared to the utilitarian critics to lack an ideology, as he did not recommend a particular course of action to bring about social change, nor, unlike Dostoyevsky or Tolstoy, did he propound a moral code of behaviour. This absence of 'message' is perhaps what continues to be perceived as Chekhov's 'elusiveness'. In 1888, Pleshcheyev criticized *The Name-Day Party* – a story that explores the state of mind of a heavily pregnant woman, her reaction to events at a party, her sudden insight into her husband's behaviour and realization of how pretentious he is – for lacking an ideological stance. Chekhov replied:

> You told me once that my stories lack an element of protest, that they have neither sympathies nor antipathies. But doesn't the story protest against lying from start to finish? Isn't that an ideology? It isn't? Well I guess either I don't know how to bite or I'm a flea.
>
> (Chekhov 1973: 112)

He further defined his views in another letter to Pleshcheyev ' ... my aim is to kill two birds with one stone; to depict life correctly and besides to show how far this life deviates from the norm', adding that he did not know what the 'norm' was. 'We all know what a dishonourable deed is, but what is honour? – we do not know' (Chekhov 1976b 3: 186).

Beyond the aspiration for a life of 'freedom from coercion, from prejudices, ignorance, the devil; freedom from passion', Chekhov felt unable to define what he called 'the norm' – an ideal standard of moral or principled behaviour – and considered that it was not necessary for an artist to offer moral guidance. Discussing the charge that in writing *Lights* he had raised, but not solved, the problem of pessimism, he wrote to Suvorin:

> The artist is not meant to be a judge of his characters and what they say: his only job is to be an impartial witness ... Drawing conclusions is up to the jury, that is, the readers ... It's about time that everyone who writes – especially genuine literary artists – admitted that in this world you can't figure anything out. Socrates admitted it once upon a time, and Voltaire was wont to admit it. The crowd thinks it knows and understands everything; the stupider it is, the broader it imagines its outlook. But if a writer whom the crowd believes takes it upon himself to declare that he understands nothing of what he sees, that alone will constitute a major gain in the realm of thought and a major step forward.
>
> (Chekhov 1973: 104)

The Ancient Greek philosopher Socrates (469–399 BC) gave as the reason for his philosophy that the 'unexamined life is not worth living'. In his view, people sought fame, money or pleasure without considering whether these were valuable pursuits. They were in danger of wasting their lives or living at some sort of cost to themselves unless they questioned and continued to question their beliefs and actions (Gottlieb 2000: 140–42). The function of a philosopher, Socrates contended, is to bring to light the implicit beliefs, the assumptions that people make about their world, themselves, their values, as Chekhov also attempted in his writing.

Though Chekhov believed there are no absolute values, he thought it necessary to live as productive a life as possible. Chekhov admired French writer Voltaire's empiricist philosophy. Voltaire's

Candide, or Optimism, written in 1758, is a sardonic exploration of
the philosophy of optimism, as set out by German philosopher
Gottfried Leibniz. Leibniz asserted the harmony of the universe,
that God's creation is as good as it can be and that all is for the best
in the best of all possible worlds, despite problems encountered by
human beings. Voltaire satirizes this idealistic viewpoint adopted
initially by his hero Candide and his philosophical adviser. At the
end of the novel, stripped of all of his illusions, Candide finds true
optimism – an understanding of life's cruelty and unfairness yet
the commitment to live a useful life, without giving way to despair.
He abandons his former grand plans and sets to work cheerfully
on the small farm that has become home to his wife and friends.
' ... We must cultivate our garden', he says, finally (Voltaire 2005:
94). This phrase entered Chekhov's lexicon (Rayfield 1975: 252), as
a metaphor for living a productive life, with realistic expectations.

Chekhov's 'objectivity'

Chekhov aspired, like other writers of his period, to write 'objec-
tively' and developed techniques of doing so (see Chudakov 1983:
1–63). While achieving complete objectivity would not be possible,
it was important for Chekhov, as the author, to maintain a position
of ambiguity with regard to the ideas expressed in his work. This
was necessary for his stated artistic purpose of 'posing the question
correctly' so that audience members or readers can draw their own
conclusions. Chekhov's heuristic approach offers two or more sides
to a question through the characters' opinions, emulating the
Socratic method, which was to ask a series of questions in order to
provoke insight. For example, in *My Life*, Misail rejects his philis-
tine, bourgeois background and goes to work as a manual labourer.
His flouting of rank and social convention scandalizes and fascinates the provincial town of his birth. His father, the town architect, disowns him, but Masha, the daughter of a rich engineer,
marries him. They set up home in the country and begin to build a
school for the peasants, who mistrust them and frequently sabotage
the project. When the school is finished, the peasants recognize that
the project is intended to help them, but Masha's Tolstoyan ideal of
simplification (*oproshchenie*), immersion in a peasant way of life, is
shattered and she has come to despise the peasants. She leaves

Misail and goes abroad to pursue a more glamorous life as a singer. She tells him about the ring she has had engraved with the same inscription as that of the biblical figure King David, 'Everything passes.' Everything passes, she says, even life, so nothing is necessary, except 'knowing that you are free'. Misail writes:

> If I had wanted to order a ring for myself, I should have chosen the following inscription: 'Nothing passes.' I believe nothing passes without leaving a trace, and that the slightest step we take is of significance in our present and future life.
>
> (Chekhov 2003: 361)

The rings encapsulate the difference between Masha's view of freedom as a hedonistic life in pursuit of artistic success and Misail's view of personal responsibility, which means he lives a life of poverty.

Similarly, different points of view are juxtaposed in the plays. In *The Seagull*, one character chooses suicide while another chooses to struggle on against the odds; *Uncle Vanya* presents religious faith in counterpoint to existential despair. Contrasting views on working for a better future for Russia are presented in *Three Sisters*, and socialist ideas opposed to capitalism in *The Cherry Orchard*.

Chekhov drew on his training as a doctor and his study of the natural sciences in developing his objective approach (Kelly 1999: 179). He said himself that his training 'significantly broadened the scope of my observations' and gave him 'knowledge whose value for me as a writer only a doctor can appreciate'. It helped him avoid mistakes in his aim of 'depicting life correctly' as he did not wish to be one of those writers 'who believe they can figure out everything for themselves' (Chekhov 1973: 367). At medical school he studied a method of questioning patients developed by Zakharin. Under his influence, Chekhov planned a course of lectures intended to '"draw his audience as deeply as possible into the world of the patient's subjective feelings", i.e. to juxtapose objective data about an illness with the subjective anamnesis' (Kataev 2002: 95). Each patient was to be treated individually; the doctor should create an environment in which the patient could express their concerns as fully as possible, setting their own opinions aside. Chekhov took the same approach to his fictional characters, treating them as individuals, aiming 'to distinguish important testimony from unimportant, to place my characters in the proper light and to speak with their language'. He said, 'I heard two Russians in a muddled conversation about pessimism, a conversation that solved nothing; all I am bound to do is reproduce that conversation exactly as I heard it. Drawing conclusions is up to the jury, that is, the readers' (Chekhov 1973: 104).

His view of nature and the relationship between human beings and their environment was influenced by Darwin's rejection of determinism, his demonstration that human beings do not have dominion over nature, but are subject to its laws and processes, like all other animals. Chekhov presents nature as indifferent, though human beings seek meaning in it as symbolic of eternal values of beauty and permanence. The processes of nature, the cycles of time are juxtaposed with the problems experienced by individuals at fixed points in space and time. Inexorable nature provides a perspective, in that human beings must find their own answers, rather than waiting for the purpose of life to be revealed through religion or scientism.

Chekhovian 'objectivity' does not equate to disregard by the author of the problems the character is trying to resolve. He aimed to write with compassion and not to make judgement, saying of *Ivanov*, 'I did not depict one evil-villain, nor one angel ... I blamed no-one nor did I justify anyone' (Chekhov 1975b 2: 138). He wrote to Suvorin:

> You tell me off about objectivity, calling it indifference to good and evil, lack of ideals and ideas, and so forth. When I depict horse thieves you want me to say: the stealing of horses is bad. But surely this has been known for a long time without my saying it. Let the jury pass judgement on them; my business is only to show what they are like. I write: if you are dealing with horse thieves, then you should know they are not beggars but well-fed people, that they belong to a cult and that horse-stealing with them is not just theft but a passion. Of course it would be pleasant to combine art with preaching, but for me personally this is extremely difficult, and almost impossible because of technical considerations. In order to depict horse thieves in seven hundred lines, I must all the time think and speak as they would, and experience their feelings, otherwise, if I add a note of subjectivity, the characters will dissipate and the story will not be as compact as all short stories ought to be. When I write

I rely entirely on the reader, assuming that they themselves will add the subjective elements to the story.

(Chekhov 1976b 4: 54)

The plays tell stories of inner crises and the catalytic events in them force the characters into new recognitions. Chekhov saw depicting this as important and he does not offer a view on how the characters should act. Much is left for the reader or audience to decide. This approach revolutionized writing for theatre in Russia; in it, he both drew from and subverted existing models of playwriting.

Chekhov and Russian theatre

Russian theatre had not flourished as Russian literature of the nineteenth century had. This was, in part, due to the existence of a state monopoly on theatre until 1882, forbidding the existence of any public theatres in Moscow or St Petersburg except those controlled by the Imperial Court, limiting development in theatre production (Braun 1982: 59). The usual repertoire consisted of European classics in translation, such as plays by Shakespeare and Schiller, romantic dramas such as those of Victor Hugo, comedy, operettas and sentimental melodramas such as those by German writer August Kotzebue. In addition, in the first half of the nineteenth century, historical drama, in particular the sentimental dramas of V. A. Ozerov and Nestor Kukolnik, had been important, as had the work of historian and playwright Nikolai Polevoy, writer of historical drama, romantic tragedy, comedies and vaudevilles. Viktor Krylov's comedies and dramas were also popular. Chekhov saw much of this theatre in Taganrog as a boy, and when established in Moscow, continued to see classical theatre and opera, and popular vaudevilles and farces.

New dramaturgies were introduced with Turgenev's plays, notably *A Month in the Country* of 1855, in which were the seeds of a more psychologically based drama with less emphasis on plot. Alexei Pisemsky, Alexei Potekhin and Leo Tolstoy wrote realist plays on the peasant theme from the mid-nineteenth century (see Marsh 1999: 146–65). Potekhin also wrote comedies and Viktor Dyachenko wrote melodramas famous in the 1860s. Alexei Tolstoy was very successful as a writer of history plays in the 1860s–1870s.

There was also a tradition of Russian plays involving satirical comment on *poshlost'* in Russian society: in particular the work of A. S. Griboyedov and Nikolai Gogol in the early part of the nineteenth century, and later that of the major writer of histories, dramas and comedies, Alexander Ostrovsky, the less well-known M. Y. Saltykov-Shchedrin and A. V. Sukhovo-Kobylin. Some of the work of these writers was not actually performed during their lifetimes, because of censorship.

As Chekhov's work as a playwright was beginning to become known towards the end of the 1880s, the main repertoire continued to be the classics, comedies and melodrama but there was growing recognition of the need for theatrical reform. Other new writers were emerging, such as Pyotr Nevezhin, whose melodrama *Second Youth* became well known. There was also the work of Chekhov's editor Suvorin, Nemirovich-Danchenko, Prince Sumbatov (known as Yuzhin, as an actor), Maxim Gorky, Sergei Naidyonov, Nikolai Gnedich and Pyotr Boborykin. After 1882, a number of privately owned commercial theatres opened, paving the way for the opening of the MAT theatre in 1898 by Stanislavsky and Nemirovich-Danchenko. They were committed to the development of new plays and to raising the standard of acting. Russian theatre had a number of actors of acclaim, such as Pavel Mochalov, Aleksandr Fedotov, Glikeria Fedotova and Mikhail Shchepkin, all connected with the Imperial Maly theatre and its tradition of realist acting. Stanislavsky drew on this and his own experimentation in the development of his system, which was also prompted by the need to find a psychologically veracious style of acting for the plays of Chekhov.

Chekhov's theatre writing forced reconsiderations of what 'drama' is as well as new ideas about acting. One of his methods was to take conventional forms and subvert them, aiming to challenge the audience's expectations. He emphasized the importance of provoking his audiences into self-reflection, voicing the thought in his notebook, 'everybody goes to the theatre to see my play, to learn something instantly from it, to make some sort of profit, and I tell you I have not the time to bother about that canaille' (Chekhov 1967: 62). In 1891, he wrote to Suvorin, 'what is the point of explaining anything to the audience? One must startle it, that's all; then it will get interested and start thinking things over again' (Chekhov 1976b 4: 332). His vaudevilles and short plays often took

Figure 2.1 Chekhov at the Moscow Art Theatre: read-through of *The Seagull*

elements from existing plays and changed them; he transformed traditional melodramatic plots in the major plays and drew from the Russian satirical tradition. He was also influenced by trends in new writing for theatre in Europe.

Chekhov and the new drama: naturalism and symbolism

Chekhov's plays are considered part of a movement in 'New Drama', the transitional stage from nineteenth century drama to modernism. Naturalism was part of this movement: his major plays have been discussed as 'true examples of naturalism' (Innes 2000: 21) and Styan asserts that he is 'The most natural of the naturalists … the first truly dark comedian' (1968: 74). French novelist Emile Zola was naturalism's chief advocate (see Innes 2000: 3–27). Influenced by Darwinism, naturalist writers opposed romanticism and attempted to portray scientifically the underlying forces determining people's behaviour, that is, heredity or environmental factors. Writers such as Henrik Ibsen, August Strindberg and

Gerhart Hauptmann were also linked with naturalism. The major plays of these writers, like Chekhov's, also display, in different ways, elements of symbolism. Their works were not performed in Russia initially when they were written in the latter part of the nineteenth century, but Chekhov read and drew from them.

The new plays aimed to convey life's complexity. They were characterized by:

> an atmosphere of general unease ... not just social forms and institutions, but the basis of society, the family and the formerly peaceful worlds of work and everyday life (*byt*), where everything is upside down, in ferment, undefined ...
>
> (Shakh-Azizova 1966: 30)

The playwrights examined traditional and conventional values, aimed to expose cruelty in human relationships and to raise questions of social responsibility. Comparisons can be made between Chekhov's families and Strindberg's depictions of family situations, in, for example, *The Dance of Death*, characters in Chekhov and Hauptmann's *Lonely People* struggling to find an ideal and Ibsen's heroes in conflict with their stultifying bourgeois surroundings. Psychological complexity, the revelation of interiority, the depiction of states of mind and changing perceptions were the subjects of Chekhov's theatre, as they were, in different ways, that of the other writers. Chekhov valued Hauptmann, Strindberg and Maeterlinck but was critical of Ibsen, dubbing his play *Dr Stockmann* 'conservative' (Chekhov 2004a 1: 162). For the anti-didactic Chekhov, perhaps the clarity of Ibsen's morality was insufficiently complex (see Papernyi 2007: 43–97). Ibsen's *The Wild Duck* was written in 1884 and performed in Russia in 1901 at MAT, where it was not a great success but provoked much discussion. Chekhov had read the play not long after it was written. Despite Chekhov's view of Ibsen, an influence can be seen in *The Seagull* in 1896, where the central image of a bird shot down is connected to characters who are hurt by life, like the character of Hedwig in *The Wild Duck*. When Chekhov's play was first presented to the Theatrical Literary Committee, which approved plays for production at the Imperial theatres, it was criticized for 'Ibsenism' – which the Committee equated with symbolism – perceiving this as 'decadence' in art (Stanislavsky 1952: 12–13).

Rather than imitating Ibsen, he had taken the image of the bird and treated it in a different way, but neither his nor Ibsen's work was much appreciated at first by the literary establishment in Russia.

Chekhov's plays are 'naturalist' to the extent that they question how social environment contributes to the individual's development. His subject matter encompasses struggles for equality such as the emancipation of the serfs and the women's movement that characterized the late nineteenth century. In naturalist plays ordinary people, rather than romantic heroes, are the protagonists. In Chekhov, these are peasants, servants, the middle classes, soldiers, teachers and civil servants. He has also been described as bringing about 'a complete re-evaluation of the scope and even the tenets of naturalism in the early twentieth century' (Emeljanow 1981: xix). Chekhov himself rejected being categorized as a naturalist writer and positioned himself as a realist. He corresponded in 1887 with Maria Kiselyova, a friend of his who wrote children's stories, about his story *Mire*. This is about a Jewish woman, Susanna Moiseyevna, who is promiscuous and fraudulent. Kiselyova referred to the story as 'disgusting', a 'pile of manure', and said that the writer should lead the reader through such material to show them 'a pearl'. By this she meant, presumably, a moral, or an uplifting ending. Chekhov replied that to do so would be 'negating literature altogether', as the purpose of art was to depict 'life as it actually is. Its aim is the truth, unconditional and honest.' He added that 'the writer is not a pastry chef, a cosmetician or an entertainer, but must "sully his imagination with the grime of life"' (Chekhov 1973: 60–66). His story was based on a woman he had encountered; he maintained that his writing was always from life, in 1988 stating about *Ivanov* 'I am telling you sincerely … that these people are the result of observation and study of life' (Chekhov 1976b 3: 115–16).

While Chekhov's writing has affinities with the aims of naturalist writers, and is realist to the extent that his models were from life, in his own time, his work was described as 'poetic realism', indicating that his writing was informed by a unique artistic vision.

Chekhov's 'poetic realism' and symbolism

Chekhov used poetic images and symbols to convey inner experience, the ways in which his characters gain insight and shift their perceptions of life. There are varying views on the use of the symbol in his work (see Redmond 1982: 227–58). Towards the end of his life, he became increasingly interested in Belgian playwright Maurice Maeterlinck, who developed his plays using symbols to explore the meaning of life and death, drawing from the symbolist literary movement, which started in France in the mid-1880s. Chekhov, in turn, became a significant influence on Russian symbolist theatre of the first decade of the twentieth century, fuelling the rebellion against naturalism that characterized Russian theatre of the revolutionary period. Avant-garde artists such as Vsevolod Meyerhold, Andrey Bely and Leonid Andreyev hailed the symbolist aspects of his work.

Symbolist work has an experiential dimension:

> Symbolic images invite the spectator to participate in a particular adventure that will not explain but rather suggest or evoke new perspectives in human experience.
>
> (Konrad 1982: 32)

French poet and critic Stéphane Mallarmé (1842–98), whose work was well known in Russia, was one of the mainsprings for the movement, asserting that a writer should not treat a subject directly but should use words evocatively:

> there must only be allusion … *To name* an object is to suppress three-quarters of the enjoyment of the poem, which derives from the pleasure of step-by-step discovery; to *suggest*, that is the dream. It is the perfect use of this mystery that constitutes the symbol: to evoke an object little by little, so as to bring to light a state of the soul or, inversely, to choose an object and bring out of it a state of the soul through a series of unravellings.
>
> (Dorra 1994: 141)

Symbolists sought to express a second reality, using developing ideas of the unconscious. Chekhov, unlike the symbolists, or Strindberg, who moved from naturalism to an expressionist exploration of the human psyche, did not use symbols to indicate mystical experience or the dream world of the unconscious, wary as he was about discussion of experiencing anything other than that of the material world. Dreaming features in Chekhov as a distraction from, not an abstraction of, reality. Nina's 'dream' of her relationship with Trigorin in *The Seagull* is not founded on an understanding of what kind of man he is, and the relationship becomes destructive for her. The significance of symbols and images in Chekhov is in the allusive meaning they have for the characters, revealing their internal world. The seagull in the play of the same name is of importance mainly because the characters attribute symbolic significance to it, Konstantin and Nina at times seeing themselves as victims of life, like the dead seagull. Similarly, the cherry orchard in Chekhov's last play is an allusive image of natural beauty, but more important as the holder of a range of views: some characters seeing it as holding their aristocratic heritage, others as a reminder of a feudal past which must be destroyed to allow economic and political progress. The symbols and poetic images have a role to play in Chekhov's characters' search to understand life. The only occasion in the plays when a symbol has significance for the audience – beyond what it means to the characters – is in *The Cherry Orchard*, where at the end the audience only hear a sound, described as that of a 'breaking string'. This suggests that this play begins to break the boundaries of realism previously observed.

If Chekhov's imagery serves to throw light on the everyday concerns of the characters, conversely, the way Chekhov portrays the details of everyday life (*byt*) points to a wider, philosophical perspective on life in general. Bely said of Chekhov's characters, 'in the trivialities by which they live a kind of secret code is revealed to us – and the trivialities cease to be trivial', defining him as a realist artist who weaves a fabric of moments:

> Thus represented life is a delicate almost transparent lacework. If one absorbs oneself in it, a given moment of life becomes in itself a door to eternity.

> (Green 1986: 132–33)

Chekhov expands the context of his plays from that of the concerns of his characters, to one that has continued relevance by constant references to the dimension of time. The characters may be absorbed in everyday life but are made aware that 'time's running out for us' as Polina says in *The Seagull* (Chekhov 2005: 169), and there is an urgent need to find something of value in life rather than to drift along. This preoccupation with the idea of human beings as responsible for their own finite lives in a world which supplies no ready-made answers has led to perceptions of Chekhov's 'fundamental existentialism' (Senderovich and Sendich 1987: 7). Gorky wrote to Chekhov that his was 'a new kind of dramatic art, in which realism is made spiritual and raised to the level of a thoroughly thought-out symbol ... Other plays do not lead a man from reality to philosophical speculation – yours do' (Chekhov 2005: 547).

Structure and form

One way Chekhov extends the perspective of his plays from a particular historical moment to that of the temporal flow of life in general is by making the action of the plays incomplete – the beginnings take us into the world of the characters, and the audience has to deduce, from hints given, some of what has led to the current situation. Chekhov wrote of his stories, 'characters must be introduced in the middle of a conversation so the reader has the impression they have been talking for some time' (Chudakov 2000: 8) and the same is true of the plays. The endings are not a resolution of the action but are structured, for example, with departure scenes that create ambiguity about what might happen next. Similarly, many of the stories use epilogues that go beyond the time frame of the story (see Turner 1994: 26, 34). *The Seagull* ends not with Konstantin's suicide but Dorn announcing it to Trigorin and urging him to take Arkadina away, emphasizing not the death but how others will cope with it. Sonya's speech at the end of *Uncle Vanya* and Vanya's silence pose the question of how they will live their lives now that the crisis has passed. Chekhov advised that writers should 'strike out the beginning and the end' (Gorky *et al.* 2004: 46). There are characters who never appear but affect the action such as Protopopov in *Three Sisters*, and there is the continued influence on characters of parents who have died before the action begins, such as General Prozorov in the same play.

Chekhov stages social and family events, such as dinners, games of lotto. He said:

in life people are not every minute shooting each other, hanging themselves and making declarations of love. And they are not saying clever things every minute. For the most part they eat, drink, hang about and talk nonsense; and this must be seen on the stage.

(Jackson 1967: 73)

Banal conversation is juxtaposed with discussion of philosophical ideas. He wrote 'with me the serious always alternates with the trivial' (Chekhov 1975b 2: 206). Objects on stage are often apparently incidental, but their purpose, as with conversation and external events, such as they are, is to reveal interiority through the characters' attitudes and reactions to them, as is the inclusion of literary allusion and quotation.

Maeterlinck asserted that 'speech is not the communication of real inmost thought – silence is' (Huneker 1905: 374). Chekhov presents moments when characters do not speak, but as in *Three Sisters* watch a spinning top, or in *The Cherry Orchard* are transfixed by the sound of a breaking string far away in the distance. At these points the characters experience a sight or a sound together, seeming to be conscious of being alive yet unsure of what it all means. The world of Chekhov's plays exists on several planes at once – the events in the play, the characters' inner life and the suggestion of life's continuation beyond that of the characters, connecting with human life as a whole.

Chekhov's 'comedy' of life

Chekhov resisted the label 'tragic' in relation to his work and saw comedy as an essential to his writing. He wrote of his methods as a doctor: 'First of all, I'd get my patients in a laughing mood, and only then would I begin to treat them' (Chekhov 1973: 44). Gilman sees a similar intent in the writing, drawing parallels between Chekhov's plays and Dante's *La divina commedia* and Balzac's *La comédie humaine*, which, like Shakespeare's comedies, function not just to provoke laughter but 'to restore, to heal, to embolden' (1995: 73). It is in his short plays *Swan Song*, *The Wedding* and *The Harmfulness of Tobacco* that Chekhov begins to develop his complex view of genre, subtitling *The Seagull*, despite the suicide at the end, as a 'comedy'. The desire to break the boundaries of genre resulted from the desire to portray the complexities of life. He is reported as having said: 'in life there are no clear-cut consequences or reasons; in it everything is mixed up together, the important and the paltry, the great and the base, the tragic and the ridiculous' (Lafitte 1973: 16).

In *Uncle Vanya*, as Yelena and Serebryakov prepare to leave, Astrov says '*Finita la commedia*!' – 'The comedy has been played out!' (Chekhov 2005: 235). There is much that is ridiculous in forty-seven-year-old Vanya's pose as thwarted lover and his attempt to shoot the professor he holds responsible for his unfulfilled life, but there is also pathos. This has led many to classify Chekhov's work as 'tragicomedy'. The comedy is essential; there is no tragic inevitability in the situations of the characters. Gottlieb states that debate about genre and Chekhov

> becomes a philosophical and political debate … the tragic view of human impotence in the face of seemingly inevitable forces, implies an *acceptance* of the world order as it manifests itself and works out its design in the characters on stage … complete anathema to Chekhov …
>
> (Gottlieb 1993: 153)

In an article on 'the absurd' philosopher Thomas Nagel wrote:

> humans have the special capacity to step back and survey themselves and the lives to which they are committed. … Without developing the illusion that they are able to escape from their highly specific and idiosyncratic position, they can view it *sub specie aeternitatis* and the view is at once sobering and comical.
>
> (1971: 720)

Chekhov's worldview as expressed in his writing was, in the phrase first used by Spinoza, *sub specie aeternitatis*, literally, from the 'perspective of the eternal', or in other words, 'objective'. He presented the human predicament as comical in many ways – in its triviality and in the human propensity for self-delusion – and also seriously, in the imperative to search for meaning in life in order to live fully.

Part II
Plays and productions

3 Vaudevilles and one-act plays

Some of the short plays written by Chekhov between 1885 and 1903 continue to be performed as frequently as Pinter's or Beckett's short plays (Gottlieb and Allain 2000: 57). However, these one-act plays are not as widely known as the major plays, and the depth and range of Chekhov's comedy is still not fully appreciated. These plays, some of which Chekhov referred to in his letters as 'vaudevilles' (Chekhov 1975b 2: 206), are important to a consideration of Chekhov's style of humour in the major plays. They also indicate how Chekhov used stock characters and plots from nineteenth century drama but developed them, as he did in the full-length plays, to become a means of dramatically framing his particular social, psychological and philosophical analysis, in a way which went far beyond what most of his contemporaries offered for the stage. Thus, for example, relationships between the male and female protagonists in *The Proposal* (1888–89) and in *The Bear* (1888) presage the farcical elements in the relationship between Varya and Lopakhin, the 'lovers' in *The Cherry Orchard,* where the element of farce heightens the social and psychological complexity of the relationship. Similarly, *The Wedding* is an example of Chekhov's examination of *poshlost'* – the notion of a society dominated by false ideals and superficiality. The satire typified in *The Wedding* becomes a more in-depth and humane exploration of the difficulties of living in the sterile environment of the Russian provinces in the major plays. Other plays, such as *The Evils of Tobacco* (of which six versions were written, the final one being completed in 1902), were contemporaneous with the major plays and arguably offer, in miniature, a comparable depth and complexity. In this short play,

Chekhov develops his consideration of *futlyarnost'*, how people become entrapped in habit, fulfilling social roles, while cut off from genuine human relationships. Some of the short plays are purely comic and in others, such as this one, a character has a moment of insight and understanding, the major theme of Chekhov's work.

Chekhov was familiar with vaudeville from his youth, and part of its appeal to him was as a miniature form. In 1888, he wrote, recommending the writing of vaudevilles, 'After all, the only difference between a full-length play and a one-acter is one of scale' (Chekhov 2004b: 167). Critical analyses, therefore, tend to focus on the relationship of the short plays to the rest of Chekhov's dramatic writing (see Gottlieb 1982). Zingerman discusses vaudeville as the key to Chekhov's dramaturgy, pointing out similarities between the environment of *poshlost'* in the short plays and the environment of Konstantin in *The Seagull,* Astrov in *Uncle Vanya* and that in *Three Sisters* (2001: 193). The short plays are also stylistically related to Chekhov's early short stories, where he frequently wrote 'little scenes' (*tsenki*), stories in dialogue form, such as *Drama* and *After the Benefit,* often on themes of theatre itself. He did, in fact, adapt some of these stories, such as *A Tragedian in Spite of Himself* and *The Jubilee,* for the stage. Chekhov's expression of the human condition through metatheatre is exemplified in *Swan Song.*

The best-known plays are *Swan Song (Calchas), A Dramatic Study in One Act* (1886–87), *The Bear, A Joke in One Act* (1888), *The Proposal, A Joke in One Act* (1888–89), *The Wedding, A Play in One Act* (1900), *The Evils of Tobacco, A Monologue in One-Act* (1902). Plays such as *The Bear, The Proposal* and *The Jubilee* (1891) are the most comic; the other plays acquire the mixture of pathos and comedy that is Chekhov's hallmark.

Chekhov and vaudeville

Chekhov wrote that he could write a hundred vaudevilles a year. 'Vaudeville subjects gush from me like oil from the Baku depths' (Papernyi 1982: 236). His use of the form was very different from traditional vaudeville, which was a popular form in eighteenth century France. It originally included songs (one development was operetta in the late nineteenth century), and was often satirical. Many translations of French vaudevilles were performed in Russian theatre of the early nineteenth century, but by the 1840s, Russian writers, such as P. A. Karatygin, were using the form to comment on Russian life (see Karlinsky 1985: 269–77). Late nineteenth century vaudeville satirized society, particularly the landowning and merchant classes. A favourite theme was backstage life, parodying the melodramas and bourgeois dramas on the same bill (Senelick 1997b: xii).

Russian director Nikolai Gorchakov describes Stanislavsky working at the Moscow Art Theatre in 1925, on a typical vaudeville, *Her First Night (Lev Gurych Sinichkin or The Provincial Actress's Debut)*, written in 1840 by Dmitry Lensky. *Sinichkin* comments on the social behaviour of aristocrats and actors, using the plot of a rich aristocrat who attempts to seduce a young actress, Lisa. The machinations of her actor father, Sinichkin, enable her to take the role in a play usually played by a famous actress for one night. The play is Lensky's satire of the popular melodrama *The Maiden of the Sun* by the popular German writer Kotzebue. Lisa thwarts the vengeful aristocrat and has a great success. This was a recognizable melodramatic theme and, typically for vaudevilles before Chekhov, one which, despite the satire, ended sentimentally with virtue triumphing over evil.

Many Russian actors, such as V. N. Asenkova and V. I. Zhivokini, gained fame as performers in vaudeville and Chekhov wrote some of his plays for particular comic actors. Stanislavsky played in many vaudevilles as an amateur actor. He emphasizes the 'realism' of Russian vaudeville, in that it was situated in the contemporary social milieu and about ordinary people.

> The world of vaudeville is a perfectly realistic one but the most unusual incidents occur in it every step of the way ... Characters in vaudeville are ordinary and realistic ... Their only strangeness is their absolute credulity about everything.
>
> (Gorchakov 1973: 204–5)

He gives, as an example, the way in which vaudeville characters fall in love unquestioningly, at first sight. Gorchakov notes that Stanislavsky also emphasized the 'naïveté of approach to objects' as well as relationships, giving as an example *The Bewitched Omelette,* where the entire action is based around a series of characters wanting to eat an omelette, but prevented from doing so until the complications in their relationships are resolved (1973: 224).

Vaudeville, in Russian theatre, 'formed a bridge between Russian neoclassical and realist drama' (Karlinsky 1985: 277). Chekhov embraced vaudeville as a popular form and took from it its exuberant comedy, also its satirical comment and focus on the lives of 'ordinary people' rather than 'heroes' – that is, in Chekhov's time, landowners, servants, merchants, the middle classes and artists – in the characters of his major plays. He developed the form further, experimenting with form and genre, and subverting the usual themes and sentimentality of traditional vaudeville, in order to question received norms of behaviour as he did in the major plays.

The short plays

Chekhov's first vaudeville, taking the humorous predilection for alternative titles in vaudevilles such as *Sinichkin* even further, was entitled *The Sudden Death of a Horse, or The Magnanimity of the Russian People*, and subtitled *A Statement Made on Compulsion*. Akaky Tarantulov proffers his play as a statement of protest about the conduct of the Society of Dramatic Writers and Opera Composers. This Society in fact existed and Chekhov is poking fun at the pretensions of minor dramatists. *The Fool or the Retired Captain*, published in 1883, is described as a 'scenelet from an unproduced vaudeville'. *Unclean Tragedians and Leprous Playwrights, A Horribly-Dreadfully-Excitingly-Desperate Trrragedy* is a parody of an adaptation of German melodrama (Chekhov 2006a: 272).

Not all the short plays were comic: *Along the Highway* of 1884, a dramatization of a story *In Autumn*, written in 1883, has a melodramatic end, where a drunken vagrant attacks the wife of an impoverished landowner, but realizing what he has done, pleads for pity from 'good Christians' (Chekhov 2006a: 248). Chekhov's experiments at this stage still included elements of melodrama, as *Ivanov*, one of his early full-length plays, also did.

The plots of the short plays, like the major plays, revolve around social gatherings and rituals that mark significant events in everyday life: marriages, parties, anniversaries such as *The Jubilee* (also translated as *The Anniversary*). This is the fifteenth anniversary of the opening of a commercial bank. The event, as such, is generally subverted; the celebration in *The Jubilee* turns into chaos and in *The Proposal*, no proposal takes place. Instead, the interaction or conflict between characters is one of the main strands of the comedy. As in the major plays, Chekhov reveals character through reaction to situations and events. In *The Evils of Tobacco*, the title refers to a lecture that is not given; instead the lecturer, Nyukhin, tells the audience about his unhappy life. Similarly, in *Swan Song*, an elderly actor performs soliloquies to his prompter, reflecting on the realities of his life as an actor. Again, like the major plays, the short plays often begin with an arrival, and the endings are not a resolution. Offstage characters such as Nyukhin's wife, or characters who have previously died, such as Popova's husband in *The Bear,* exert an influence on the happenings on stage.

The comic characters are consumed by trivia, have an inflated self-image and go to extremes to impose this view on others. They are prone to swift changes of attitude if they see it is in their own self-interest. Chekhov gives comic characteristics to archetypes: the widow Popova's grief is a pose, the would-be bridegroom Lomov is a hypochondriac rather than a dashing suitor. Chekhov makes stock characters original by giving them idiosyncrasies and often individualized speech patterns. Like his satirical forebears, Pushkin, Ostrovsky and Gogol, Chekhov gives his characters grotesque and comic sounding names (see Peace 1983: 142) and the plays often include specialized vocabulary indicating Chekhov's knowledge of all sorts of trades and interests. For example, *The Bear* includes discussion of Smith and Wesson guns, *The Proposal* the anatomical features of hunting dogs.

Chekhov embraces the corporeal in the gestural language of his short plays, as his characters get drunk, faint, cough, have facial tics or fall over and break the furniture. This features in the major plays: in *The Seagull*, Masha's leg 'goes to sleep', Olga in *Three Sisters* has constant headaches, in *The Cherry Orchard* Simeonov-Pishchik falls asleep and snores and Yepikhodov gets a 'frog in his throat'. The emotional reactions of the male characters are often expressed in comic physical behaviour and movements, as when Petya Trofimov rushes out of a room, upset after an argument, and falls downstairs (Tait 2002: 82). There are farcical elements like this in the short and longer plays – particularly in *The Cherry Orchard* – but as Gottlieb notes, farce in Chekhov is a far remove from the dehumanized chaos of farces in the tradition originating with French writers such as Eugène Scribe, Georges Feydeau and Eugène Labiche (2000: 236). Chekhov's work has more in common with Russian tragifarce, the satirical work of writers such as Gogol (see Listengarten 2000: 56–72).

The Bear – A Joke in One Act

Chekhov's success in breaking previous stage conventions, even in light comedy, was indicated when this play was initially forbidden by the censor, who wrote 'The unfavourable impression produced by this highly peculiar theme is increased by the coarseness and impropriety of tone throughout the play, so that I would have thought it quite unsuitable for performance on the stage' (Gottlieb 1982: 63). This decision was overturned at a higher level on condition that some cuts were made. It was first performed at the Korsh Theatre in Moscow in October 1888 and became highly successful. The plot derives from *Les Jurons de Cadillac, une comedie en une acte* by Pierre Berton, which Chekhov had seen translated into Russian as *Conquerors Are Above Criticism* (in which the famous comic actor Nikolai Solovtsov played), and also from Petronius' ancient Roman story 'The Widow of Ephesus' (see Senelick 1985: 57).

Smirnov, a middle-aged landowner, visits Popova, a 'dimpled' young widow. Chekhov subverts the image of the mourning widow through Popova's comic self-dramatization. She refuses to leave the house despite the fact that her dead husband was unfaithful to her, she is determined to be faithful to his memory in order to 'show him I know how to love' (Chekhov 2005: 5). She talks to his portrait and requests that Toby, her former husband's favourite horse, should be fed extra oats to show her dedication to everything he held dear. Her attitudes are echoed with pathos as well as comedy in characters in the major plays: Varya in *The Cherry Orchard* and Popova say they want to enter a nunnery, but do not do so – in Varya this is more than a pose as it is understandable that she wants to escape from the difficulty of her current life. Masha in *The Seagull* casts herself as 'in mourning for her life' and therefore always wears black (Chekhov 2005: 136); underlying her dramatic pose, unlike Popova's, is depression.

Smirnov, like characters in *Ivanov* and *The Cherry Orchard*, is desperate for cash to pay off the interest on the mortgage of his estate. Popova refuses to pay off her husband's debts in her bereaved state and says Smirnov must wait until the return of the bailiff. Their quarrel reveals their indignation at the way they have been treated by the opposite sex. Counterbalancing Popova's pose, Smirnov takes that of a woman-hating Don Juan – he has fought three duels over women, twelve women have left him and he has left nine. He says he has supported women's emancipation but knows that every woman's soul is that of a 'common or garden-variety crocodile' (Chekhov 2005: 11). Traditional ideas of femininity and masculinity are humorously subverted – the 'bear' who threatens he will toss the old servant Luka 'like a salad' suddenly clutches his heart and feels faint whereas Popova fearlessly accepts Smirnov's challenge to a duel. Smirnov says, 'Shooting at one's fellow human – that's what I call equality, women's rights!' (Chekhov 2005: 14). He has to show her how to use the gun and, putting his arms round her to do so, falls in love with her. Intense hatred is rapidly transformed into romance and Smirnov proposes. The characters' pretensions to mourning and to misogyny are debunked and there is a final bathetic moment, when a 'prolonged kiss' – how a conventional vaudeville would end (Gottlieb 1982: 61) – is witnessed by the servants, who have entered armed with pitchforks to fight off Smirnov. Popova tells Luka that today there will be no oats for Toby, signalling the transference of her affections from her husband's horse to Smirnov, a comic subversion of a traditional romantic ending as she pronounces on trivial matters in a self-important manner.

Guns feature in all the full-length plays, an example of allusiveness of the objects Chekhov places on stage. Firearms are used by Chekhov 'to bridge the gap between conventional melodrama and the emerging Symbolism of the 1880s' (Woods 1982: 254). Chekhov parodies melodramatic convention, where duels were fought on stage, often over a woman, in his use of the duel. The romanticized duel in 'defence of honour' was also often depicted in relation to the 'superfluous man' in Russian literature by writers such as Pushkin, Lermontov and Turgenev, and Tolstoy also described duelling scenes. Chekhov uses the duel for comic effect here. He also explored it as social convention, using it to express deep conflicts and subverting its dramatic effect in stories such as *The Duel* and in the plays. In *Ivanov*, Lvov insults Ivanov in public, provoking Borkin to challenge him to a duel (Chekhov 2005: 82). There the idea of the duel focuses differing ideas about morality as in *The Duel*, where it highlights two different philosophies: the Social Darwinist is pitted against the 'superfluous man'. In *The Seagull*, Konstantin tries to call Trigorin out to a duel, expressing his feelings about Trigorin's relationship with his mother and with Nina. In *The Wedding,* the corrupt social ethos is encapsulated in the fact that the honourable elderly sea captain, when insulted, says 'If you were respectable people I could challenge someone to a duel but now what can I do?' (Chekhov 2005: 108). In *Three Sisters,* a duel is fought offstage, which has tragic consequences in the death of Tusenbach, the unloved lover of Irina, who is called out by Solyony, who also loves Irina. His supposed duel of honour is revealed to be an insane act.

As in the major plays, Chekhov extends the frame of reference by the unobtrusive presence of servants. Luka is not a traditional comic servant, but an old man. He witnesses much of the action and has a good insight into the true nature of his mistress. The servants in *The Seagull*, the nannies in *Uncle Vanya* and *Three Sisters* patiently watch the drama of the gentry being played out while getting on with practical matters of keeping the household going.

The Proposal

The Proposal was written initially in 1888 and had its first production in St Petersburg on 12 April 1889. Later that year it was played at Tsarskoye Selo for Alexander III. This vaudeville, in seven scenes, satirizes the conventional comedy plot of lovers whose path to the altar involves overcoming parental opposition. Lomov visits his neighbour Chubukov with the intention of proposing to his daughter Natasha. As Popova's dimpled cheeks belie her tragic self-image, Lomov's image as a romantic suitor is debunked by his description as a 'healthy, well-fed hypochondriac'. (Characters in the major plays are also given wider dimensions through contradictions: Lopakhin, the successful businessman, has 'delicate, gentle fingers like an artist' (Chekhov 2005: 364), and Sonya, the warm-hearted Christian in *Uncle Vanya*, has 'shrewd, suspicious eyes' (Chekhov 2005: 216).) Lomov reveals in a monologue that he thinks a well-regulated married life will be good for his health. As with Smirnov, his masculinity is subverted; he feels faint: he has to keep drinking water, has a ringing in his ears, and a twitch. Chubukov thinks at first that Lomov has come to borrow money and so, far from opposing the marriage, when he finds out the purpose of the visit, greets the idea with glee. Again the idea of romantic love is satirized as he assures Lomov that his daughter is 'in love like a cat', and sends her in to see him, telling her cryptically that 'a dealer has come for the merchandise' (Chekhov 2006a: 436–37).

Lomov, formally dressed in a tailcoat and white gloves, meets Natasha who is prosaically wearing an apron, as she has been shelling peas. He begins his proposal by recalling the friendly, even familial relationships between the Lomov and Chubukov clans. He mentions how their land adjoins at Bullock Fields, precipitating an argument with Natasha about the ownership of the fields. The argument escalates: Chubukov enters. Lomov threatens legal action and insults are traded about each family, satirizing the ideal of noble families:

LOMOV: Every member of the Lomov clan has been honorable and not a single one has been tried for embezzlement like your beloved uncle!

CHUBUKOV: But every member of your Lomov clan has been crazy as a loon!

NATALIYA STEPANOVA: Every one, every one, every one!

CHUBUKOV: Your grandfather drank like a fish, and that young auntie of yours, you know the one, Nastasiya Mikhailovna, ran off with an architect and so on …

LOMOV: And your mother was lopsided.

(Chekhov 2006a: 442)

Lomov becomes increasingly incapacitated, claims that his left leg is paralysed, that he has spots before his eyes and staggers out. Chubukov reveals that Lomov had the gall to propose marriage. In a comic reversal, Natasha, fainting hysterically, demands that Lomov is brought back and father and daughter turn on each other. Lomov returns and Natasha is prepared to concede her purportedly deeply held and principled stance, if it will get her a husband. She changes the subject to hunting, to allow Lomov time to bring himself to propose. The conversation again becomes an argument about whether Dasher, Lomov's hunting dog, is superior to Splasher, the Chubukov's dog. Palpitations ensue for Lomov, Chubukov re-enters in scene eight but becomes so heated he appears to faint, Natasha has hysterics and Lomov passes out, at which point Natasha fears her potential husband is dead. Chubukov demands a knife or pistol to kill himself, to escape from the torment. The couple kiss and claim to be happy, though Lomov's leg has gone numb. They recover to carry on the argument about the dogs, while Chubukov attempts to shout over them for champagne, the main irony being that Lomov has not actually proposed.

The situation reflects social actuality: issues of marriage and property in the landowning classes. Chekhov questions 'nobility' here as he does in *The Cherry Orchard*. Marriage is a major theme in numerous stories from more satirical early stories such as *Before the Wedding* (1880) and *The Trousseau* (1883), to *Anna on the Neck* (1895) and *A Marriageable Girl* (1903). Rather than using it as a plot device signifying reconciliation, a traditional comedy ending, Chekhov's depiction of marriage as an institution has its antecedents in Gogol's comedy *Marriage,* in which the main character Podkolyossin cannot decide whether he should marry. Chekhov did not marry until he was forty-one and accounts of his previous relationships and his letters demonstrate an ambivalence towards the institution as a whole. In *The Proposal*, the arguments indicate that the future of the relationship will be constant bickering. The expectation in *The Cherry Orchard* is that Varya and Lopakhin will marry, but the proposal never takes place. *The Wedding* is about the party after a wedding, which is certainly not a love match. Masha, in *The Seagull*, marries Medvedenko in the attempt to forget Konstantin who does not love her. In *Three Sisters*, one sister is unhappily married; the two others desire marriage and one agrees to marry a man she does not love, who dies the day before the wedding. Andrey, the brother, makes a marriage he comes to regret. The gesture in *Ivanov* is the most extreme, with the suicide of the groom just before the ceremony. At the same time, Chekhov often indicates how marriage for a woman meant social and financial security. In *The Lady with the Little Dog* (1899), for example, it is clear that if the heroine Anna left her husband to be with the man she loves, she would be socially ostracized.

The Wedding

This play was first performed in Moscow on November 28th in 1900 at the Hunt Club for the Society of Art and Literature. Chekhov described it as *A Play in One Act*, distinguishing it from the earlier *Jokes in One Act*, signalling that this play was to be more than pure comedy. *The Wedding* presents a merchant society in which husbands and status can be bought. The 'wedding' is, in fact, the reception after the marriage of Dashenka, daughter of retired civil servant Yevdokhim Zakharovich Zhigalov and Nastasya Timofeevna, to Epaminond Maksimovich Aplombov. 'Aplombov' indicates salesmanship; Zhigalov has connotations of 'cunning rogue'. The comedy centres on the characters' pretensions. Nyunin, an insurance agent, has been given money to bribe a general to attend the wedding so that it can be seen as a social event with high-ranking guests. Zmeyukina, one of the guests, quotes poetry, sings and seeks 'atmosphere'. Chekhov notes in contrast to the romantic 'aristocratical' image she wishes to present of herself that she is 'a midwife, about 30, in a crimson dress', and Yat, another guest, points out that she is sweating (Chekhov 2005: 100). Aplombov represents himself as a good catch for Dashenka, describing himself as a 'respectable person with good references' and aiming to appear cultivated in his use of French (Chekhov 2005: 98). Like Natasha in *Three Sisters*, he mispronounces this to comic effect, and his true status is revealed as an appraiser in a pawnshop. Nastasya and Dashenka debunk money-grabbing Aplombov's claims to be educated, the rejection of education being the epitome of *poshlost'* in Chekhov:

DASHENKA: The gentleman's just trying to show off his eddication, talking about what nobody understands.
NASTASYA TIMOFEEVNA: We've lived all our life without education, thank God, and this is the third daughter we've married off to a good man.

(Chekhov 2005: 102)

The ignorant Zhigalov views electricity, a symbol of hope of Russia's modernization, as 'swindling the common man'. His hypocrisy is revealed in his attitude to a guest, Kharlampy Spiridonovich

Dymba, a Greek caterer: 'Greeks are like Armenians or Gypsies. Can't sell you a sponge or a goldfish without trying to put one over on you' (Chekhov 2005: 100–1). He claims that he and his family are simple, ordinary and decent people, a claim that is undermined as the true preoccupation of the characters is revealed. Aplombov says his mother-in-law promised him two lottery tickets as part of the dowry, and that if she does not produce them, he will make her daughter's life 'a living hell. On my honor as a gentleman!' Natasya Timofeevna ignores this; later she answers Yat's statement that the couple must be marrying for love, as the dowry is skimpy, by listing the dowry as 'a thousand roubles cash money, three lady's coats, a bed and all the furniture' (Chekhov 2005: 102).

The 'general', Fyodor Yakovlevich Revunov-Karaulov (whose name has connotations of 'calling for help'), arrives; he is an elderly deaf gentleman who talks incessantly about ship manoeuvres, using nautical vocabulary. When it is revealed that he is not a general but a retired naval captain second class the comedy turns to pathos. He realizes that Nyunin was given money to bribe a general to appear and has kept the money. The old man is shocked and disgusted. The characters' claims to 'decency' are unmasked; Revunov says 'To insult an old man this way, a navy man, an officer who has seen active duty! ... If you were respectable people I could challenge someone to a duel.' In despair, he shouts 'Waiter, show me the way out!' The Russian word for waiter, *chelovek*, also means 'person' or human being, so the old man includes the audience in his cry for help (Chekhov 2005: 109).

Swan Song – *a dramatic study in one act*

Swan Song was first written in 1886–87 and performed at the Korsh Theatre in Moscow in February 1888. It was written for Vladimir Davydov, a popular comic actor, as was *The Evils of Tobacco*. An actor performs in a theatre: Chekhov's metatheatrical presentation of the human condition. Arkadina and Nina both perform in *The Seagull*, which is structured around a play written by Konstantin. Chekhov also wrote a number of stories where the subject is the Russian stage, between 1880 and 1889, including *Calchas, Stage Manager Under the Sofa (a story from the wings), A Tragic Actor, A Comic Actor, A Critic, Death of An Actor, After the Benefit, The Jubilee.*

There is also *After the Theatre* (1892) and more serious stories feature the theatre and theatre people including *The Darling, A Dreary Story*, *In Moscow* and *The Lady with the Little Dog*. The piece was based on the story, *Calchas*. Chekhov changed the name of the play to *Swan Song*, in Russian, *Lebedinaya Pesnya*, of which he wrote 'A long bitter-sweet name, but I couldn't think of another' (Chekhov 1976b 3: 43).

Calchas, in Greek mythology, was a seer. The name of the main character is Svetlovidov, which has connotations of 'light' and 'sight' or 'view'. The play presents the Chekhovian theme of gaining insight and the language used refers to seeing. Svetlovidov, who is wearing the costume of Calchas from Offenbach's *La Belle Helene,*[1] has given his benefit performance. This was an evening in Russian theatre where a leading actor was allowed to select the plays and to take the box office profits. After the performance, he gets drunk and later wakes up in the theatre, where Nikita Ivanych, the theatre prompter, an old man, secretly spends each night, as he has no home. Svetlovidov describes to Nikita how he was of a noble family and had served in the army before becoming an actor. He fell in love with a beautiful young woman, whom he wanted to marry, but she refused to marry an actor, as the profession was seen as disreputable. He 'saw the light': the stage, which he had seen as 'sacred art', now seemed to him nothing but vulgar entertainment, in the eyes of the public he was 'practically a whore! ... To flatter its vanity, it makes my acquaintance, but won't stoop to let me marry its sister, its daughter.' He gave up, 'put no stock in anything', played clowns and cheapened his talent. Now he has a different insight; he sees sixty-eight years have passed and perceives that his life is over (Chekhov 2006a: 311).

Nikita attempts to comfort him. Svetlovidov recalls how he has been moved by the work of great writers and performs speeches from Pushkin's *Boris Godunov*, *King Lear*, *Hamlet*, Pushkin's *Poltava*, with Nikita in supporting roles. All the plays refer to the plight of elderly men. He is inspired and declares that his life isn't over yet: 'Old age can go to hell! ... Strength is gushing through my veins like a fountain – there's youth, vigor, life!' Petrushka and Yegorka, the theatre watchmen, are heard. Svetlovidov sees Nikita crying and his exaltation fades. He questions his life again: he is 'a squeezed lemon, a dripping icicle, a rusty nail', he is only useful in minor parts in serious plays and Nikita is 'an old theatre rat'. Then he rallies himself and Nikita, reciting from *Othello* and making his exit as Chatsky in Griboedov's *Woe from Wit*, a bitter goodbye, as Chatsky was alienated from his social milieu (Chekhov 2006a: 313–15).

The symbolism of the provincial theatre setting after the audience have gone home – with the dark hole of the auditorium and Nikita's appearance like a ghost in a white dressing gown – suggests death. In this poignant tragicomedy, Svetlovidov faces the thought of death, unsure whether his life has been worthwhile while declaiming to an empty theatre, dressed in a comedy costume.

The Evils of Tobacco – *scene-monologue*

In *The Evils of Tobacco*, also translated as *On the Harmfulness of Tobacco*, Chekhov makes use of the comic stereotype of the hen-pecked husband and also the 'little man', an image from nineteenth century Russian literature. The 'little man', who figured in the works of Pushkin, Gogol, Dostoevsky and Turgenev, was depicted as the submissive product of a repressive and hierarchical society, often meeting a tragic end because of his inability to assert himself against authority. The 'little man' also occurred in Russian vaude-ville, as a sentimentalized and sometimes ridiculous version of the type (see Obraztsova 1993: 49–50).

Nyukhin (the name has connotations of sniffing) is described as 'the husband of his wife', who runs a music school and a girls' boarding school (Chekhov 2006a: 318). Chekhov's original version of this 'scene-monologue', written in 1886, parodied public lectures given on improving themes, which the government promoted in the 1880s. He rewrote it in 1887, 1889, 1890 and 1902 and completed the final version, one of his last works, in 1903. In the first version, Markel Ivanych Nyukhin is speaking at a provincial club and begins 'pompously', saying that 'true scholarship is modest', but his wife agreed he would give this lecture in a good cause. His 'scholarship' is in question immediately as he says he is 'a stranger to academic degrees' and he derides the idea of the public lecture which imparts to the public, as he says, a 'sense of superior knowledge'. He begins his lecture describing the chemical properties of tobacco but then has an asthma attack. His pompousness disappears and his true situation is revealed as he recalls his first attack on the day the sixth of his ten daughters was born. He speaks about his plight as a hen-pecked husband, whose wife has taught the school pupils to regard him as a 'stuffed dummy'. In taking snuff Nyukhin finds that the children have substituted some noxious powder. The daughters never laugh (he now says there are nine of them) and none are married but 'just by looking at them, one could guarantee that they would make the most splendid wives'. Finally, Nyukhin cries about how he has failed his wife (Chekhov 2006a: 323).

In the final version, performed first by A. I. Kuprin in Moscow in 1901, Ivan Ivanovich Nyukhin wears a threadbare tailcoat. The monologue is more absurd and rambling – there are segues about insects, which recur as a theme throughout, and all the daughters were born on the 13th of the month, they live at number 13, a house with 13 window panes and that is why Nyukhin says his life is such a failure. His wife's stinginess and her abusive behaviour are emphasized. When she is in a bad mood she calls him 'dummy, viper or Satan' (Chekhov 2006a: 968). She deprives him of food and he is always hungry. He fears his wife and thinks his daughters have not married because they are shy and meet no one, as his wife puts off visitors.

A key difference from the first version is that Chekhov presents Nyukhin as a comic figure initially, but then draws the audience into an understanding of his plight. He wants to run away from this 'shabby, vulgar, despicable life, which has turned him into a pathetic old idiot'. In this version he makes a gesture that indicates, like the actor in *Swan Song*, he has some new insight into his situation. He tears off the threadbare tailcoat he wore to be married in thirty years ago, the symbol of his unhappy marriage, and defiantly stamps on it (Chekhov is here referencing Gogol's classic story of a 'little man', *The Overcoat*). When he sees that his wife has arrived and is waiting for him, he asks for complicity from the audience, they should tell his wife that 'the dummy behaved with dignity'. His final words in Latin are a reminder of the pomposity with which Nyukhin began his monologue '*Dixi et animam levavi!*' but the pomposity has been revealed to conceal his anguish (Chekhov 2006a: 970). The phrase means 'I have spoken and my soul is the easier for it'. The audience have been cast in the role of confidant to a struggling, unhappy man, who once studied at the university, and has now been consumed by *poshlost'*. Other Chekhov characters, like Lebedev in *Ivanov*, see themselves as having not lived up to the promise of their time at university.

Other 'little men' in Chekhov include Tolkachov from the comic short play, *An Involuntary Tragedian (From The Life of Vacationers)*, written in 1889. Tolkachov, 'the father of a family', describes himself as a 'doormat' and is worn out carrying out his family's demands. As with Nyukhin, comedy and poignancy are blended in Medvedenko, the impoverished schoolteacher in *The Seagull*, devoted to Masha, who marries him though she does not love him. Also, Telegin (Waffles) in *Uncle Vanya* sacrifices his life in loyalty to his wife, who left him for another man on his wedding day. Chekhov uses the image of the 'little man' to question the institution of the family and family loyalties.

Key productions

After their initial reception in Russia, the short plays were performed widely and were staged in Europe and America. The first British production of *The Bear* was in 1911, in America 1915. Directors used them in experimental productions after the Russian revolution, recognizing how far Chekhov broke with theatrical convention even in the short plays. There was *The Wedding* in Evgeny Vakhtangov's production at the MAT Third Studio in 1920 and Meyerhold's *33 Swoons* in 1935. In addition, Hallie Flanagan, who became director of the Federal Theatre Project in America, staged *A Marriage Proposal* in 1928, using a different style for each of the three acts: realism, expressionism and Meyerhold's constructivism for the third act.

The Wedding

In 1920, Vakhtangov, one of Stanislavsky's most brilliant and innovative students at the MAT, staged a studio production of *The Wedding, The Jubilee* and a dramatization of Chekhov's story *Horse Thieves*. He reworked *The Wedding* in 1921, producing it along with Maeterlinck's one-act play *The Miracle of St Antony* in what became the Third MAT Studio. Vakhtangov asserted that Chekhov's work was more tragic than lyrical but this was tragedy of the everyday, of lives consumed by triviality (*poshlost'*). He had planned a double bill with Pushkin's *Feast in Time of Plague*, demonstrating the difference between heroic tragedy and what he saw as Chekhov's tragedy. He wrote, 'When someone shoots themselves it is not lyrical. It is either *poshlost'* or a heroic deed. And both ... have their tragic masks' (Vakhtangov 1959: 188). He defined Chekhov's 'supertask', using Stanislavsky's term, as 'the struggle with *poshlost'*, petty bourgeois philistinism and the dream of a better life' (Simonov 1969: 72). In *The Wedding*, he wished to demonstrate this struggle to affirm the new ideals of the Revolution and the rejection of the former way of life under the autocracy of the Tsars. The tragicomic production was a vehicle for Vakhtangov's 'imaginative realism', the techniques he developed to marry Stanislavsky's 'truth as in life' with imaginative expression. He took the play into the realm of the grotesque. Ruben Simonov, who played the part of Dymba, noted that the distortion of reality in the grotesque and in 'eccentric' acting was intended to heighten the audience's understanding of life (1969: 24). A bleak picture of humanity was painted and the isolation, the *futlyarnost'*, of each of the characters was emphasized. Gorchakov noted that the production suggested that the characters thought they were living life, celebrating the wedding, dancing and making merry: 'they think they live, but in reality someone is pulling the strings and telling them; "That's how it should be".' (Gorchakov 1960: 29).

The production was widely recognized as a new, post-revolutionary interpretation, 'the angry pen of a clever satirist – not caricature but a deepened realism, condensing, exaggerating the internal, plastic sketch of the show to the utmost expressiveness, to the grotesque' (Litvinenko 1981: 68). Vakhtangov was successful in marrying his vision with Chekhov's in a way that went beyond the political circumstances of the time. 'Chekhov the satirist acquired a power no one had previously imagined. True the satire's target was bourgeois vulgarity, this time viewed not as an Aunt Sally for Marxist denunciation, but rather *sub specie aeternitatis* (Senelick 1997a: 120–21).

33 Swoons

In 1935, Meyerhold produced *The Jubilee, The Bear* and *The Proposal* at GosTIM as *33 Swoons* in Moscow for the seventy-fifth

Figure 3.1 33 Swoons by Meyerhold (reproduced by permission of the
A. A. Bakhrushin State Central Theatrical Museum)

anniversary of Chekhov's birth. Like Vakhtangov, he attempted to
find a way to link the plays with the politics of the Revolution. At
this point in his career, as artists were becoming more and more
constrained by Stalin's policies on art, Meyerhold was under attack
for 'formalism', that is, seen as emphasizing aesthetic form rather
than content which should further the causes of communism. He
therefore asserted the social significance of the plays, for example,
adapting *The Jubilee* so that the bank director Shipukhin was more
central, implying that he had been fraudulent and noting that
Chekhov had written the piece to point out an actual case of fraud
at the Skopinsky bank (Hoover 1974: 225). The characters were
'neurasthenics', possessing 'the lethargy, the loss of will-power that
is typical of Chekhov's characters', and Meyerhold said that his
research had confirmed 'the unusually high incidence of neur-
asthenia amongst the intelligentsia of the eighties and nineties', of
Chekhov's society, the former regime providing the social pre-
conditions for such a phenomenon (Braun 1998: 283). He aimed to
strengthen the satire in order to provide a critique of that society,

noting the importance of satire in vaudeville since the time of Karatygin and Lensky. He aimed to expose the shallowness of the characters, such as the 'soap bubble' Shipuchin and the hypocrisy of the characters in *The Bear*.[2]

As a comic routine (or *lazzo*, from *commedia dell'arte*, as Meyerhold referred to it) that would unite the three vaudevilles, Meyerhold identified thirty-three occasions when the characters fainted or nearly fainted in the three. Placards were shown showing what number faint or swoon it was so 'the audience know they will get their money's worth – if there are only 32 they should get their money back'.[3] There was an orchestral accompaniment, carefully arranged for each swoon, including music by Grieg and Tchaikovsky for *The Bear*, Strauss and Offenbach for *The Jubilee*. The set made use of screens, a staircase which reminded one commentator of Meyerhold's constructivist sets, and the set was brightly lit (Sitkovetskaya 1993: 147). Meyerhold introduced Masha, a maid, in *The Proposal*. She stood holding a broom, looking from one character to another as the arguments escalated. Two other characters ran on at the end to present flowers to the engaged couple, dancing a comic quadrille with them, the traditional end of a vaudeville. He also introduced elaborate stage business, for example Lomov's antics trying to get his glove off. Chubukov wore baggy underclothing and a dressing gown to contrast with Lomov's formal frock coat (which had a collar that was too small to further comic effect). Each swoon was carefully choreographed, with Lomov pouring water into a glass, 'sensing a swoon coming on', feeling his heart becoming more and more agitated, panting and speaking his words in an agonized way.[4]

Meyerhold is reported as saying that too much physical action stopped the flow of the text: 'we tried to be too clever and consequently lost sight of the humour ... the result was a disaster' (Braun 1998: 284). It is difficult to know to what extent Meyerhold was attempting to ward off criticism by saying this, as political hostility towards him increased. Contemporary commentators tend to echo Meyerhold's self-evaluation: 'Like Vakhtangov, Meyerhold was reducing Chekhov's people to puppets, but unlike Vakhtangov, he was unable to infuse them with deeper meaning' (Senelick 1997a: 129). Reviews at the time indicate that the productions were far from a 'disaster', some criticizing the productions on ideological grounds, that it was 'not true to life', whereas others defended Meyerhold's interpretation, referring to the fact that the same could be said of many of Chekhov's stories which had unusual, even eccentric features. One reviewer wrote that Meyerhold's 'inventive' staging was faithful to Chekhov, while providing a contrast to the usual interpretations.[5] Another judged this to be a successful production, a 'tragicomedy, pathetic satire on the mortal illness of a class-based society'.[6]

Talia Theatre

The connection between Meyerhold and Chekhov was explored more recently by Talia Theatre in Manchester, England. In 2004, the group mounted a production of Chekhov's vaudevilles (*The Evils of Tobacco*, *The Bear* and *The Proposal*) directed by Gennadi Bogdanov, director of the Moscow School of Theatrical Biomechanics and teacher of Biomechanics at the Russian Academy of Theatre Arts (GITIS). Bogdanov studied with Nikolai Kustov, who was trained by Meyerhold and kept alive the teaching of Biomechanics, Meyerhold's physical theatre training technique, while Meyerhold's work was suppressed in the Soviet Union. Working with Bogdanov, Talia attempted to find a balance between using Biomechanics to physicalize the text, producing exaggerated characters, and allowing character to emerge from the relationships in the text.[7]

The Sneeze

The Sneeze is an adaptation by Michael Frayn of *The Bear*, *The Harmfulness of Tobacco*, *The Proposal*, *Swansong* and several short stories: *Drama* 1887, *The Alien Corn* (adapted from *In a Foreign Land* 1885), *The Sneeze* (adapted from *The Death of a Government Official* 1883), *The Inspector-General* (adapted from *An Awl in a Sack* 1885). In *The Death of a Government Official*, a clerk sneezes on the bald head of an official of high rank and goes to extreme lengths to apologize, eventually dying from panic about what might happen as a result of his sneeze. The story owes a debt to Gogol's *The Overcoat*, which also treats disaster befalling a 'little man' in Russia's hierarchical society, and was also based on an incident that took place at the Bolshoi Theatre, so was related to Chekhov.

British comic actor Rowan Atkinson, famous from the TV show *Blackadder* and *Mr Bean*, first performed the show at the Aldwych Theatre, London, in 1988 with Cheryl Campbell and Timothy West each playing a series of roles. Theatricality was emphasized, and the skill of the actors in performing the swift *volte-faces* of the vaudeville characters, physical comedy routines such as Atkinson's elaborations of the clerk's role, performing 'suicidal cleansing operations on the gleaming bald head'.[8]

Frayn's conception of the production emphasized 'farce'; he saw the plays as similar to English and French farces where 'their characters are reduced by their passions to the level of blind and inflexible machines'.[9] Darker aspects of the comedy were suggested: West brought out the 'comedy of death' in *Swan Song*, and the government clerk's antics acquired a pathos as it was clear he was heading for disgrace and starvation.[10] Reviewers commented on how the production revealed Chekhov as entertainer in a way that remains unusual for the British stage.

Conclusion

A variety of approaches have been taken to Chekhov's short plays exemplifying their versatility, as vehicles for comic actors or for highly physicalized, even grotesque performances. The fact that they are so often revisited is an indication that they offer a view of humanity which transcends the social conditions of the time when they were written, as Vakhtangov demonstrated. In most of the short plays, Chekhov's view of how the serious and the comic are entwined in life is apparent. He once said that he had an idea for a vaudeville where the hero dies at the end: after all, this was 'true to life. Isn't that the way it happens? People are laughing and joking, and suddenly – bang! Curtain!' (Kataev 2002: 186).

4 Suicide and survival
Ivanov and *The Seagull*

Both *Ivanov* and *The Seagull* feature individuals in provincial
Russia of the late 1880s–1890s who refuse to settle for a banal existence (*poshlost'*) and instead pursue their desires for social change
or artistic fulfilment. Nikolai Ivanov pioneers new farming methods
and aspires to bring about social reform. In *The Seagull*, Konstantin
Treplyov wants to revolutionize the theatre of his time and Nina
Zarechnaya wants to transcend social norms for upper-class women
and become an actress. Chekhov rejects the stereotypical depiction
of heroes struggling within an oppressive environment typical of
much Russian literature and offers a complex study; Ivanov and
Treplyov's own lack of understanding of the realities of their
situation and a lack of understanding by those around them of
their visions and ambitions lead to self-destruction. Both plays end
with a suicide. In 1887, Chekhov's adviser Grigorevich had suggested, after a wave of suicides by young people in Russia, that
Chekhov should prove his commitment to social concerns by
addressing this topic. Suicide occurs as a theme in stories such as
Volodya, and all the major plays as well as *Ivanov* and *The Seagull*.
In *The Wood-Demon*, Uncle Zhorzh commits suicide. In *Uncle
Vanya*, Vanya takes a bottle of morphine with the intent to commit
suicide, but is dissuaded. In *Three Sisters* Vershinin's wife regularly
attempts it. In *The Cherry Orchard* Ranevskaya has attempted
suicide in the past. As the plays progress, the act of suicide or
attempted suicide moves offstage or into the play's prehistory, but
that does not reduce its importance in Chekhov's depiction of
characters seeking to find the purpose of their lives. Ivanov verba-
lizes the existential problem: 'Who am I, why am I alive, what

do I want?' (Chekhov 2005: 81). Among Chekhov's characters, there are those who are imprisoned by pessimistic attitudes and cannot find a reason to go on living, whereas others, even in difficult circumstances, find a way to go on and shape their own destiny.

IVANOV – A DRAMA IN FOUR ACTS (1887–89)

Nikolai Alekseevich Ivanov is thirty-five years old and owns a provincial estate in central Russia. Inspired by populist ideals of the 1870s, he has experimented with radical farming methods and is in charge of the district Council for Peasant Affairs. He has defied convention by marrying a Jewish woman, Sarra, who takes the name Anna Petrovna. She dies of tuberculosis between Acts 3 and 4, neglected by her husband and isolated from her family, who did not accept her marriage. Ivanov's farming experiments have failed and he is in substantial debt. Borkin, a relative and Ivanov's estate manager, proposes dishonest moneymaking schemes but Ivanov refuses to collude with this. Ivanov was one of only three university-educated men in the district until the recent arrival of Dr Lvov; the others are Count Shabelsky, Ivanov's uncle, who lives with him and Pavel Kirillych Lebedev, a neighbour, who runs the local *zemstvo*. Shabelsky and Lebedev were at university in the 1860s, the period of reform and optimism, but are now demoralized. Ivanov, too, is disappointed, exhausted to the point of breakdown, and cannot cope with his wife's illness.

Like Astrov in *Uncle Vanya*, he finds a temporary diversion from his problems in romance. Sasha, Lebedev's daughter, thinks herself in love with Ivanov and defends him against Lvov, who condemns Ivanov for his unkindness to Anna and his attentions to Sasha. Ivanov is the subject of gossip among his neighbours, who lead trivial lives, playing cards, drinking, preoccupied with money – the portrayal of these characters adds a comic dimension to the play. In the last act, after Anna's death, Ivanov is about to marry Sasha, though he knows that her love for him is a romantic fantasy. He decides that he will ruin Sasha's life if he marries her, that he is nothing but a bad influence on those around him and shoots himself.

The 'superfluous man'

In *Ivanov*, Chekhov problematizes the concept of the individual in conflict with social norms. This was a major theme in Russian literature, including Pushkin's *Evgeny Onegin*, Griboyedov's Chatsky in *Woe from Wit* and Lermontov's Pechorin in *A Hero of Our Time* (see Chances 1978, 2001). Turgenev's Chulkaturin in *The Diary of a Superfluous Man* (1850) perceives himself to be at odds with his society, blaming fate. He writes, 'It is quite clear that nature did not count on my making an appearance in this world; subsequently, she has treated me like an unexpected and uninvited guest' (Turgenev 1984: 20). Other figures include Goncharov's *Oblomov* (1859), a nobleman, who is so paralysed by indecision that he does not get out of bed for the first 150 pages of the novel. The 'superfluous man' in literature was a member of the nobility, an idealist and a politicized figure, whose tragic indecision arose partly from political restrictions and partly from a fatal flaw of character.

For Chekhov, the 'superfluous man' was not a tragic figure but a romantic cliché. In 1891, he wrote *In Moscow,* a story about an aristocrat who sees himself as a 'Moscow Hamlet'. The figure of Hamlet here is not Shakespeare's but a Russian image, linked with the 'superfluous man' discussed in Turgenev's lecture of 1858, *Hamlet and Don Quixote*; someone who lacks the will to act (see Gottlieb and Allain 2000: 234). Chekhov's Moscow Hamlet is no victim of fate but responsible for his own situation; his boredom and his cynical and nihilistic stance are rooted, as he himself acknowledges, in the need to conceal the fact that he is uneducated, though he passes himself off as 'very clever and unusually important'. He knows that he could have chosen to live his life otherwise, 'studied ... built wonderful bridges in Moscow, traded with China and Persia, brought down the death rate, fought the ignorance, corruption and vileness which stops us living ... ' (Chekhov 1982a 7: 502, 506).

Chekhov subverts the image of the 'superfluous man' further in *Ivanov*. His aim in writing the play was to sum up:

> everything written thus far about whining, despondent people, and of having my *Ivanov* put a stop to this sort of writing. It

seemed to me that all Russian novelists and playwrights feel a need to portray dejected men and that they all write by instinct, without a clear-cut picture or position on the matter.

(Chekhov 1973: 84)

Chekhov's position is that it is too easy to blame society or faults of character for a lack of action. Instead, he attempts to give a detailed depiction of the breakdown of a talented and dedicated man who has attempted to contribute to the modernization of Russia, presenting moral, psychological and philosophical problems. However, Chekhov's play was so radical as to be widely misunderstood.

The rewriting of *Ivanov*

The first version of the play was written in 1887, at the request of E. P. Karpov, the owner of the Korsh Theatre, Moscow, where light comedies and vaudevilles usually played, and the premiere took place on 19 November. Chekhov's portrayal of Ivanov's behaviour towards his wife met with a shocked reaction and the play confounded the expectations of audiences used to a moral: one critic wrote, 'Where would you meet such scoundrels, such soulless rascals? ... What coarse ignorance of psychology, what an unpardonable slander of human nature!' (Papernyi 1982: 56). The first performance, according to Chekhov, provoked screaming, yelling, clapping, and hissing (1973: 73–75). Mikhail Chekhov also describes the mixed reception of the first night, some expecting a farce from a writer they knew from the comic stories in *Fragments*, others something new and serious (1981: 120). Chekhov attributed some of the problem to the acting; the play was under-rehearsed and the leading actress distracted by her daughter's fatal illness at the time of the performance. Chekhov wrote to his brother that the second performance with another actress went well, jokingly signing the letter 'Schiller Shakespearovich Goethe' (1973: 75).

Misunderstanding centred on the character of Ivanov; many saw him as a womanizing villain and Lvov as the hero of the play, and so Chekhov reworked it. The changes included the ending: Ivanov died of a heart attack in the first version but as audiences had seen this as just retribution for wrong-doing, Chekhov changed the death to a suicide to make it clear that Ivanov was not being punished by fate and wanted to free Sasha from what he perceived to be his pernicious influence on her. Chekhov attempted to clarify how in Dr Lvov, he was subverting the figure of the young reformer and populist, a 'positive hero' found in utilitarian fiction. A comparable female figure is portrayed in the wealthy Lida, in *The House with the Mezzanine – An Artist's Story*, of 1896. She is a zealous member of the *zemstvo*, sure of her own moral rectitude. Lvov's constant refrain is about his own decency, leading Sasha to dub him 'Mr Decent Person' (Chekhov 2005: 52). Lvov declares, 'I am outraged by human cruelty' (Chekhov 2005: 64); he is piously indignant at Ivanov's treatment of Anna. In fact, he makes the situation worse for Ivanov, who finds his wife's illness unbearable. Shabelsky points out Lvov's narrow-mindedness: Lvov condemns peasants who live well as 'money-grubbing exploiters' and condemns Shabelsky, who owned serfs before emancipation, as a 'low-life and a slave-owner' (Chekhov 2005: 47–48). He does not see the extent of Shabelsky's guilt and self-condemnation. Shabelsky says of Lvov that he thinks he is a 'second Dobrolyubov', referencing narrow-minded utilitarian views.

Chekhov, however, condemns no one

> If my Ivanov comes across as either a blackguard or superfluous man and the doctor as a great man, if no one understands why Sarah and Sasha love Ivanov, then my play has evidently failed to pan out …

He adds that Lvov is

> the model of an honest, straightforward, hot-headed but narrow-minded and limited man … he's a stereotype personified, a walking ideology … he wants either saints or blackguards … such people are necessary and for the most part likeable.
>
> (Chekhov 1973: 76, 79)

Chekhov presents the conflicts between the characters as a way to reveal their lack of understanding: Lvov's easy moralizing and Ivanov's failure to see that his goals as a social reformer were too idealistic.

'A type that is encountered only too often in life ... '

Some critics connected Ivanov with a nihilistic socio-political position – the abandonment of overt, even revolutionary social protest
in the reactionary 1880s (Turner 1994: 57). However, Chekhov's
view was that to blame one's environment or adopt the pose of a
'superfluous man' as a reason for abandoning the struggle for
change, would in fact be dishonest. In a passage added to the
second version, Lebedev says, 'Your surroundings, my boy, have got
you down!' Ivanov says this is 'stupid and stale', thus rejecting the
stance of 'the superfluous man' as victim of society (Chekhov 2005:
63). Chekhov attempted in Ivanov a complex psychological analysis
of what he saw as a 'type that is encountered only too often in life',
a volatile intellectual who has taken on too much. 'By the age of
thirty such a man is bored, ready to espouse right-wing beliefs,
reject the *zemstvo*, scientific farming and love.' Ivanov's problems
are weariness, boredom and guilt; he is also isolated, living in the
provinces, surrounded by drunks, card players or people like Lvov.
Also, 'life doesn't care and ... people like Ivanov don't solve problems; they fall under their burden'. Chekhov distrusted the changing enthusiasms he perceived in the intelligentsia, a theme he had
treated in *On the Road,* in 1886, seeing in them an absence of a
considered stance, and political convictions that changed with fash-
ion. He commented while working on the play, 'the socialists have
got married and are criticizing the *zemstvo* ... Where is liberalism?'
(1973: 78).

The theme of non-understanding

Chekhov notes that, his enthusiasms having waned, 'the straight-
forward Ivanov, however, openly admits to the doctor and the
audience that he doesn't understand himself' (1973: 78). *Ivanov* is a
'a play about *non-understanding*' (Kataev 2002: 78); the phrase
occurs as a refrain throughout. Ivanov has lines introduced in Act 3
in the second version, 'I don't understand, I don't understand, I
don't understand!' He tells Lvov,

> Clever man, think of this: in your opinion, nothing's easier than
> understanding me! ... I don't understand you, you don't

understand me, we don't understand one another. You may be an excellent general practitioner – and still have no understanding of people.

(Chekhov 2005: 64, 65)

Ivanov's dilemma is that, unlike fellow *intelligent* Lebedev, he cannot give up on his ideals and conform and live as his neighbours do. Lebedev urges him: 'Calm your mind! Look at things simply, the way everybody else does! In this world everything is simple. The ceiling is white, boots are black, sugar is sweet' (Chekhov 2005: 80). But Ivanov cannot anaesthetize himself with alcohol, food and gambling as other characters do, or agree with the other characters' pursuit of money, status, or romantic love as the way to live life – he seeks a knowledge and understanding of life that the other characters do not. However, there are barriers to his understanding: his exhaustion prevents him from thinking clearly and he also dramatizes his own situation, perceiving it to be hopeless. The culminating act of self-dramatization is when he commits suicide at his own wedding (see Senelick 1985: 41). Chekhov introduced, in the attempt at clarification, an image that encapsulates Ivanov's perception of his own situation. Ivanov compares himself in Act 3 to a workman, Semyon, who wanted to show off his strength by hoisting two sacks of rye on his back, giving himself a hernia, which killed him. Ivanov states that farming, district schools, projects and his marriage were the sacks of rye that he hoisted on his back, so that his back, metaphorically, broke (Chekhov 2005: 63). Ivanov persuades himself that his life is finished.

Sasha also has illusions and dramatizes her situation; her idea that love will conquer all is her barrier to understanding. Chekhov wrote that 'she loves Ivanov because he is a good man. In the land of the blind the one-eyed man is king', but expands, 'she doesn't love Ivanov, she loves her mission.' She does not realize that life is not a novel (1973: 80).

Like Masha and Nina in *The Seagull,* her view of life is obscured as it comes from literature rather than actual experience. Lebedev attributes his daughter's problems to ideas from books: 'Principles, Schopenhauer!' (Chekhov 2005: 80).

The theme of 'non-understanding' is developed further in relation to Anna's illness and how the characters relate to it. Shabelsky, as well as Ivanov, is cruel towards Anna, his cruelty masking his lack of understanding, his fear of death. He admits, 'I cannot abide the thought that a living human being suddenly, for no reason at all, can up and die!' (Chekhov 2005: 58). Shabelsky, like Ivanov, has a moral dilemma; he is tempted to behave like the 'lowlifes' around him and marry Babakina for her money. In the final act, he is moved by the memory of the good-hearted and honourable Anna and realizes that he cannot honestly take such a step. Ivanov similarly realizes that to marry Sasha would be an unprincipled act. This is only a partial insight; he cannot find a way out of his existential predicament and chooses to end his life. Chekhov presents us with the fact and makes no moral comment.

A new dramaturgy

The subject matter of the play was new to the Russian stage. It demonstrated Chekhov's interest in mental health, similarly to the stories *A Nervous Breakdown*, *The Name-day Party* and *The Black Monk* (1894), and was new in dramatizing nervous exhaustion. The Jewish theme was also groundbreaking and controversial. Shabelsky and Anna joke in mock-Jewish accents. Ivanov loses his temper and calls his wife a 'kike bitch', telling her brutally that she is soon to die (Chekhov 2005: 71). In marrying her, Ivanov has broken social convention. This was topical, as in the reactionary 1880s the Russian government, in an attempt to assert Russian nationalism, had changed its policy towards Jews from that of assimilation into the Russian nation to designating Jews, along with nomads and Central Asian Muslims, as aliens. Anti-Jewish pogroms, as part of the wave of reactionary government after the assassination of Alexander II, took place in the Pale of Settlement, an area in western and southern Russia populated by Jewish people (Hosking 2001: 341–44).

Also topical were the ecological questions raised by Borkin's behaviour; he sees the land solely as a source of income, there to be plundered rather than nurtured. In Act 1 he wishes Ivanov to buy a strip of land so that he will own both sides of the riverbank and then to announce that he will dam the river to build a mill. The two factories and the monastery that depend on the river as a water supply will pay them not to go ahead with the plan (Chekhov 2005: 28). In Act 2, it is revealed that Borkin planned to infect animals in order to gain compensation, and that Ivanov was falsely blamed for this. Ivanov rejects his dishonest schemes and has given up on his own over-ambitious ones. The relationship between the health of the characters and the health of the environment is symbiotic. Ivanov says, 'The estate goes to rack and ruin, the forests topple beneath the axe. (*Weeps*) My land stares at me like an orphan' (Chekhov 2005: 64).

Chekhov was unable to go fully beyond melodramatic convention in this play, ending each act with *un coup de théâtre*: Anna seeing Ivanov and Sasha kissing, Ivanov shouting abuse at Anna, and finally the suicide. However, the play offers a new concept of dramatic conflict. In classical drama, the will of the main hero conflicts with that of others, but Chekhov's Ivanov does not will or desire anything: he does not want to work, to 'turn cartwheels in the hay' with his wife, as they used to in the happy days of their marriage, to stay at home in the evenings or to go out in the evenings or, in the final event, to marry Sasha. Ivanov's conflict is within himself (Zingerman 2001: 225). As regards the other characters, Chekhov speaks of their originality, adding there is 'not one villain nor an angel – but I couldn't resist clowns' (Chekhov 1975b 2: 138). The slanderous talk in Zyuzyushka's drawing room, where Ivanov is often the main subject, has aspects of social comedy, and there are comic scenarios. For example, Zyuzyushka's miserliness drives her guests to go through her cupboards in search of something to eat. The combination of vaudeville elements with serious subject matter presages *The Cherry Orchard*, but in *Ivanov*, the comedy is juxtaposed with the drama, rather than blended with it – the characters are either serious or comic, albeit darkly so, rather than possessing elements of each. Kosykh, a neighbour, is obsessed with card playing, as Gayev in *The Cherry Orchard* is with billiard playing; the reactions of others to his blow-by-blow descriptions provide humour, but the more detailed aspects of characterization present in the later plays in even the minor characters are missing in Kosykh.

Pavis discusses *Ivanov* as the 'invention of a negative dramaturgy', identifying a 'hesitation between naturalistic writing and symbolist vision ... two sides of the same coin and *Ivanov* is the "negative" dramaturgy at the source of this revelation' (2000: 70). The dialogue is far more explicit than in the later plays, with characters pouring out how they feel and much exposition through dialogue. On the other hand, the structure, language and rhythm of the play are also highly original. As with the major plays, events that have preceded the play, that is, Ivanov's career, marriage and the fact that he has exhausted himself, dictate the course of the action. Everyday events are presented on stage – a game of cards, conversations over vodka, a social gathering.

The play was produced again at the Imperial Alexandrinsky Theatre, St Petersburg on 31 January 1889 (see Senelick 1997a: 19–24), but despite the changes, misunderstandings continued. This was partly because audiences continued to seek in Ivanov either a melo-dramatic villain or a tragic hero, and partly because Chekhov was still working out his dramaturgical techniques.

Productions of *Ivanov*

Nemirovich-Danchenko produced the play at MAT in 1905, its last production in Russia until the 1950s, as *Ivanov* was seen as irrele-vant in a Soviet Russia where communism had purportedly resolved issues between the individual and society. However, the play found resonances in demoralized Russian society under Leonid Brezhnev in the 1970s with several productions (see Senelick 1997a: 208–12). The play was also revived in the 1970s in Britain after a couple of previous productions; since then it has been regularly performed on the world stage.

The adaptation of *Ivanov* by David Hare premiered in 1997 at the Almeida Theatre, London, with Ralph Fiennes as Ivanov, which also toured to Moscow. Hare saw the major theme of the play as 'honesty'. He felt Chekhov had revealed some of his own personal conflicts in the play (Chekhov 1997: ix) as Chekhov had a relation-ship with a Jewish woman, Dunya Efros, whom he at one point thought of marrying. The British critical reception indicated that Fiennes' performance had successfully conveyed the contradictions within Ivanov: 'He is full of despair and ineffectualness, yet he also implies that Ivanov has an honesty and intellect that has been despoiled by circumstance.' Jonathan Kent's production also rea-lized the comedy and its darker side, with the laughter at anti-Semitic jokes and the comic yet debasing pursuit of money depicting 'the pettiness and vulgarity of Russian provincial life with Gogolian fervour'.[1]

Figure 4.1 Ralph Fiennes and Harriet Walter in *Ivanov* at the Almeida
Theatre © Ivan Kyncl

THE SEAGULL (1896)

In *The Seagull*, Chekhov returns to questions of aim in life, focusing
on ideas about art and the life of the artist in *fin-de-siècle* Russia.
The celebrated actress Arkadina and her lover Trigorin, a famous
writer, are visiting the country estate where her son Konstantin
Treplyov lives with Arkadina's brother Sorin. The play opens as
Konstantin (Kostya) is preparing for a performance of a symbolic
drama he has written which is to be staged by the lake on the
estate. Medvedenko, a local schoolteacher, loves the estate manager's daughter, Masha. She, however, is desperately in love with
Konstantin, who in turn loves Nina Zarechnaya, a young woman
from a neighbouring estate, who is to act in his monodrama. There
are old and young people in this play – confronting the challenges
of different stages of life. The young rebel in their relationships with
their parents, against social and artistic norms; their dilemmas are
about finding expression and fulfilment in life, finding partners,
having children, the future, whereas the older characters are aware
that life is passing by all too fast, while their desires remain

unfulfilled. Sorin is ill, and reflecting on his lack of achievement in life, calls himself '*L'homme qui a voulu*' ('The man who wanted to') (Chekhov 2005: 173). Arkadina fears the loss of her youth and sexual attractiveness; having a son Konstantin's age, as he says, is a constant reminder to her of this. There is a middle-aged love triangle as Polina, Masha's mother, has had a long-term affair with Dr Dorn and it is hinted at the end of Act 1 that he is Masha's father, rather than Shamrayev the estate-manager. (This was stated overtly in Chekhov's first version of the play, but afterwards only hinted at as Chekhov moved away from melodramatic endings to each act.) Polina wishes to live with Dorn, to escape her overbearing husband, but Dorn claims that at fifty-five he is too old to change his way of life.

The young people are deprived emotionally and also impoverished financially. Money is a major theme in the context of changing economies; the estate is in difficulty and the area is becoming depopulated, yet women such as Arkadina are earning substantially. Arkadina (a miser, like Zyuzyushka in *Ivanov*) has 'seventy thousand in a bank in Odessa' but will not give Konstantin money to travel or even to buy a new coat (Chekhov 2005: 139). Ironically, he begins to earn money from his writing just as the events that lead to his suicide are triggered. Medvedenko, surviving on a teacher's salary, talks constantly about money and claims that Masha does not love him because he is poor. Nina's father has deprived her of her inheritance from her deceased mother and Shamrayev, whose wife is unfaithful to him and whose daughter dislikes him, asserts himself by constantly exercising control over spending on the estate, which Sorin claims is a waste; as in Ivanov, the efforts at reform are insufficient to counter the depressed farming conditions. Dorn is the only character to spend money for pleasure, using his savings on a trip to Europe.

The younger people experience confusion about their identity, where they belong and why they are alive. Masha asks Trigorin to send her a copy of his new book inscribed 'To Masha, who can't identify her family,[2] and lives in this world for no apparent reason' and Konstantin struggles to find a place in society. He is a *raznochinets,* the son of an actor who was a Kievan *meshchanin*, a provincial bourgeois, a term used derogatively of her son by Arkadina.

He has been compelled to leave university because of his political allegiances and is now attempting to write.[3]

In Act 1, his experimental play is interrupted by Arkadina's mockery. Konstantin calls for the curtain and storms off. Later, he lays a gull he has shot at Nina's feet, saying that he will soon shoot himself like the bird, as Nina no longer loves him but loves Trigorin. Next, Trigorin finds the seagull and is inspired to write a story about a young woman who lives by a lake and is 'happy and free like a gull. But by chance, a man comes along, sees her, and having nothing better to do, destroys her, just like this gull here' (Chekhov 2005: 160). In between Acts 2 and 3, Konstantin has attempted to kill himself. In Act 3, on the day Arkadina and Trigorin are to depart, an intimate scene, where Arkadina bandages her son's head, escalates into a terrible argument. Then, Trigorin asks Arkadina to release him from his commitment to her so he can be with Nina. She persuades him to stay with her, kneeling before him, flattering him, and thinks she has recaptured him. At the end of the act, Nina tells Trigorin she has decided to run away from home and come to Moscow to find work as an actress; he arranges to meet her there secretly.

Between Acts 3 and 4, two years have passed. Arkadina and Trigorin are visiting the estate again, as Sorin is ill. Dorn has been away travelling and asks Treplyov to tell him what has become of Nina. Konstantin explains that she had an affair with Trigorin, and had a baby, which died. Trigorin maintained a relationship with both Nina and Arkadina for a long time but eventually abandoned Nina, leaving her in despair. Konstantin relates that she had been working as an actress but has shown only glimpses of talent. In the meantime, his own writing is being published. Nina appears at the house, in a state of distress, and meets Konstantin. She keeps repeating that she is the seagull, reiterating Trigorin's story, and says that she still loves Trigorin. She calms herself and states that she has found her vocation as an actress. Konstantin begs her not to leave him, says he has no goal in life and when she does leave, systematically destroys his writing. The play ends as, during a game of lotto, Shamrayev presents Trigorin with the seagull, stuffed and mounted. Trigorin claims not to remember it, then a shot is heard. Dorn tells the group that a medicine bottle has exploded, but taking Trigorin aside, tells him that Konstantin has killed himself.

'Dreadful violence to stage conventions ... '

Chekhov worked on the play from 1892, referring in his letters to working out new techniques. The extent to which Chekhov drew from life in developing *The Seagull* has been well analysed (Rayfield 1975: 203–5, Magarshack 1980: 177–80, Golomb 2000). Particularly, he drew from his own experiences as a writer, the affair of one of his lovers, Lika Mizinova, with the writer I. N. Potapenko and the attempted suicide of Isaac Levitan, an artist and friend of Chekhov's. In 1895, Chekhov wrote in a letter to Suvorin, 'I'm enjoying writing it, although I'm doing dreadful violence to stage conventions. It is a comedy, with three parts for women, six for men, four acts, a landscape (view of a lake); many conversations about literature, hardly any action, and 185 pounds of love' (Chekhov 2004a: 336). In that year he wrote *Three Years*, which also discusses love and art – the characters question what love is beyond sexual attraction and debate modernism and utilitarianism in art. He said of the play that he had begun with an interesting subject for a comedy for which he needed to find an ending (Magarshack 1980: 174). As a 'comedy' that ends with a suicide the play intentionally confounds audience expectations. Chekhov, using politicized language unusual for him, wrote of positive heroes and happy endings as 'lulling the bourgeoisie into its golden dreams' making 'them feel at ease with the idea that you can hoard capital while maintaining your innocence, be a beast and yet be happy' (Chekhov 1973: 276).

The actual events of the play, the suicide, seduction and abandonment and the death of Nina's baby, are conventionally melodramatic. However, Chekhov's treatment of these events was new. As in *Ivanov*, there are neither villains nor positive heroes. Unlike plays on the Russian stage that Konstantin says 'try to extract a moral – not too big a moral' (Chekhov 2005: 139), *The Seagull*, like *Ivanov*, asks questions about morality within a changing society; the treatment of the breakdown of traditional family ties and sexual freedoms is comparable to that in Hauptmann and Ibsen (Rayfield 1975: 210).

'Hardly any action ... '

Chekhov developed techniques he had begun to use in *Ivanov* to convey interiorized action, abandoning melodramatic devices (see

Pitcher 1985: 38–39 and Magarshack 1980: 160–63). The suicide in *Ivanov* takes place on stage as the climactic ending to the play, whereas the suicide happens offstage in *The Seagull*. Dramatic tension is provided by internal action: Konstantin's anxiety about his play drives Act 1. Also, in early versions of the play Nina reacted in a startled way to Trigorin's story of the young woman who is destroyed like the seagull, and said 'You mustn't say that' (Chekhov 1982a 12: 266). In the final version, all that is scripted is a pause, though the way Nina later identifies herself with the seagull demonstrates that the story has a profound effect on her. There are other internal shifts and changes where nothing is said or done. For example, the interaction between Nina and Trigorin in Act 1 reveals a gulf between them in their views on art, but as they converse the curtain on Konstantin's stage is taken up, indicating symbolically that Konstantin's relationship with Nina is over and 'the drama of Nina and Trigorin is about to begin' (Senelick 1985: 82). In *Ivanov*, the dialogue is more direct and explanatory, but in *The Seagull*, the language is more poetic and allusive. The opening lines spoken by Masha, who when asked why she is wearing black replies, 'I'm in mourning for my life', and her statement 'I feel as if I were born ages and ages ago; I lug my life around like a dead weight, like the endless train on a gown … ' present images as a key to understanding Masha's view of herself rather than direct information about the character (Chekhov 2005: 136, 150).

Another technique is the reportage on certain characters by others and how this fits with the images the characters present of themselves. In Act 4, Konstantin relates Nina's story to Dorn. This report gives information, moreover it enables the characters to tell stories about each other, about the past and to voice what is going on internally. Crucially, what they say has to be read in juxtaposition with other parts of the text. For example, Konstantin's story of Nina's affair, the death of her baby and her acting career is contrasted with the plot of Trigorin's story of the girl who is happy and free like a seagull, but destroyed by a man, like the seagull who has been shot. Nina's construction of her self-image in relation to this is an innovatory way to reveal character, part of the originality of the play.

More recent critical works emphasize that inner action is still action; in response to the long-held perception of Chekhov's plays as lacking action and peopled by passive characters, Flath writes that Chekhov's drama is 'packed with action'. There is an interesting opposition between words uttered and the actions carried out offstage:

> What characters say serves in a revelatory function to reveal hidden truths, to express reactions to events, or to express desires that may lead characters to take action; but the actions themselves are generally hidden from us.
>
> (1999: 494)

Kataev emphasizes the importance of inner action, viewing the change in Nina and Konstantin as the 'main event' in the play (2002: 174). The play is more than a 'psychological' play, as it has been designated (Pitcher 1985: 3–4). As in *Ivanov*, the desires and aspirations of the characters attain a metaphysical significance within the broader questions asked by the play about purpose in life.

'Many conversations about literature … '

The play questions literature – what is art and what is an artist – and examines the characters' ideas and illusions about this. Two different kinds of theatre are represented in the content of the play – the traditional and new. Konstantin says that the theatre of the day is 'trite, riddled with clichés' and accuses his mother of being in 'pathetic third rate plays' (Chekhov 2005: 139, 165). Sorin's opinion differs: 'You've got to have theater'; despite its shortcomings, it was a forum for the intelligentsia (Chekhov 2005: 139). Arkadina plays in the Imperial and provincial theatres, in melodrama and French comedies, European romances and classics. Her descriptions paint a picture of the life of an actress in that period: having to pay for her own costumes; sitting in hotels on tour and learning a part; the reactions and gifts of her fans. Her lifestyle defies respectability and convention; Konstantin longs for 'an ordinary' mother and Nina is not permitted by her parents to come to the estate they think of as 'bohemian' (Chekhov 2005: 141). Konstantin calls for new forms, reflecting a point of view of his times, as Stanislavsky and Nemirovich-Danchenko set up the Moscow Art Theatre to develop a new repertoire and reform stereotyped melodramatic acting.

Konstantin's experiments reflect French avant-garde theatre and anticipate Russian symbolist theatre, which began in about 1900.

Nina is not interested in his work; the traditional theatre epitomizes her ideal as an actress. German romanticism, so influential in nineteenth century Russia, had posited that the artist had a sacred task, to serve 'truth', and Belinsky had also maintained the idea that the artist had a spiritual vocation: to bring about the improvement of society (see Andrew 1980). Chekhov reveals the idealization of art, the processes of creativity and the realities of celebrity: in the play there is an established actress and a raw beginner, a famous writer and a tyro. The notion of 'sacred' art is consistently undercut: Dorn tells Konstantin that if he ever got the chance 'to experience the spiritual uplift artists feel at the moment of creation' he would let go his material shell, and 'let myself be wafted far away from earth into the empyrean' (Chekhov 2005: 149). Konstantin, however, more anxious to find Nina than listen to Dorn, ignores this panegyric. Likewise, in Act 2, Nina expresses an exalted view of Trigorin as an artist devoted to the public, whose happiness lies in being 'yoked to the artist's chariot'. She would 'live in a garret and eat nothing but black bread' in order to experience fame (Chekhov 2005: 159). Then Arkadina is heard, calling Trigorin to pack, claiming him and placing him in the realm of the prosaic, as opposed to Nina's fantasy of him. Masha's description of her romanticized image of Konstantin, reciting with a 'beautiful, mournful voice and the look of a poet', is greeted comically by Sorin's snoring (Chekhov 2005: 152).

The idealized figure of the artist is contrasted with the realities of the artists' lives. Dorn tells Polina that 'If society loves actors ... it's ... idealism' (Chekhov 2005: 143). At the beginning of *The Seagull*, Medvedenko says of Konstantin and Nina and Konstantin's play, 'They're in love and today their souls will merge in an attempt to present a joint artistic creation' (Chekhov 2005: 137). By the end of the play, it is clear that their relationship is a factor in Konstantin's suicide and, simultaneously, the realities of the situation for women deciding to join the theatre are presented. The role of the actress was connected with prostitution. Nina, in Act 4, is going to Yelets, a provincial town, travelling third-class with peasants. She knows that there, 'art-loving business men will pester me with their propositions' (Chekhov 2005: 180).[4] So far from being spiritual leaders of society, Arkadina and Trigorin are flawed individuals: Arkadina is cruel to her son; Trigorin's treatment of Nina is paralleled by the man in his story who destroys a young woman's life 'having nothing better to do' (Chekhov 2005: 160). However, all the characters revere them in some way: Shamrayev, trying to impress and entertain Arkadina, tells theatrical anecdotes, which fall flat. Senelick discusses how the word 'talent' is the touchstone by which the characters evaluate themselves and one another, though for Chekhov to be talented is not to be a superior person (Senelick 1985: 78). Chekhov does not make clear whether any of the characters are talented are not; Arkadina is famous but her acting may be crudely melodramatic. Her assessment of Trigorin as 'our greatest living writer' is countered by his own: 'Charming, talented ... Charming but a far cry from Tolstoy' (Chekhov 2005: 167, 158). Konstantin describes Nina's acting as having moments of greatness; we only have his opinion on this. Dorn knows nothing about theatre, he says, but is moved by Konstantin's play and encourages him to go on writing, but to define clearly his aims. Chekhov's concern rather is how the characters construct themselves in relation to the notion of 'the artist', to literary images. The characters' viewpoints are shaped by art; Arkadina says to Trigorin 'You are the last chapter in my life story' (Chekhov 2005: 167). Masha, in her desperate attempt to 'rip her love' for Konstantin 'from her heart', says unconvincingly, 'Unrequited love – that's only in novels' (Chekhov 2005: 160, 171).

The intertextuality of the play, the use of cultural narratives identifiable by the Russian audiences of the time gives further cues to understanding the characters.[5] For example, the passage from Maupassant read aloud by Arkadina in Act 2, describing how women pursue novelists, points to an aspect of Arkadina's relationship with Trigorin which she vehemently denies. Trigorin's monologue about writing is almost a paraphrase of Maupassant's *Sur l'Eau*. Rayfield explores the characterization of Trigorin and expressions of a 'philosophical duality common to the two writers' (1975: 149). Senelick discusses the relationship of Nina to the character of the young woman, seduced and abandoned in Russian works by Karamzin, Ostrovsky, Potekhin, Turgenev and Pisemsky (1985: 75–76). There are allusions to *Hamlet,* of which there are many in Chekhov's works including *Ivanov* (see Winner 1956,

Stroud 1958, Porter, 1981, Golomb 1986). *Hamlet* contains a play within the play as *The Seagull* does; Arkadina and Konstantin exchange lines from *Hamlet* in Act 1, pointing to tensions in the son's relationship with the mother. Konstantin's father, like Hamlet's, is dead. Here, the main point of the allusions is that Konstantin, like Shakespeare's Hamlet, questions why he is alive and, like Ivanov and the Moscow Hamlet, dramatizes his existence to the extent that he thinks others would be better off without him.

Masha's 'mourning for her life', Nina's tragic view of herself as the seagull, or as a character from Pushkin's *Rusalka*, are attempts to communicate emotional experiences.

> *The Seagull* is not simply a play which exposes the illusions of romantic longing; instead it reveals the powerful operation of theatrical and literary representation of love within the imagination of its fictional characters and its impact on their lives.
>
> (Tait 2002: 30)

Moreover, as in *Ivanov*, self-dramatization is part of the lack of understanding of life, which Chekhov examines. A romantic view of art is a romantic view of life: only by ceasing to identify their experiences with the experiences of fictional characters and defining practical aims in life can the characters grow and develop. Konstantin has an insight that his writing is not about his self-image as an avant-garde theatre maker, but that writing should 'pour freely out of your soul' (Chekhov 2005: 179). He gives up on life before he has explored this insight.

Papernyi defines Trigorin's story of the seagull as a 'micro-subject', like the image of Semyon in *Ivanov*, linked with development of action and fates of many of the characters (1982: 63).[6] Pitcher, among others, identifies Nina with the seagull as a victim (1985: 64), and others have suggested Konstantin is the seagull (Magarshack 1980: 194). The image works on several levels throughout the play – the fictionalized image in Trigorin's story and the object in the play, the shot seagull, which is later stuffed and can be read as indicating the way in which Trigorin and Treplyov objectify Nina. In Act 2, as Konstantin throws the seagull at Nina's feet in a nervous state, she recognizes that he is talking 'in code, symbols of some kind' (Chekhov 2005: 156) but claims she cannot understand him. She rejects Konstantin's self-dramatization, his attempt to communicate his pain, by means of the shot seagull. In Act 4, two things happen: Nina has enacted in her own life the image of the victimized seagull in Trigorin's story but finally rejects that image of herself. On the prosaic plane there is the bird that was shot. A final bizarre juxtaposition is of the stuffed seagull, which Shamrayev attempts to present to Trigorin, with the shot, which is heard off-stage. The author of the story about the seagull, which is had such a powerful effect on Nina, is presented with a travesty reminder of the fiction and its consequences. At the same time Konstantin fulfils the action he warned about in shooting the seagull, 'I'll soon kill myself, the very same way' (Chekhov 2005: 155).

'A landscape (view of a lake) … '

Like the seagull, the image of the lake exists on two planes within the play – as part of the setting and metaphorically in terms of what it represents to the characters and therefore reveals about them. Konstantin poeticizes it: his play is site-specific and must start at a particular time when the moon is reflected on the lake. In the play, the world soul talks poetically about the silent fish and starfish inhabiting the waters. Arkadina remembers how years ago there was music and singing every night from the country houses along the lake and one love affair after another, indicating how she sees life. This also shows how desolate the area has become as people have moved to the towns and how the life she knew is disappearing. In Act 1, Nina says to Trigorin 'I've spent my whole life on the shores of this lake and I know every islet on it'. She is young, close to nature, and knows nowhere else. Trigorin remarks on what a lot of fish there must be in the lake – though he is purported to be a famous and talented artist, his attitude is unromantic. Dorn the doctor says ironically ' … all this love … Oh, spell-binding lake' (Chekhov 2005: 160, 147, 150).

At the same time no one wants to be on the estate of which the lake is a part: Sorin wants to get into town; Nina wants to get away to Moscow; Treplyov is trapped there; Arkadina uses the word 'boring' when referring to country life on the estate several times. Yet they return to the estate as birds return to the lake. Nina says 'I am drawn here to the lake, like a gull' (Chekhov 2005: 141). The characters have a need to come back together and work through relationships again – destructive though they are, with arguments between Arkadina and Konstantin recurring. The argument over the provision of horses for Arkadina in Act 2 ends with Shamrayev resigning and Arkadina saying she is leaving and that 'Every summer it's the same thing!' (Chekhov 2005: 154). Nina returns in Act 4 with the intention of resolving the past. Konstantin and Nina's trajectories in *The Seagull,* one towards death, and one towards self-determination in life, are linked with Konstantin's play set by the lake; the vision of the world soul.

The world soul

Konstantin's play has been variously read, for example, as a creation myth, a metaphor for the artist's journey and a disguised Oedipal confession. Jackson describes it as 'terrible ... a concoction of melodramatic posturing and mannered symbolism' (Barricelli 1981: 3–4). Reid suggests it 'should be read as an amusing parody of the mystical ideals of Solovyov's followers' (Reid 1998: 610). Poet-philosopher Vladimir Solovyov was a symbolist and a believer in a 'world soul'. Konstantin's play provides a framing device for the discussions of art and aim in life. It has a structural purpose; references to it run through *The Seagull.* Masha quotes the play in Act 2 and in Act 4 the stage and its tattered curtain remain, a symbolic suggestion of how Konstantin's play and the events connected with it continue to hold significance for the characters. Everyone responds characteristically to it. It foregrounds the relationship between Arkadina and Konstantin; the tension between them over his play in Act 1 prefiguring the row in Act 3 where their differing views on art again become the locus for the expression of their troubled relationship. Arkadina calls her son a 'decadent' who has not 'got what it takes to write a miserable vaudeville sketch'. ('Decadent' was a name for artists in the symbolist and other avant-garde movements – unlikely people to write vaudeville sketches.) Konstantin's play is a vision of a post-apocalyptic world. It is odd, immature work. Nina describes it as having little action and no love interest, denigrating it in comparison with traditional theatre, but she repeats lines from it when she returns in Act 4, recalling it as something innocent and fresh. Trigorin is not interested in the play but in Nina: 'I didn't understand a word. Still, I enjoyed watching it. Your acting was so sincere. And the scenery was gorgeous' (Chekhov 2005: 147). Only Dorn is enthused by the idea of the play and describes an experience in Genoa where he was part of a crowd, which 'you merge with psychically', and started to believe that there may in fact be a world soul, as in the play (Chekhov 2005: 173).

The setting for the play reflects the French symbolists' interest in experiment with theatrical space (Deak 1993: 18) and a view of nature as mystical. As Rayfield suggests, Chekhov is anticipating, not parodying, the Russian symbolist movement, which took as one of its themes fighting the spirit of evil (1975: 204–5). Moreover, the play can be considered as a reflection of attitudes current in Chekhov's time to pessimistic philosophies, in its use of Schopenhauer's ideas, which recur in Chekhov's other works (see Skaftymov 1972, Durkin 1981, Ischuk-Fadeeva 1997). Chekhov is not engaged in philosophical polemic, but, as in all Chekhov's work, the ideas function both to reveal character and *zeitgeist*.

Konstantin's play deals with the struggle to establish the kingdom of the world soul, also called Brahma, in the Buddhist philosophy espoused by Schopenhauer. The world soul is the one absolute and real entity, whereas human beings' subjective experience of self and the world is an illusion (*maya*) (see Nicholls 1999: 183). Our lives, according to Schopenhauer, are permeated by suffering, because of our desires – our will – for fame, money, love and so on which can only ever be temporarily satisfied. Striving for personal fulfilment is pointless. The attainment of peace and insight is nirvana – unity with the world soul and the recognition that we are nothing. The origin of the will of the world, which dictates human lives, is in a sinful act of Brahma, the world soul. In Konstantin's play the world soul is at war with the forces of the devil, in the hope of establishing the 'kingdom of the will of the world', where human life is united with the world soul. The world soul suffers and strives. The play refers to the sad 'cycle' of life, a reference to the Buddhist wheel of suffering (Chekhov 2005: 144). Life must be lived and reincarnated until nirvana is achieved. For some, Schopenhauer's philosophy implied a nihilism that denies all value in existence; for others it opened up the possibility of understanding the true nature of life.[7] It is one of the schools of thought encountered by Chekhov and his characters, and Chekhov suggests the young man's struggle with current ideas, in the attempt to make sense of his troubled life and rationalize his depression.

In *The Seagull*, Nina chooses survival, whereas Konstantin chooses to kill himself, believing that what he wills, his desires, can never be fulfilled. Konstantin's hopes and dreams are thwarted by his mother's actions and Nina's rejection of him, and he continues to be thwarted throughout the play. Nina's trajectory is from naïvety and illusion to disillusion, identifying herself, after Trigorin's rejection and the death of her baby, as 'the seagull', a victim. Finally, she rejects this idea of herself, realizing that what is important in acting or writing is not fame or glamour, the things she used to dream about, but knowing how to endure. When she thinks of her calling as an actress, she is not afraid of life. Nina speaks of faith and bearing her cross, using religious terminology. Chekhov references the philosophy of the Stoics with the idea of 'endurance'. Konstantin travels from illusion to disillusion to despair, to seeing himself as 'nothing'. Flath discusses the leitmotif of nothingness, non-entity (*nichtozhestvo*), in the language used of himself and by others to refer to him (1999: 497–501). He says he has no faith, no calling. Seeing finally that Nina will never be his, he rips up all his manuscripts and goes to shoot himself.

'One must have an aim in life ... '

This play is about survivors and non-survivors. In the last act, after two years, all four young people have changed. Masha, Medvedenko and Konstantin are more hopeless in their outlooks. Masha still loves Konstantin but has married Medvedenko, whom she does not love, repeating her mother's situation. She neglects her child, as she would rather stay at the house to be near Konstantin than go home to see her baby. Chekhov wrote that there were '185 pounds of love' in the play but questions, as he does in all the plays, what love is. Nina is the one person who possibly has the determination to take control over her life, unlike Masha, whose aim is to be loved by Konstantin and whose actions are reactions to the fact that he does not love her.

Some see no hope in *The Seagull* (Brahms 1976: 47–48); Volchkevich asserts that it is only Konstantin's view that Nina has 'found her way' (2007: 12). However, Magarshack contrasts Nina with Katya in Chekhov's *A Boring Story*, who also became an actress and was abandoned by her lover after having a baby (1980: 176–77). Katya gives up on her career and purpose in life whereas Nina's decision to continue her struggle is emphasized by the fact that the final words she speaks in the play are as an actress, asserting her chosen identity. Hollosi quotes the correspondence of Komissarzhevskaia, the first actress to play Nina, with Chekhov, ' … her sufferings and fate are so ardent that she will compel many others to have faith'. Karpov reported that Chekhov said to him 'Nina's part means everything to me in this play' (1983: 118, 120). Chekhov does not offer conclusions and his characters are not his mouthpiece, but in his correspondence he consistently stressed the importance of aims in life. The writer Sazonova, criticizing Chekhov's work, argued that the purpose of life is life itself; that the artist must value that which is, and that all 'our troubles boil down to the fact that we all seek lofty, remote goals'. Chekhov wrote in response:

> if that's not female logic, it certainly must be a philosophy of despair. Anyone who sincerely thinks man has no more need of lofty goals than do cows and that those goals 'cause all our troubles' can do nothing more than eat, drink, sleep or when he's had his fill, take a flying leap and dash his head out against the corner of a trunk.
>
> (Chekhov 1973: 246–47)

He also noted:

> Treplyov has no definite aims and that has led to his destruction. His talent is his undoing. He tells Nina in the final scene – you have found your road, you are saved but I am done for.
>
> (Chekhov 1980a 17: 116)

Nina has asserted herself against her father and established her independence, whereas Konstantin does not resolve his relationship with his mother – the play begins with his putting on his production for her, wanting to impress her. His last words are about her – not that she might be distressed by his death, but she might be distressed if she caught sight of Nina. As for many of Chekhov's

characters, there is a disjunction between their perceptions of themselves and their environment and their actual situation. In order to
arrive at a valid perception of self and world they must reject
socially conditioned roles and literary models. Nina rejects the safe
and respectable role defined for her by her family – that of the
daughter of the house on a country estate – and eventually also her
idealized vision of the artist. She has the possibility of authenticity
and some freedom as she abandons her father and mother and her
stultifying environment and leaves behind Trigorin, asserting her
right to a career and her own identity despite a patriarchal society.
Whether she will succeed or be crushed is not known, but she at
least has created a possibility for herself.

Dreams

Nina has moved from illusion to knowledge of the harshness of
reality. The motif of dreaming, trance and delirium recurs
throughout *The Seagull*. The play references a symbolist slogan
about theatre portraying life 'not the way it is, and not the way it's
supposed to be, but the way it appears in dreams' (Chekhov 2005:
142). There are references to dreams and dream-like states all
through the *Seagull*. Nina intoxicates herself with her vision of an
artist's life in a garret so that her 'head is spinning'. At the end of
Act 2 after her conversation with Trigorin she says 'It's all a
dream'. Trigorin says that when he is writing he is in 'some sort of
trance and often I don't even understand what I'm writing' (Chekhov 2005: 159–60). The word for 'trance', 'haze' or 'fumes' recurs
again in the name of a play Arkadina has performed – *Chad Zhizni,
The Fumes of Life*[8] – and again, with Pashka Chadin, a comedian
mentioned by Shamrayev. There is Masha's use of substances,
vodka and snuff, to escape reality, and Sorin's cigars and alcohol,
which Dorn says depersonalize him: 'your sense of self, your "ego"
gets fuzzy round the edges and you start talking about yourself in
the third person – as "that other fellow"' (Chekhov 2005: 153).
Arkadina says to Trigorin when he talks to her of his need for
Nina's love, 'you're a little tipsy, sober up' (Chekhov 2005: 166).
Konstantin is the subject of Masha's fantasy life whereas his dreams
are of Nina and art. In dismissing his work as 'decadent delirium',[9]
'asphyxiating us with sulphur', in Act 1, Arkadina is destroying

Konstantin's dreams (Chekhov 2005: 145–46). Trigorin affirms her opinion, saying in Act 4 that there is something delirious about Konstantin's writing. Nina says in Act 4 she dreams that Konstantin does not recognize her, perhaps indicating a sense of guilt towards him. Nina wakes up to reality and is learning how to cope with life but Konstantin remains trapped in a world of dreams. He says to Nina that he is 'still drifting in a chaos of day dreams and images, without knowing what or whom it is for' (Chekhov 2005: 181–82). Those who live in dreams and maintain illusions about what life should be may find themselves in conflict with it, and either seek escape, bring harm to others or perish.

Key productions

Detailed discussions of the first productions of *The Seagull* can be found in Senelick (1997a), Allen (2000) and Chepurov (2006). The première took place on 17 October 1896, at the Alexandrinsky Theatre in St Petersburg, and was received badly, prompting Chekhov to swear he would never write another play. As with *Ivanov*, the director and actors struggled to understand the play, it was under-rehearsed, and again some of the audience's expectations were of a traditional comedy. However, further performances were very successful and the actress Kommisarzhevskaia gained fame for her portrayal of Nina. Chepurov, re-assessing the critical reception, notes that the harshness of the reviews of the first performance indicates recognition of Chekhov's revolutionary approach, a new concept of dramatic conflict and of moral and aesthetic values (2006: 242).

MAT production

In 1898, the play was produced at the Moscow Art Theatre, the second production of the new theatre. Stanislavsky struggled with what was cryptic, deliberately inexplicit in Chekhov (Stroeva 1973: 35). Existing methods for developing characterizations were inadequate for the inner drama of the characters, and this was one of the prompts for the development of Stanislavsky's 'system' (see Merlin 1999, Allen 2000: 47–64). The theatre billed the play as a 'drama' rather than a 'comedy'. Chekhov objected to this and other aspects of the production, particularly the 'blubbering' of Maria Roxanova, who played Nina, and also Stanislavsky's portrayal of Trigorin, but wrote 'it wasn't bad on the whole ... quite gripping in fact' (1973: 357). What was important for Stanislavsky was the 'mood' or 'atmosphere' of the play, what he saw as the 'sad, monotonous life of the characters' (Stanislavsky 1952: 139). At that point in his career as a director Stanislavsky focused on establishing mood, using sound and staging effects as a means of communicating emotion to an audience (Stroeva 1973: 127). Unfortunately, this reading became characterized in the west as 'Chekhovian', the purported passive and mournful mood of the pre-revolutionary intelligentsia in Russia, a clichéd interpretation, which has persisted in the history of productions.

Later, Stanislavsky revised his perception of the play and made plans to restage it in 1917, insisting on energized performances, to suggest that the characters, rather than being mournful, desire to live life to the full (see Senelick 2004). In working on *Uncle Vanya,* he decided that the key to Chekhov's characters was how they struggle against their oppressive environment (Stroeva 1973: 48–49). He expressed this as, in his view, the main aim or supertask of Chekhov's work: 'Chekhov fought against vulgarity and petty-mindedness and dreamed of a better life. The struggle, this striving towards it became the Supertask of many of his works' (Stanislavski 2008b: 307).

Three British Seagulls

The main debate in reading the play has continued to be whether it is ultimately tragic, portraying the futility of the characters' lives, or whether it can be read positively. Three recent British productions (Trevor Nunn's at the Royal Shakespeare Company, Katie Mitchell's at the National Theatre and Ian Rickson's at the Royal Court Theatre) illustrate this debate. They also demonstrate the move away from western perceptions of 'elegiac' Chekhov to new emphases, Mitchell focusing on the cruelty of the characters' behaviour to each other, whereas Nunn and Rickson both highlighted the theme of endurance. Nunn's production was paired with *King Lear* with Ian McKellen as Lear and Sorin (doubling in this role with William Gaunt) and Nunn explored the themes, in both plays, of conflict between generations and the need to develop the power of endurance in life. Edgar's stoical 'Men must endure / Their going hence even as their coming hither; Ripeness is all' (v 2, 9–11) was paralleled with Nina's decision to embrace life while Konstantin chooses death.

The Seagull *at the National Theatre*

Mitchell saw Nina's future as bleak, an untalented actress having to prostitute herself. The National Theatre production saw the major themes of the play as 'Unhappy love, the family, the arts and destroyed dreams'.[10] In keeping with this view, Mitchell worked on the image of the seagull as scavenger, flying above refuse sites; the symbol accrues meaning, 'the final image of stuffed bird in a glass case crystallizes what the gull symbolizes – destroyed dreams'.[11] Mitchell wished to update the play: writer Martin Crimp, working from a literal translation, removed nineteenth century references and theatrical conventions such as the monologues. She believed that the alterations revealed both Chekhov's modernity and also a vision of a world of cruelty, comparing him in this with British writer Sarah Kane.[12]

Acts 1 and 4 were set at the back of the house so that the auditorium became the imaginary lake. This avoided reproducing a lake on stage and developed the symbolism of the house, a crumbling, dilapidated mansion. The set had intentionally anachronistic items such as an electric lamp, a microphone, a wind-up record player and plastic raincoats, alongside objects from the 1890s, and the characters danced tangos. Mitchell explained that the intention was 'to get a younger audience to watch the play without distancing themselves, thinking that it was all about old people in bustles and funny hats'.[13] The innovations were widely praised, though one critic wrote that altering the play's social context meant that 'loosed from its fin de siècle setting it floats uneasily'.[14] Crimp's contemporized version introduced direct contact between characters. In Act 1, Polina viciously ripped up flowers given by Nina to Dorn in front of Nina, whereas this action is usually more covert; Masha danced to Konstantin's piano playing in front of him, making his ensuing rejection of her more direct and cruel. Other aspects of relationships were also more overt; Dorn picked Masha up at the end of Act 1, reinforcing the hint in the text that she is his child. Political references were heightened; in staging Konstantin's play, the cast imagined the atmosphere of empty houses on the other side of the lake because of economic changes, so that the play was making a point politically, as well as lyrically, in its setting. Chekhov could only hint at the fact that Konstantin has been expelled from university for political reasons because of censorship, so Crimp wrote this in:

> Konstantin: No special skills. No money. And because I'd been stupid enough to play politics at university, not even a degree.
>
> (Chekhov 2006b: 7)

The result divided critical opinion. One critic wrote that 'it always requires a sure grasp of history – theatrical as well as political and social – to play with a text in this way ... Get it wrong, as Crimp has done, and you breach disciplines that are sacred.'[15] Others described it as 'a terrific revision'[16] taking 'bold liberties ... but the changes almost always seem to work'.[17]

The significant aspect of this interpretation of the play was the view of Nina as a crude and untalented actress. Her future was therefore seen as bleak: a life of prostitution in Yelets. In the original, in translation, Nina's speech in Act 4 reads:

> Now I'm a real actress, I like acting, I enjoy it. I'm intoxicated when I'm on stage and feel that I am beautiful. And now that I'm living here, I go walking and walking and thinking and thinking and feel everyday my spirit is growing stronger ... Now I know, understand, Konstantin, that in our work – it doesn't matter whether we act or we write – the main thing isn't fame, glamour, the things I dreamed about, it's knowing how to endure. I know how to shoulder my cross and have faith. I have faith and it's not so painful for me, and when I think about my calling, I'm not afraid of life.
>
> (Chekhov 2005: 181)

In Crimp's version this became 'But now I can really act – yes – really command the stage – feels amazing, like a drug' (Chekhov 2006b: 63), suggesting that Nina deludes herself about her acting talent and cutting the text about endurance seen as crucial by the other directors.

The Seagull *at the Royal Court*

Rickson chose to direct Christopher Hampton's version of *The Seagull* at the Royal Court Theatre to mark the fiftieth anniversary of the theatre famous for producing new writing, because he saw the play as essentially about the act of creation, the difficulties of being an artist, whether aspiring or a celebrity.[18] He saw Arkadina as a good actress within traditional theatre and Konstantin and Nina as promising beginners. The artistic desires of the other characters were acknowledged: Sorin's unfulfilled aspiration to be a writer, Dorn imagining what it would be like to write beautifully, Masha's poetic mode of expression.

The action of the play was oriented urgently towards Konstantin's suicide, balanced with Nina's journey to become an actress. The action of the first act centres around staging Konstantin's play, which Rickson saw as 'ambitious and beautiful', and the emotional reactions that it provokes, which Rickson noted parallel Chekhov's own experience in some ways. The climax of the first act was when Dorn is on stage alone saying 'I liked that play' (Chekhov 2007: 26), balancing the mockery it has received with a positive view. The significant moment in Act 4 is when Konstantin realizes that writing must flow from the heart: 'He's made a breakthrough. And at that moment, Nina is at the door and the play unravels'.[19] 'The moment on stage when he is tearing up his writing which was bold at the time, and really bold now, minutes of wordless action.' Rickson sees Chekhov's modernity in this boldness and also draws a comparison with Sarah Kane. In his view, Konstantin's suicide deprived the world of a potentially major writer as Kane's did. Rickson suggested Hampton refer to Kane's *4:48 Psychosis* when working on Konstantin's play, as both plays have a similar 'linguistically bare existential strangeness'.[20] Konstantin commits suicide, but for Rickson, the important thing is the depiction of Nina's journey from naïvety and her self-destructive love for Trigorin to the point where she changes her ambition from wanting to be famous to wanting to be a good actress. At this point, her depression lifts. Rickson said:

And when she says 'I know now, Kostya, that it's not the fame, the glory, but the ability to endure', I always burst into tears because I think what an amazing revelation to have. I spent fifteen years at the Royal Court watching writers and actors grapple with that – from experiencing initial moments of fame to thinking the important thing is to try to sustain and endure a career – and anyone can identify with that, from an estate agent to a painter.[21]

In Rickson's view, Chekhov shows that though a person may have damaging experiences, there is still the possibility of growth and understanding arising from them. This human journey means the play continues to resonate for audiences. Critics recognized this as the main emphasis in the production. Nina 'delivers the play's most fortifying message, following her convincing conversion from innocent to broken woman – that it's the ability to endure that counts in art as in life. Young writers, take heart.'[22] Critics also noted the theme of celebrity as a trap in the production, and how Trigorin

Figure 4.2 Mackenzie Crook as Konstantin in *The Seagull* at the Royal Court Theatre © Johan Persson

and Arkadina have become limited by it – 'Art has nothing to do with celebrity.'[23]

Rickson believed that the play would resonate most strongly for a contemporary audience if it was placed in its original time and setting, and so immersed himself in Russian culture to find the opposite of the traditional lyrical and sad English Chekhov. 'He gives the play strong socio-political pointing ... Hildegard Bechtler's handsome design is something different. A forlorn pair of birch trees and a grey back wall remind us that Sorin's estate and the life of the landed gentry is fading out in bleak poverty.'[24] The result was a production that was widely recognized as achieving a balance between humour and poignancy, one that succeeded in conveying Chekhov's tragicomedy.

5 Space and confinement

Uncle Vanya

Uncle Vanya was probably completed in 1896 after *The Seagull*, and first produced in 1899. While Chekhov's ironic subtitle to the play, *Scenes from Country Life*, suggests pastoral comedy, his reflection on Russian provincial life in the 1890s is anything but idyllic. He examines the situation of members of the intelligentsia, who, inspired by the ideals of the 1860s, have worked for reform to no avail, as they reach middle age in the early years of the reign of Nicholas II. Misplaced loyalties and unexamined idealism are presented as a way in which people can collude with situations in which they are oppressed. The difficulty of 'wringing the slave' out of oneself in a repressive social environment is seen. In this most poetic play, Chekhov uses a series of metaphors related to space and confinement to convey the predicament of people who are gifted but thwarted in seeking a way forward in life. Furthermore, his exploration of concepts of time and space widens the perspective from the specific historical moment to present a view of existence in general.

UNCLE VANYA – SCENES FROM COUNTRY LIFE

Again, a traditional melodramatic plot, where a young and beautiful woman is unhappily married to an old man and has two suitors, is transformed in Chekhovian style. Yelena Andreyevna, married to Professor Serebryakov, a retired professor of literature, is the object of the attentions of both Ivan Petrovich Voinitsky (Vanya), Serebryakov's brother-in-law by his first marriage, and Mikhail

Lvovich Astrov, the local doctor. Act 1 begins in the garden of the Serebryakovs' country estate, which is maintained by Vanya and Sonya, Serebryakov's daughter by his first wife, Vera Petrovna, who died nine years previously. Serebryakov and his second wife Yelena are visiting the estate for the summer. Ilya Ilich Telegin, an impoverished local landowner, is a constant visitor. As characters arrive to take tea, various frustrations are voiced: Marina complains that Serebryakov and Yelena's presence disrupts the daily routine, as they eat fine meals at times customary for high society rather than those usual for the household. Astrov complains to Marina about his hard life and reveals that a patient in his care recently died under chloroform when he was operating, exhausted by dealing with a typhus epidemic. Vanya has two obsessions: the beautiful Yelena and the professor, whom he resents. Vanya and Sonya have worked on the estate, Vanya for the past twenty-five years, encouraged by his mother, Mariya Vasilyevna, in order to enhance the professor's income for his research on literature. Vanya once believed this work to be important; he now finds it empty and pretentious.

Act 2 is set in the dining room of the house past midnight that night. A storm is brewing and the atmosphere is stifling. The frustrations of the characters begin to be voiced more openly. Serebryakov is in pain and argues with the exhausted Yelena. He has refused to let Astrov examine him. Vanya and the doctor have been drinking and Vanya makes a pass at Yelena, which she rejects. Astrov despises himself for drinking and is encouraged to stop by Sonya. Yelena and Sonya have not been speaking to each other but now have a tête-à-tête, in which Yelena assures Sonya that she married her father because she then thought she loved him, not from wrong motives, as Sonya has suspected. She now knows she does not love him. Sonya confesses her love for Astrov and Yelena expresses her admiration for him. Yelena wants to release her emotions by playing the piano and Sonya goes to ask her father's permission for this. He refuses and the act ends with this image of the women being forbidden their music.

Some time passes until Act 3, which takes place in September. There are various turning points, rather than dramatic climaxes. The professor has called a meeting for one o'clock in the dining room. Vanya annoys Yelena and goes to fetch flowers for her as a peace offering. Sonya expresses her desperation to Yelena; Astrov does not notice her, though he now visits daily to see Yelena. Yelena promises to question Astrov discreetly about his feelings for Sonya and asks him to show her his drawings of the district, which show the deforestation of the last twenty-five years. He is passionately committed to preserving the forests. Yelena asks him directly about his feelings for Sonya. Astrov says that a month or two ago he might have considered a relationship with Sonya but not now (the implication being, since he has met Yelena). He suggests Yelena has engineered the conversation to manipulate him and kisses her as Vanya enters with a bunch of roses.

Oblivious to the acute emotions of the rejected Sonya, humiliated Vanya and mortified Yelena, Serebryakov begins the meeting and proposes to sell the estate to buy a cottage in Finland (near St Petersburg), for himself and Yelena. Vanya is incensed, as the estate in fact belongs to Sonya, bought as a dowry for her mother. Vanya worked to pay off the mortgage and relinquished his inheritance for his sister and her husband, taking only a small salary. He accuses Serebryakov of ruining his life and goes to get a gun, which he fires at Serebryakov. He misses and collapses in exhaustion.

The final act, of departures but not resolutions, is set shortly afterwards in Vanya's study. Serebryakov and Yelena are leaving for the provincial city of Kharkhov, where they are going to live. Everyday routines are being re-established: Marina is winding wool with the help of Telegin and looking forward to eating ordinary food again. There is a concern that Vanya may kill himself: Astrov asks Vanya to return the morphine he has taken from the doctor's bag. Vanya says he cannot face the rest of his life. Astrov shouts at him to rouse him from his self-pity. Sonya persuades Vanya to return the morphine and she and Vanya prepare to get back to work on the estate accounts. Goodbyes are said; Serebryakov accepts Vanya's apologies and asks his forgiveness. Vanya replies that everything will be as before as regards the allowance. Astrov leaves, saying he will not call again, unless needed, until next summer. Left with his niece, with Marina knitting, Telegin playing the guitar and his mother reading a pamphlet, Vanya tries to work, though he is in despair. Sonya attempts to comfort him with her religious vision, assuring him in an emotive speech that though in their lives they have to labour for others, they will bear their fate with patience, and after death, God will take pity on them and they will rest.

The Wood Demon

Uncle Vanya had its genesis in an earlier play, *The Wood Demon* (also translated as *The Wood Goblin*). In 1888, Chekhov had begun to write a comedy with Suvorin, which he completed by himself in 1889, when he was also reworking *Ivanov*. It was staged by Maria Abramova's company in Moscow, but was not received well. One critic wrote that if Chekhov wanted to put real life on stage, he should first consider that no one wanted to see it. 'We want extra-ordinary occurrences' (Schuler 1996: 221 n 91). This indicates expectations of drama of the time; as compared with the later plays, *The Wood Demon* has 'dramatic' events. Zhorzh, the prototype for Vanya, commits suicide in Act 3 and the play ends with two engagements: that of Sonya to Dr Khrushchov, and that of two other characters, Yuliya and Fyodor Ivanovich Orlovsky. Dr Khrushchov, from whom Astrov's character was derived, is nick-named 'the Wood Demon' because of his passion for conserving the forests. The basic plot is much the same: Professor Serebryakov has retired with his young second wife Yelena to the estate belonging to his daughter Sonya and his brother-in-law, Zhorzh. Serebryakov plans to sell the estate, which is not his to sell. This precipitates Zhorzh's suicide, which is comparable to Ivanov's in that Zhorzh, like Ivanov, has been subjected to social opprobrium and gossip; it is believed that he has had a sexual relationship with Yelena. In reworking the plot so that Vanya, unlike Zhorzh, does not actually commit suicide, and having Astrov reject Sonya rather than having a conventional romantic end to the play, Chekhov turns his 'comedy' into a complex drama of mid-life crisis.

It is generally recognized that in *The Wood Demon*, Chekhov was experimenting with Tolstoy's Christian philosophy of loving one's neighbour (Magarshack 1980: 121, Papernyi 1982: 84–85, Senelick 1985: 43). Khrushchov says to Sonya:

> If you knew how oppressive and stifling it is here! An environ-ment in which everyone sidles up to a man, peers at him out of the corner of their eye and pigeonholes him as a populist, a psychopath, a windbag – anything at all other than a human being.
>
> (Chekhov 2006a: 621)

This is a sentiment expressed by Chekhov himself in a letter he wrote while working on the play: 'respect, trust and absolute honesty are necessary in relationships' (Chekhov 1976b 2: 256). The lack of understanding and the malice of those around him prompts Zhorzh's suicide. Characters' problems are resolved when they see the importance of sincerity and lack of judgement in their relationships with each other; so, for example, the profligate Orlovsky is reformed by Yulya's love.

Chekhov widens the focus from moral issues by the inclusion of a deeper political perspective in *Uncle Vanya*. In both plays, Serebryakov uses a motto of 1860s liberalism, 'one must take action' (Chekhov 2006a: 605, 2005: 236), a statement made also in the later play by Mariya Vasilyevna, urging commitment to social causes. In *The Wood Demon*, Chekhov indicates that Serebryakov's liberal stance and his utilitarian literary work are insincere and that Krushchov's work is of more value, as he has Serebryakov disdaining Krushchov's commitment to the environment and to providing medical care for the peasants. In *Uncle Vanya*, however, the difference in political points of view is more complicated: Serebryakov's purported liberalism has brought about no change but neither has the programme of social action initiated by reformers such as Krushchov, in his twenties in the earlier play. Astrov says at the beginning of *Uncle Vanya*, 'In ten years time I've turned into a different man' (Chekhov 2005: 197), indicating that over the course of the past decade, idealistic Krushchovs in Russia have turned into disillusioned Astrovs. Astrov's campaign for the forests and his tireless work as a doctor now appear to him to be a drop in the ocean. He says to Vanya:

> In the whole district there were only two decent, cultured men, you and I. But it took no more than ten years for humdrum life, despicable life to drag us down; its pestilential fumes poisoned our blood and we have become just as vulgar (*poshlyi*) as everybody else.
>
> (Chekhov 2005: 233)

In *Uncle Vanya*, Chekhov considers the condition of people living such a life, without proposing solutions. This most medical of the major plays, with the predominance of the doctor figure in Astrov and its inclusion of themes of sickness and health, provides a diagnosis of the condition of Russia in the 1890s.

Space and confinement

The play has been construed as a play about false ideals. Depperman identifies the central theme as 'the disillusionment of the idealists' (Chekhov 2005: 549). Chekhov explores how people respond to the loss of ideals, whether political or personal, by means of the characters' self-dramatization and use of literary references, by a series of poetic images and metaphors which recur through the play, and also by the characters' discussions about their situation, work and the future.

Self-dramatization

In *Uncle Vanya*, as in *Ivanov* and *The Seagull*, Chekhov's characters react to the frustrations of their environment through melodramatic behaviour. This aspect of the behaviour of Chekhov's characters has been variously discussed: Morson writes that histrionics is Chekhov's central theme (1993: 214). Kramer notes that there are characters who are determined to see the drama in their own lives, but who at the same time debunk one another's dramas (1999: 512). Tait discusses Vanya's outburst in Act 3 in terms of gendered behaviour:

> the representation of emotion in Chekhov's play is socially aligned with the ways in which hysterical talk is conflated with femininity, which therefore make Vanya seem emasculated.
>
> (Tait 2002: 43)

Through Vanya's self-dramatization, Chekhov develops both the theme of suicide and his dramatic technique. Unlike Ivanov and Konstantin, Vanya does not kill himself; his is an inner drama of someone toying with the ideas of murder and suicide. This is a source of the play's dark humour, from Act 1, where Vanya responds to Yelena's comment on the lovely weather that it is 'good weather for hanging oneself … ' (Chekhov 2005: 203), to the tragi-comic debacle of Act 3, where he fires the gun offstage then runs into the parlour and shoots again, missing Serebryakov though he is firing at close quarters. His intention to commit suicide is no stronger; he meekly hands over the morphine he has stolen from Astrov when Sonya requests it. Vanya differs from both Ivanov and Konstantin in the 'undramatic' outcomes of his self-dramatizing, which are more comic but still poignant. There is no condemnation of the characters for this behaviour; with his psychological insight, Chekhov shows how with self-dramatization goes self-denigration and distress that the characters are trying to communicate. In *The Seagull,* Konstantin's self-deprecation escalates to his perception of himself as 'nothing'; Ivanov describes himself as 'no-good, pathetic, insignificant'; and Vanya's 'stabbing sense of shame can't be compared to any pain there is' (Chekhov 2005: 63, 232–33).

Tait, pointing out how the characters use shared cultural narratives in their self-dramatization, notes:

> Self-dramatisation is recognised as a motif in Chekhov's depiction of social behaviour but the intertextuality is much more significant to the meaning of the plays than most commentaries indicate.
>
> (Tait 2002: 21)

Vanya's poignantly comic 'If I had had a normal life, I might have evolved into a Schopenhauer, a Dostoevsky' (Chekhov 2005: 228) – comic partly because Schopenhauer and Dostoevsky's lives were anything but normal – should also be read in the context of Chekhov's attitudes to their philosophies. Schopenhauer's pessimism is connected with misguided ideas in *Ivanov* and *The Seagull* and Chekhov, on the whole, did not admire Dostoevsky's orthodox Christian philosophy.[1] He wrote to Suvorin in 1889 that Dostoevsky's work was 'all right, but much too long and lacking in modesty. Too pretentious' (Chekhov 1973: 331). Vanya is thinking about his life in the wrong way, blaming others for his lack of achievement, but unclear about what he thinks he should have achieved. Telegin pronounces that Vanya's outburst in Act 3 is 'A subject worthy of Aivazovsky's brush' (Chekhov 2005: 231). Aivazovsky was a Russian nineteenth century painter of dramatic sea battles and storms. Telegin aggrandizes Vanya's anti-climactic misfire by the reference. The citing of famous writers and artists serves to underline that the events of the characters' lives are those of the everyday (*byt*).

Serebryakov makes literary references, including a joke that falls flat, when he begins the meeting he has called in Act 3 by stating 'I have invited you here, my friends, to inform you that we are about to be visited by an Inspector General' (Chekhov 2005: 225). This is the first line spoken by the Mayor in Gogol's *The Inspector General,* an exposé of the corruption of bureaucracy under the Tsars. The use of a literary joke, and the characters' lack of response to it, is an indicator of how out of sympathy they are with Serebryakov's academic credentials. Other characters also use literary images of themselves to self-dramatize. Yelena says, 'Mine is a dreary walk-on part ... In the field of music and in my husband's house, in any of life's dramas – no matter where, in short, I've only had a walk-on part' (Chekhov 2005: 217). She complains of boredom in Act 3 and Sonya suggests she does some work: getting involved in managing the farm, teaching, or nursing. Yelena responds

> I don't know how. Besides, it's not interesting. Only in social-purpose novels do people teach and tend peasants, and how am I, out of the blue, supposed to go tend them or teach them?
>
> (Chekhov 2005: 219)

In dramatizing her situation as that of someone on the sidelines of life and in dismissing working for social improvement as a fiction rather than a practical possibility (though it is what Astrov does), Yelena reveals that she thinks she has been born for something greater. Similarly, in *My Life,* Masha, a beautiful and musical woman, marries Misail and 'goes to the people' with him, but eventually looks as though

> she were coming out of a coma and was now wondering how she, who was so intelligent, cultured and so fastidious, could have fallen into this pitiful provincial hole among a band of petty, worthless people ...
>
> (Chekhov 2003: 346)

As he says goodbye to Yelena, Astrov pronounces '*Finita la commedia*!' The Italian phrase signifies that the comedy-drama of the characters has been played out; in Chekhov's metatheatre, the inner drama of his plays is partly created through the self-dramatizing of the characters. Moreover, Chekhov's use of imagery, throughout this play in particular, expresses the inner life of the characters and their relationships.

Breath and suffocation

Polarized imagery of space and confinement, suffocation and breath indicates relationships between people and with the environment. Chekhov makes use of 'pathetic fallacy', where the weather reflects the emotional atmosphere. 'It's stifling', says Astrov, in Act 1, echoed by Vanya (Chekhov 2005: 197, 199). The storm building in Act 2 symbolizes Vanya's mounting anger and frustration and Serebryakov says he is suffocating (Chekhov 2005: 206). When the storm is over, Yelena opens the window to let in the fresh air and Vanya says that though everything in nature will be refreshed, he will not be: 'Day and night, like an incubus, the idea chokes me that my life has been wasted irretrievably.' The metaphor of suffocation and breath pervades the play: Vanya says of Serebryakov: 'I lived, I breathed for him' (Chekhov 2005: 210, 211). In Act 4, Vanya says how hard it is for him: the Russian '*Tyazhalo mene*', meaning literally 'It is heavy on me', 'I feel weighed down' (Chekhov 2005: 238). At the very end, Sonya's 'We shall rest', in Russian, '*my otdokhnyom*', is etymologically related to *dushno*, the word for 'stifling', and connotes breathing freely (see Senelick in Redmond 1982: 244–45, Senelick 1985: 95).

The house itself suffocates and confines the inhabitants. Yelena says 'there is something oppressive about this house'. Serebryakov states in Act 3, 'I do not like this house. Just like a labyrinth. Twenty-six enormous rooms, everyone scatters and you can never find anyone.' He also refers to the house as a 'mausoleum', in which he is 'in exile' (Chekhov 2005: 209, 225, 208). The house and estate are isolated: at the end of the play, Astrov says that he will not come until the spring, indicating, as well as his choice to be away from Sonya, that during the winter months travel to the estate will be difficult. The settings of the play move from outdoors into the house and finally into Vanya's office, which is also his bedroom. No doubt for reasons of economy, much of Vanya's life, waking and sleeping, is in this one confined space, despite the size of the house. Astrov connects the imagery of the house with how its inhabitants are trapped in negative attitudes, saying:

> I wouldn't last a month in this house, I'd suffocate in this atmosphere ... Your father all wrapped up in his gout and his books, Uncle Vanya with his biliousness, your grandmother, and lastly your stepmother ... a life of idleness cannot be pure.
> (Chekhov 2005: 213–14)

The characters see themselves as trapped: both in themselves (Yelena refers to herself as 'inhibited'), and by each other. The caged starling in Vanya's room in Act 4 forms a contrast with Yelena's image of freedom: 'If I could fly like an uncaged bird away from you all'. Astrov sees himself caught by Yelena, like a sparrow by a fox or a weasel (Chekhov 2005: 221, 223). The professor begs not to be left alone with Vanya in Act 2, saying 'he will talk me blue in the face' (Chekhov 2005: 208).

Construction of gender

Traditional masculine and feminine roles form an aspect of the way the characters are entrapped. The play has been discussed as a crisis of masculine identity (Tait 2002: 37) and Serebryakov, Vanya and Astrov seen as forming a 'tense masculine triangle' (Bjørnager 2005: 54) in their relationships with each other and with Yelena. Vanya's 'ineffectuality as a male protagonist' has been ascribed to the network of emotional ties that bind him to his dead sister, her family and his mother (Vitins 1981: 35). He idealizes Vera, his dead sister, describing her as a 'pure angel', believing that somehow his situation would be different 'if only she knew!', though it is hard to see in what way it would make a difference, as Vera, from Marina's description, also devoted her life to the Professor, and was full of anxieties about him (Chekhov 2005: 200, 213, 209). Vanya's loyalty to Vera, his relationships with his mother – who colludes in the sacrifice of Vanya's life to support Serebryakov – and Sonya have enslaved him, frustrated him as a lover and emasculated him.

In counterpoint to the male triangle, there is a female triangle of a different kind, of Yelena, Sonya and her deceased mother Vera.

Their names all evoke Ancient Greek 'virtues', particularly linked to female images: 'Sonya' signifies wisdom, and 'Vera' faith, Yelena's name suggests beauty, after Helen of Troy.[2] Yelena's beauty is a problem, both for her and other characters. Others compare themselves with her unfavourably: Sonya repeats throughout the play that she is unattractive (Chekhov 2005: 220), and the men, while admiring Yelena, comment on their own perceived ugliness. Telegin introduces himself in a self-deprecating way, saying he is called 'Waffles' on account of his 'pock-marked appearance'. Serebryakov says he disgusts himself and everyone must be disgusted to look at him. Astrov compares himself to an Ostrovsky character: 'a man long on moustache and short on brains' (Chekhov 2005: 202, 207, 203–4).

The men objectify Yelena because of her beauty and it both defines and limits her. She regrets her marriage and her husband limits even her opportunities to express herself artistically.[3] Vanya thinks he is in love with her; he continually makes demands on her, but rarely listens to her. His fantasy about how he would comfort her, if they were married, during a storm, when she would nestle, in fear, in his arms, is an image that does not accord with reality. Yelena is clearly not afraid of storms and has a practical streak to her nature. She struggles to take the gun from Vanya in Act 3; her action in the situation is purposive, whereas Vanya's is not. The men, as well as constructing images of her feminine fragility, also view her as a sexual predator. Vanya, using sexualized imagery, urges her to be a 'water nymph' (Chekhov 2005: 219). Yelena finds male attitudes towards her, their desire to possess her, destructive. In contrast, Astrov reflects on the meaning of 'beauty' in relation to Yelena, indicating that in his opinion her beauty is skin deep as 'everything about a human being should be beautiful: face, dress, soul, ideas' and Yelena's idle life cannot be 'pure' (Chekhov 2005: 206, 213). Aspects of the male characters' negative view of Yelena have been echoed in those of male critics. Magarshack sees her as a 'predator' (1972: 87); see also Styan (1971: 136).

Yelena's lassitude could also be a form of depression; she, like Vanya, is disillusioned, having dedicated her life to a man she wrongly believed to be great. The wife of a provincial doctor, Pobedimskaya, wrote to Chekhov asking whether she was right to interpret the character not as ' ... an apathetic idle woman, incapable of thinking or even loving', but as a 'reasoning, thinking person, who is made unhappy by her dissatisfaction with her present life'. Chekhov replied that Pobedimskaya was right:

> Yelena Andreyevna may produce the impression of being incapable of thinking or even loving, but while I was writing *Uncle Vanya* I had something completely different in mind.
>
> (Chekhov 1973: 446)

Sonya's name is connected with 'wisdom'. By the end of the play she has developed: she has experienced unrequited love and rejection but is established as a force within the household and finds a way to go on; perhaps, in this sense, she has gained 'wisdom'. Her final speech is intended to comfort Vanya; women frequently take the role of 'wise comforter', particularly with the men. The play begins with Marina sympathizing with Astrov, allowing him to drink vodka because she understands that he drinks to mask his pain, and ends with Sonya overcoming her own tiredness and disappointment to find words of encouragement for her uncle. Sonya and Yelena try to soothe Serebryakov in Act 2 and though he rejects them, he allows Marina to take him to bed. Marina also counsels Sonya, who cannot turn to her father or her uncle. Marina offers her own homespun wisdom along with food and drink and comforts Astrov, Serebryakov and Telegin with the assurance of God's mercy and understanding (Chekhov 2005: 198, 209, 231). Sonya also asserts in her final speech:

> We shall hear the angels, we shall see heaven all diamonds, we shall see how all earthly woes and all our sufferings will be submerged in a compassion that will fill all the world and our life will be peaceful, tender and sweet as a caress ... We shall be at rest!
>
> (Chekhov 2005: 238–39)

The topic of Chekhov and religion has been widely discussed (see Jackson 1993, Sobennikov 1997, de Sherbinin 1997, Swift 2004). Chekhov presents a variety of views of priests and orthodox religion in his writing; sometimes satirized as in the story *In the Ravine*. In *The Student* (1894), and here, he presents the profundity of some people's religious belief. There is no authorial comment; this is Sonya's 'wisdom', not Chekhov's, and her way of surviving the difficulty of her current circumstances.

The name of 'Vera' resonates with the discourse on the meaning of 'faith' that runs through the play: there is Sonya and Marina's religious faith and Yelena's assertion that 'you must trust everyone; otherwise life becomes unliveable' (Chekhov 2005: 217). Vanya criticizes Yelena's sexual fidelity to the Professor, which he says is 'phony', adding sarcastically, 'To cheat on an old husband you can't stand – that's immoral; to try and stifle the vestiges of youth and vital feeling in yourself – that's not immoral.' Telegin objects, plaintively arguing that anyone who is unfaithful to their husband or wife is 'someone who might even betray his country!' He reveals that his wife left him the day after their marriage, but since then he has remained faithful to her, selling his estate to educate the children she had with her lover. He has no happiness, but he has his pride (Chekhov 2005: 201). The consideration of faith highlights Vanya's situation: he put his trust unquestioningly in the Professor and has been disappointed.

Lack of understanding

The characters generally are trapped in views of each other. Vanya, having lost his trust, is obsessed with the thought that he has been deceived by the professor, whom he refers to as 'a soap bubble', a 'perpetual motion writing machine' (Chekhov 2005: 211, 203). Some critics have construed Serebryakov as the villain of the piece (Magarshack 1980: 222–23). But it is possible to read much of Serebryakov's behaviour, such as his complaints about Astrov and refusal to see him, as resulting from his fear of death. He makes constant references to death and fears sleep as it may bring death with it. In this, he can be compared with Chekhov's other old men, such as Shabelsky and Sorin. The critical discussion of naturalism and realism in art in the sixties was progressive: the problem is when once radical views become ossified they are no longer relevant as times change. Comparably, in *The Name Day Party* (1888), Peter is depicted as a 'man of the sixties', now a high court judge who has abandoned his former principles and postures as an important figure in society. The portrayal of Peter, like that of

Serebryakov, is not without compassion and Serebryakov too suffers as a result of government policies and the poor pensions given to retired academics (Bjørnager 2005: 51). Vanya refuses to see anything that might condone Serebryakov's behaviour. He also condemns his mother: 'My old magpie of a *maman* goes on babbling about women's rights; one eye peers into the grave, while the other pores over her high-minded pamphlets, looking for the dawn of a new life' (Chekhov 2005: 199–200). He despises her political beliefs but has no way forward to suggest. Mariya too has had her disappointments. She takes refuge in her reading, clinging to her faith in Serebryakov, refusing to question her long-held beliefs. She is shocked to see that the writer of a pamphlet she is reading has changed his views and is writing the opposite of what he said seven years ago.

Astrov is a progressive, a talented man; his name suggests 'stars'. His efforts to bring about social improvement have been as nothing in the years of indifference and repression after the 1860s. He has worked for a better future and hoped to see some results and now believes there will be no reward for his work in his lifetime. When he is drunk, he recaptures his grand ecological vision, making plans for the future. When sober, he is disillusioned; he says several times that he loves no one, except perhaps Marina. Astrov excuses his drinking on the grounds of the life he leads, working with disease, poverty and in bad conditions. Despite his problems, he continues to live by his philosophy, interrupting his work in the course of the play only because of his attraction to Yelena. He is widely misunderstood; Serebryakov disparages him as a 'holy fool' (Chekhov 2005: 208).

Waking and sleeping

Krasner has identified how, in the language of the play, words to do with sleeping and awakening are repeated and the main gesture of the play from Vanya's point of view goes from awakening to rest (1994). Vanya enters in Act 1, having napped after lunch, saying 'Yes … (*pause*) Yes' (Chekhov 2005: 198). He is speaking in response to something he has been dreaming about, not to Astrov and Marina. The idea of dreaming is used as it is in *The Seagull* to suggest escape from reality. Vanya exists in his dreams about

Yelena, and desire for revenge on the professor. He says, 'When there is no real life, people live on illusions. After all, it's better than nothing.' He speaks 'dreamily'; he dreams of Yelena's eyes (Chekhov 2005: 212, 199). Though there are dreams, there is no restful sleep, for Vanya or other characters. In Act 2, Vanya has been sleeping in the daytime and in Act 3, he has not slept for three nights from frustration at having wasted time (Chekhov 2005: 202). Instead of restful sleep there is laziness (a word particularly associated with Yelena), torpor, numbness, in Astrov's case, assisted by alcohol. Vanya toys with the idea of putting himself to sleep forever with morphine. Serebryakov keeps others awake and no one can sleep in Act 2 because of him and the stormy environment, whereas Chekhov wrote to Knipper that in Act 4 'the atmosphere should be quiet and lethargic' (Chekhov 1980b 8: 272).

Vanya seeks a new awakening: 'If one could wake up on a bright, still morning and feel that life had begun anew, that all the past is forgotten, has blown away like smoke', but Astrov denies that such a thing is possible and says there is only one hope: 'lying in our coffins we'll be haunted by visions, maybe even pleasant ones' (Chekhov 2005: 233). At the end of the play, Vanya has in fact awoken, not to a new life but to the painful reality of his situation. He is in a liminal space: he does not share Sonya's vision and does not know how to go forward. His twenty-five years' self-imposed service to an intellectual ideal has been based on an illusion and there is nothing, at the moment, to give him a direction in life.

Darkness and light / blindness and sight

Images of darkness and light and of blindness and sight further illustrate Vanya's inner journey and also the situation of other characters. Astrov, the visionary, is currently, like Vanya, in spiritual darkness.

> You know how, when you walk through a forest on a dark night, if all the time in the distance there's a glimmer of light, you don't mind the fatigue or the dark or the prickly branches hitting you in the face ... but in the distance there's no light glimmering for me.
>
> (Chekhov 2005: 214)

He has no expectations and no love for anyone. Vanya says his better feelings are 'fading away … like a sunbeam trapped at the bottom of a mineshaft, and I'm fading along with them' (Chekhov 2005: 210). He responds sarcastically to his mother who says he used to be 'a man of steadfast convictions, a shining light', 'Oh yes! I was a shining light but no-one ever basked in my rays … ' He adds that before last year (when he met Yelena as Serebryakov's wife) he, like his mother, was deliberately trying to cloud his vision with 'book learning … to keep from seeing real life … ' (Chekhov 2005: 202). He has been in the dark and thinks he now sees reality: that Serebryakov is to blame for his problems. His response to the plan to sell the estate in Act 3 is to say 'now my eyes have been opened!' (Chekhov 2005: 228).

Here, Vanya's desperate behaviour belies true insight. Like Yelena, he wants what is impossible; to start again with a new life. The desire to start a new life, to run or fly away is echoed by many Chekhov characters: Andrey in *Three Sisters*, Laptev in *Three Years*. Mariya tells Vanya that he seems to blame his former convictions, but 'they aren't to blame, you are' (Chekhov 2005: 203). Unless he takes responsibility for himself and stops blaming Serebryakov for his situation, which he entered into freely, there can be no possibilities for him. His social situation will not change in the immediate future; all that can change is the way he views his life. He can choose whether to give way to despair or to carry on. In the moving scene at the end of the play Sonya tells him with passion: 'what can be done? We have to go on living' (Chekhov 2005: 238). Yelena has described the situation in the household as 'hell' (Chekhov 2005: 228). Finke discusses Chekhov's use of *katabasis*, the archetypal motif of the hero's descent into the underworld in many works (1994). Vanya passes from living hell, the darkness of his unawareness, then the insane anger that clouds his judgement, in order, possibly, to see more clearly.

Sonya evidently gains insight. At the beginning of the play, she does not understand Yelena and does not appear to notice Astrov's fascination with her. She learns truths about both of them. The conviction with which she delivers her final speech is very different from the hesitant way she speaks about Astrov's forests in Act 1; she has found her own vision, instead of adopting Astrov's.

Sickness and health

Motifs of illness pervade the play. The theme of the destruction of environment is entwined symbiotically with that of human illness – mental and physical. There are references to clinical conditions such as typhus, angina pectoris, gout, migraine, rheumatism and ageing. The figure of the doctor and his dilemma in the social situation is examined more closely than in other plays. Astrov is haunted by the death of his patient, which signifies his failure to meet the ideal of a doctor. The doctor himself is sick and reliant on the self-medication of alcohol to function. Characters diagnose each other: Vanya says of Serebryakov: 'His poor old liver's bloated with envy and jealousy' (Chekhov 2005: 200). Astrov sees Serebryakov's medicine bottles and asks: 'Every town in Russia must be fed up with his gout. Is he sick or faking?' (Chekhov 2005: 211). Astrov tells Yelena that she and Serebryakov have poisoned them all, infecting them with idleness, and states that he himself would perish if they stayed. He also says to Vanya that this life's 'pestilential fumes poisoned our blood' (Chekhov 2005: 235, 233). Remedies do not work: Serebryakov insists he is being given the wrong medicine. Vanya wants medicine from Astrov in Act 4 but he has none to give him. Only Marina's solicitation and lime-flower tea can bring relief for some. There is discussion of psychological illness; Vanya claims to be insane but Astrov says he is not that but a 'crackpot' (Chekhov 2005: 232) and that he has come to the conclusion that this is the normal condition for a human being. Astrov complains that people consider him odd because of his vegetarianism and love of forests; he sees his hard life as having turned him, too, into a 'crackpot' (Chekhov 2005: 197, 205).

Time

Chekhov's treatment of time expands the horizons of the play. Time is important in all Chekhov's plays; the characters speak of time, discussing past time and future time (see Turner 1994). They remind each other of mortality, as Serebryakov does in this play: '*Manet omnes una nox*' (the same night awaits us all) (Chekhov 2005: 226). Events preceding the plays are significant to the temporal context of the plays. Astrov says to Marina as the play opens, 'Nanny how long have we known each other?', and talks about what has happened to him in the past eleven years (Chekhov 2005: 197–98). Timing is also important: in Act 3, Astrov talks about the old and the new life of their society and its decline; a failure to act in the past has brought about current problems. Vanya reflects on his failure to act at the right time; he believes he could have married Yelena if he had approached her ten years ago. His appearance in Act 3 with a bunch of roses for her, only to see her kissing Astrov, a moment of tragifarce, is another example of bad timing (Chekhov 2005: 211, 224).

Attention is drawn to the cyclical nature of time, the progression of days and changing of seasons in all the plays. *Uncle Vanya* begins on a summer afternoon, ending on an autumn evening that year. Hristic notes that as the events in the life of the characters are placed in the cycle of nature in this way

> they cease to be simply private unhappinesses and begin to take on that cosmic dimension which the events in a classical play, by its nature and the status of its heroes, naturally and directly possessed.
>
> (1985: 280)

Time in Chekhov lacks causality as in classical drama and the flow of time from past to present to future puts the events of the play in context. We witness what the characters make of the present moment and then life goes on. Marina says of Vanya's outburst and attack on Serebryakov in Act 3, events that, at the time, seem cataclysmic to the characters, 'Honk, honk go the geese and then they stop' (Chekhov 2005: 229).

Chekhov's ideas of time have been compared with those of philosophers; Golub compares Chekhov's with Henri Bergson's view that human beings can measure duration but experience time subjectively (1994: 19–20). *Time and Free Will* (1890) suggests that time itself brings unforeseeable possibilities. We cannot predict the future for Chekhov's characters in this time of change. Hristic refers to Heidegger's concept of being as defined by temporality (1985: 282), as propounded in *Being and Time* (1927), as only time can bring understanding. Chekhov's interest in Darwinism encouraged him to see human beings as subject to time and chance. Like Herzen, he rejected philosophical pessimism, maintaining that though human life is not pre-ordained by God, morality is nonetheless possible (Kelly 1999: 10, 349). Though Chekhov's characters are at the mercy of time, they are rarely powerless, and can take some responsibility for their lives. Despite the difficulty of circumstances, the characters are not tragically trapped in time.

Uncle Vanya reveals the reluctance of the characters to assume responsibility for the present moment. The characters live in the past and the future as if they have parallel lives in which their dreams are fulfilled. Vanya thinks he could have 'had everything that's withheld from me now by my old age' if he had not wasted his time (Chekhov 2005: 202). In Sonya's imaginary life, Astrov is always there: 'every minute I can hear him, feel the pressure of his hand; and I stare at the door and wait, I get the sense he is about to walk in' (Chekhov 2005: 220). Yelena believes her life is unfulfilled. Serebryakov, too, is 'every minute yearning for the past', his life at the university (Chekhov 2005: 208). Astrov is preoccupied with the future; he believed he was working for a better future for Russia and in his disillusionment is disturbed by the fact that the people 'we are blazing a trail for' one or two hundred years from now will not remember him (Chekhov 2005: 198).

Work and the environment

The play ends with the return to work. Astrov goes to visit his patients, Marina knits, with help from Telegin, Sonya and Vanya return to work on the running of the estate, which Vanya has been neglecting. Mariya Vasilyevna carries on with her reading. But the value of work, intellectual or manual, is under question; what kind of work can bring about change, can restore health both to people and to the environment? Chekhov has been seen in this play as exposing the idealization of romantic love, wealth and status and proposing the value of 'prosaic work', such as work on the estate and care for the peasants, 'counteracting idle and wasteful habits' (Morson 1993: 223) (see also Valency 1966: 196, Peace 1983: 57, Magarshack 1980: 223).

So much work remains to be done. The estate is isolated, Kharkov is the nearest town but there is no mention of a railway. As Astrov points out:

> The peasants are very monotonous, backward, they live in filth; and it's hard to get on with educated people ... they don't see beyond their noses ... A spontaneous, unpolluted, open relationship to nature and to human beings no longer exists ...
>
> (Chekhov 2005: 214)

In the 1830s, the state's income from forestry was far exceeded by the losses from fire and illegal tree felling. The Minister of Finances admitted knowing nothing about rural resources. Steps were taken through the 1850s and 1860s in land allocation and preservation, peasant farming practices and provision against bad harvests, but this only prepared the ground for the more substantial changes needed which did not take place as the regime lacked the personnel required to make progress in rural areas (Saunders 1992: 131–32).

In Act 3, Astrov shows with his maps how the landscape has altered as a result of deforestation since the 1830s. Waste and the environment are linked with the idea of wasted human life. Sonya asks Astrov why he draws attention to ecological problems, when he is destroying himself (Chekhov 2005: 215). He is in danger, like Ivanov, of exhausting himself, as his efforts gain so little support from the government or those around him. Vanya believes that his past life has been thrown away, but while he is not working, bemoaning this, the mown hay is rotting in the rain. There are therefore consequences for others and the environment. Astrov states that as a result of the influence of Yelena and Serebryakov's lives of idleness and the fact that he has done nothing for a month, people have fallen ill and the peasants have grazed their cattle in his forest, damaging the young trees (Chekhov 2005: 235). Astrov locates the environmental problem in a lack of reason: people are too lazy to pick up fuel from the ground.

> Human beings are endowed with reason and creative faculties in order to enhance what is given to them, but so far they have not created but destroyed. Forests are ever fewer and fewer, rivers dry up, wildlife is wiped out, the climate is spoiled and every day the earth grows more impoverished and ugly.
>
> (Chekhov 2005: 205)

The image of wasted beauty is a metaphor for Russia. Telegin is the impoverished owner of a nearby estate; as in *The Seagull*, estates are going to rack and ruin. The rivers are drying up and with them humanity: Serebryakov is described as a dried up old fish in Act 1. Chekhov writes on the environmental theme in many stories, for example, *Panpipes* (1887) and *Rothschild's Violin* (1894).

The presence of the peasants also raises issues to do with the land. Yefim, the night watchman, is tapping on his rounds at the end of Act 2. In Act 4, there is a mat in Vanya's office for the peasants to wipe their feet on. In Act 3, Marina says that the peasants have come again about the field which is being left untilled, presumably because of Vanya's neglect (Chekhov 2005: 201). Telegin relates at the beginning of Act 4 how a shopkeeper called him a 'freeloader' (*prizhival*, the same word used of Treplyov); he is seen as usurping the land on his estate (Chekhov 2005: 231). Peasants protested in various ways about land issues from the time of emancipation onwards (Fitzpatrick 1982: 16).

The image of waste is contrasted with the idea of possibilities for growth. The symbolism of trees is strongly developed in Russian literature from Turgenev and Tolstoy (see Peace 1983: 136–37). Astrov says: 'When I plant a birch tree and then I see how it grows leaves and sways in the wind, my soul is filled with pride ... ' Some commentators have seen Astrov as Chekhov's mouthpiece in this particular aspect. Fadeeva sees Astrov's philosophy as embracing love of life, in contrast to the Schopenhauerian nihilism on which Chekhov appears to comment in other works (1997: 109–10) (see also Valency 1966: 199). Chekhov's discussion of the environment in *Uncle Vanya* raises questions of the extent to which the characters' personal difficulties are in some measure due to the political situation in which they find themselves, about which Chekhov could not write directly.

Key productions

Uncle Vanya *at MAT*

Chekhov promised *Uncle Vanya* to the Imperial Maly Theatre in 1897, but withdrew it when the literary-theatrical committee of the theatre asked for changes. The committee (two of whom were professors) found Vanya firing a gun at a character with professorial

Figure 5.1 Uncle Vanya at the Moscow Art Theatre (from a private collection)

status offensive and stated that 'the change in Voynitskiy's attitude toward the professor, whom he previously worshipped, is incomprehensible' (Vitins 1981: 45). Chekhov allowed the MAT to produce the play and it opened, after successful stagings in the provinces, on 26 October 1899, with Knipper as Yelena and Stanislavsky as Astrov. Stanislavsky's rather garbled description of the play in *My Life in Art* implies that he saw the play as a drama of the dominance of people like Serebryakov in society, whom he describes as 'untalented and irrelevant', while 'men of real talent' such as Vanya and Astrov rot away in Russia's backwoods (Stanislavski 2008: 201). Other descriptions of the production reveal this to be an over-simplification; the production brought out the lyricism of the text and vibrantly drew the contrast between the characters' love for life and the difficulties of everyday life (*byt*) in Russia at the time (Stroeva 1973: 48). Meyerhold wrote to Chekhov commenting on the complementary way Stanislavsky and Nemirovich-Danchenko had worked on this production, with Nemirovich ensuring fidelity to the text, preventing Stanislavsky from cluttering the production, as was his wont, with props and sound effects: 'Not only are the basic ideas carefully preserved by not burying them in a heap of useless details, they are rather skilfully brought out' (Benedetti 1991: 58–59).

The MAT production had a mixed reception but ran for much longer than *The Seagull* and *Three Sisters* did, creating a tremendous impression in some quarters. Many, in an audience of rural doctors who saw the play, wept to see what they identified as the actuality of their lives being portrayed, and the young people who associated themselves with the liberal editor of the journal *Russian Thought* 'dedicated two weeks to a special study of *The Seagull* and *Uncle Vania* for they found in these plays an intellectual content and the hope of discovering at least a way out of the impasse of Russian life' (Simmons 1970: 560, 497).

Vanya on 42nd Street

Various versions of *Uncle Vanya* are available on film including the TV version of Laurence Olivier's 1962 production with Michael Redgrave's inspired performance as Vanya and Sybil Thorndike as Nanny. Anthony Hopkins' *August* set in Wales and Michael Blakemore's *Country Life* set in New South Wales both appeared in 1995. The film *Vanya on 42nd Street*, based on a workshop run for several years by director André Gregory with a group of actors on the adaptation of the play text by David Mamet, premiered in 1988. Workshop performances from 1990 to 1992 were for an invited audience only in the rehearsal setting, an abandoned theatre. In 1994, Gregory collaborated with Louis Malle on a film production. The film was shot in the then also abandoned and dilapidated New Amsterdam Theatre, on 42nd Street in New York City, built in 1903, and originally the home of the *Ziegfeld Follies*. The drama of *Uncle Vanya* is framed by scenes in the film with the actors and director: the film begins with Gregory and the actors (including Wallace Shawn as Vanya and Marianne Moore as Yelena) meeting up and walking to the theatre along 42nd Street, conversing with Mrs Chao (actress and food writer Madhur Jaffrey, daughter of Chekhov's Bengali translator) who has come to see the rehearsal. There is a seamless transition as the actors go into the theatre and into the first scene of *Uncle Vanya*, intended to signal the close identification of the twentieth century New York actors with the characters.

Gregory had initially intended that there should be no performance outcomes for the project, seeing it as not theatre but a spiritual quest:

> in which people search for the darkest in themselves but also for the lightest ... to sense more closely what life actually feels

like as it passes, and to see the unfolding of the human being in all its ambiguity.

(Senelick 1997a: 304)

Mamet's adaptation from a literal translation contemporizes the dialogue, interjecting comments by other characters to break up the longer speeches, so a more modern conversational flow is established. Some themes are reduced, such as the themes of time and of religion, whereas the desire for survival, to get something out of life whatever the difficulties, is emphasized. Malle and Gregory, through the use of close-ups and skilled direction of subtext, succeed in conveying an intimacy and warmth between the characters that enables them to transcend the differences between them at times and unifies them in their predicament. There is much laughter between the characters, some sardonic, self-deprecating but also moments of joy. The film successfully moves the play from its specific historical context in that it succeeds in conveying a sense of powerlessness of people in a certain social environment, with which the performers found a way to identify. One critic perceived this as a 'modern dress, demotic, American Chekhov' (French 2000: 160) and a reviewer noted: 'Despite such seemingly pervasive differences, it is indeed Uncle Vanya that we experience through Louis Malle's film'.[4]

Dodin's Uncle Vanya

Russian director Lev Dodin's landmark production of the play, while retaining the social context, also conveyed the intimacy between characters undergoing personal crisis within a situation of political decline. It premiered in April 2003 at the Maly Theatre in St Petersburg and has toured internationally. Dodin saw the main gesture of the play as gaining insight into reality and, like Gregory, saw rehearsing the play as a personal journey for the company: 'for Dodin the process of staging the play is the same as the process of gaining comprehension of life'.[5] He saw the play as the fatally ill Chekhov's depiction of the realization that can occur to anyone, at some stage in life, that their life has been unfulfilled in some ways. 'They start to see visions of other possible, but unlived life.' Such a person then rejects the present in their search for what has been missing from the past and turns to fantasy.

The more valuable you perceive life to be, the more keenly you perceive the disjuncture and this contradiction gradually becomes a tragedy. Time passes and eventually only one choice is left – to renounce life altogether or to find in yourself the courage to live the life given you by God or fate and which to some extent you have brought and bring into being yourself, by the strength of your personality.[6]

Like Gregory's film, Dodin's production emphasized the close relationships between the characters and there was much laughter and physical contact, including one scene where Yelena, played by Ksenia Rappoport or Irina Tychinina, was fighting on the floor with Vanya (Sergei Kuryshev). Vanya's mother Mariya was interpreted with an unusually sympathetic warmth; often actors play her as a cold or bitter woman, basing this on her attitude towards Vanya. The psychological depth of the characterizations gave the production breadth: the characters all 'desperately want to live' and Serebryakov's behaviour was attributed to *futlarnost'*, being 'encased', trapped in a habitual mode of behaviour (Ogibina 2004: 47–48).

Shevtsova identifies two themes central to Dodin's Chekhov work: the problem of losing one's home and the meaning of love. In Act 3, Vanya perceives that he may lose everything: his home, Yelena and his last chance of passionate love. 'This stupefying insight is precisely what makes sense of Vanya's attempt to shoot Serebryakov … Dodin and Sergey Kuryshev in the role of Vanya play it in a crazed, extraordinarily funny way that points out just how horrifying Vanya's burst of consciousness really is' (Shevtsova 2006a: 249–50).

Borovsky's minimalist set presented a wooden country house with three haystacks suspended above the stage. Light and dark were emphasized – with candlelight, twilight and a gold autumnal light reflecting the colours of the wood. The heavy rain of the storm was heard and seen in Act 2. Reviewers commented on the haystacks 'signifying the earthly life of Sonya and Uncle Vanya',[7] representing the 'base of the world-order',[8] and 'the metaphor of "hay hanging over their heads"'.[9] At the end of the play the haystacks descended, engulfing the stage: a symbol of the fact that life makes pressing demands, despite the desires of the characters for life to be other than it is. What is imperative is to get on with work in order to survive.

Figure 5.2 Ivan Kuryshev in *Uncle Vanya*, Lev Dodin's Maly Theatre.
Photograph by Viktor Vasilyev

6 Work and women

Three Sisters

Chekhov began writing *Three Sisters* in 1899 and it opened at the Moscow Art Theatre in January 1901. It has been described as a 'play about love' (Gilman 1995). The action in the play revolves around 'the question of love' (Kramer 1981: 62). It is also seen as a play about 'delusions' (Llewellyn Smith 1973: 26–28). Also, McVay writes: '*Three Sisters* is a play about happiness, or about the elusiveness of happiness' (1995: 37). Brahms, discussing Chekhov's families, states: 'The Family Prozorov are the saddest because for them fate can find no happy ending' (1976: 58). Hahn contrasts the sisters' 'bleak future' with the theme in the play of optimism about the future of the human race (Hahn 1977: 287). Styan asks: 'Is this a play of hope? Rather of resignation and endurance' (1971: 236). There are varied interpretations but essentially the play asks the questions: what is happiness? How can meaning be found in life? Bristow notes that *Three Sisters* is 'centrally concerned with the meaning of existence ... perhaps more than any other Chekhovian play' (1981: 91). Moreover, women are the main protagonists, the difficulty of their situation and search for happiness and fulfilment in life heightened by the restrictions on women in patriarchal Russian society of the time. Their story takes place against a military backdrop as the sisters are from a military family.

THREE SISTERS – A DRAMA IN FOUR ACTS

The play spans four years, beginning on the fifth of May, the name-day of Irina, the youngest, at twenty, of the three Prozorov sisters. They have lived for eleven years in the capital town of a Russian county, a town like Perm, as Chekhov wrote to Gorky (Benedetti 1995: 85); that is, a large provincial town thousands of miles from Moscow. Olga, the eldest sister, aged twenty-eight, recollects the death of their father, a general, a year ago. Olga works as a teacher at the local school; she and Irina dream of returning to Moscow, their birthplace. Olga longs to be married. Masha, the middle sister, is unhappily married to Kulygin, a teacher. Chebutykin, an elderly army doctor, lodges with the sisters and their brother Andrey. He, Baron Tusenbach, a lieutenant, and staff captain Solyony discuss the new battery commander Vershinin, who has a wife, a mother-in-law and two little girls. Tusenbach relates that she is Vershinin's second wife and that she frequently attempts suicide 'apparently in order to give her husband a hard time' (Chekhov 2005: 251).[1] Vershinin, who is from Moscow, arrives and fascinates the sisters. Irina says that she longs to work and Tusenbach also idealizes work, despising the idleness of his aristocratic upbringing. Various gifts are brought for Irina, all revealing aspects of the characters and their situation; Chebutykin presents Irina with a silver samovar, an entirely inappropriate gift, as it is usually a gift for a wedding anniversary. This and other clues in the text point to the fact that Chebutykin was in love with the deceased mother of the family, and in some way keeps her presence alive in his memory through his relationship with her daughters. Then, the sisters relate that Andrey is to be a professor and that he is in love with a local girl, Natasha, whom they view as socially inferior. Natasha arrives and the company eat lunch. Natasha is teased about her relationship with Andrey, and leaves the table in embarrassment. Andrey follows her, embraces her and proposes.

Act 2 takes place a year and nine months later, beginning at eight o'clock in the evening. It is *Maslenitsa*, the festival to celebrate the end of winter, before Lent. Natasha is checking the house, looking, she says, for candles left alight, while Andrey is sitting in his room reading. Natasha is gradually exerting control over the household, usurping the sisters. She claims that their baby, Bobik, is unwell, and so she does not want the traditional carnival mummers to call. She insists also that Bobik's room is too cold for him and Irina should share with Olga so he can have Irina's room. In the next scene, Vershinin secretly declares his love for Masha. Then

Tusenbach and Irina arrive: she is tired of her job at the post office and feels guilty that she lost patience with a grieving woman. She consoles herself with the thought of moving to Moscow in June. Andrey has been gambling and has lost money. Chebutykin has not paid his rent for eight months. Andrey is forced to explain that the mummers will not be coming, so Masha goes out with army officers Fedotik, Rode and Tusenbach. Andrey and Chebutykin leave to gamble. Solyony declares that he loves Irina and swears to kill any rival. Kulygin, Olga and Vershinin enter to find there is no party. Natasha leaves to go for a ride with Protopopov, the head of the local *zemstvo*, where Andrey now has a job. The act ends with Irina alone, saying with longing 'To Moscow! To Moscow! To Moscow! (Chekhov 2005: 280).

Act 3 takes place a year later, between two and three o'clock in the morning, in Olga and Irina's bedroom. There is a fire in the town and Vershinin's house has nearly burned down. His wife and children are downstairs and Olga is sorting clothes to give to the fire victims, with former nanny Anfisa, aged eighty. There are a series of emotional outbursts: Masha tells her sisters she is in love with Vershinin. Natasha attempts to assert further control, bullying Anfisa. Irina bursts into tears, she hates her new job, working for the *zemstvo,* and says she is old and her 'brain has dried up' (she is twenty-four) (Chekhov 2005: 288). Olga advises her to marry Tusenbach, though she does not love him. It is revealed that Andrey has mortaged the house and Natasha has taken the money, though the house belongs to all four of them. Andrey takes out his temper on the elderly *zemstvo* messenger Ferapont who is trying to get permission for the firemen to cross the garden to the river. He then attempts to assert his dignity with his sisters, defending Natasha and his choice of work. He asks their forgiveness for mortgaging the house (to Protopopov), justifying this by saying that their father left the sisters an allowance. He then breaks down: 'My dear sisters, precious sisters, don't believe me, don't believe me … ' (Chekhov 2005: 291). The act ends as Irina tells Olga that the brigade is being transferred. Rather than being left without their companions, she will marry Tusenbach, but, she implores Olga, they must go to Moscow.

In Act 4, dreams of Moscow have faded completely. The scene is the old garden at midday. The sisters have lost all control of the house. Olga is now living at the school, where she is headmistress, with Anfisa. People pass freely from the street through Prozorov's garden to get to the river. Chebutykin is sitting in the garden singing a refrain, 'tararaboomdeay' (Chekhov 2005: 293). Tusenbach, Irina and Kulygin are saying their goodbyes to Fedotik and Rode, as the unit is about to move on. Irina and Tusenbach are about to be married and she is looking forward to leaving the house. Chebutykin tells Andrey (but not Irina) that the day before Solyony provoked an argument with Tusenbach and Solyony then challenged him to a duel, which is soon to take place. In the meantime, Vershinin says goodbye to the distraught Masha. Kulygin, who has accepted his wife's affair, tries to make her laugh, as her sisters comfort her. Natasha announces that when everyone has left she will have the trees in the garden cut down. She organizes Andrey to look after Bobik and Protopopov to look after Sophie (the implication is that Protopopov is Sophie's father). Chebutykin brings the news that Tusenbach has been killed. The sisters, united in shock and grief, affirm the need to carry on living. The play ends with the sound of a military band and the news of Tusenbach's death, as it began with the image, in Olga's description, of their father being carried to his grave, to the sound of the band. The women, bereft, have to find a way forward for their lives.

Imagery

Images of an ideal life, 'lovely clean images of birds and snow, blossoms and spring warmth' (Hahn 1977: 286), are presented and also subverted throughout the play. Distance lends enchantment to Moscow, the hometown of the sisters' childhood memories. Interestingly, Chekhov described his own longing for Moscow at this time in his life when he was too ill to live in a cold climate (Chekhov 2004a 2: 304–5). In contrast to the sisters, Vershinin has a memory of an ominous aspect of the river and connects this with a feeling of loneliness (Chekhov 2005: 256). Moscow is also mythologized and given a ridiculous aspect. Ferapont says there is a rope stretched across the middle of it and that a shopkeeper died there from eating too many pancakes (Chekhov 2005: 267). The ideal is contrasted with the actuality of the provincial town and, similarly, there is a contrast between objects representing the ideal, cultivated life such as Andrey's violin, the humming top with its wonderful sound, and everyday objects: Olga's exercise books, newspapers, the fork left outside in Act 4. There are objects that do not fit with the sisters' ideas of how life should be: Protopopov's gift of cake is unwanted, Natasha's belt is 'all wrong' (Chekhov 2005: 263). Poetic layers are added to the text through literary allusions; McVay explains those that may be more accessible to a Russian audience (1995: 74–76). In addition, Bristow discusses how the concept of three is entwined in the fabric of the play in groupings of characters (1981). Peace discusses how Chekhov references and departs from classic drama and alludes ironically to the sisters as the Fates of classical drama. Their surname derives from '*prozorli-vyi*, able to see into the future', which, of course, they are unable to do, unlike the Fates (1983: 85–86). Chekhov, too, noted when he had finished writing the play, 'their future, their immediate future, at least, is veiled from me by the murk of uncertainty' (Chekhov 1980b 9: 139).

Chekhov and gender: Chekhov's women[2]

The title of the play places women at centre focus and the sisters' words to each other open and end the play. The representation of masculinity, particularly in the military, the instrument of auto-cracy, is placed in counterpoint. Stanislavsky emphasized that this was not a play criticizing the army, writing that Chekhov valued the military, who, 'in his own words, carried out a cultural mission in the backwoods, taking a new sense of enquiry, knowledge, art, happiness and joy with them' (Stanislavski 2008b: 206). General Prozorov dictated the life of the Prozorov family; from daily rou-tines, such as what time they should get up, to their education. Since his death, those structures for living are being eroded; the play examines the predicament of educated women in provincial Russia, who have no outlet for their talents in a changing society. At the end, a new order is established; Protopopov (who does not appear on stage) owns the house, is Andrey's boss, has appointed Olga as head of the girls' school, has given employment to Irina, is Nata-sha's lover and, by implication, father illegitimately of Sophie. He represents *meshchanstvo*, bourgeois philistinism, and a new kind of authority in the town, supplanting General Prozorov.

Chekhov wrote of 'impressionable, genteel women confined in oppressive and intellectually barren provincial towns' such as his birthplace, Taganrog, and used this theme in many stories such as *Three Years, Lights, Big Volodya and Little Volodya*. He noted:

> As soon as you go out onto the street and begin to observe, say, women, then life is terrible ...

Clyman adds that

> women mirror most vividly the horrors of life ... the deviations from the ideal, the 'norm', as Chekhov put it.
>
> (Clyman 1974: 26)

In much of his writing, Chekhov depicted the effects of a society where women are dependent on men economically and for their social status. The situation of abused women is considered in *Gore, Rothschild's Violin*, and prostitution in *Words, Words and Words, Anyuta, The Chorus Girl, A Male Acquaintance* and *A Nervous Breakdown*. *The Darling* describes a woman who has no opinions of her own and takes them from the men in her life. Single women, like Varya in *The Cherry Orchard*, and Olga in *Three Sisters,* struggle with life; women who have chosen to marry such as Yelena in *Uncle Vanya* and Masha in *Three Sisters* regret the constraints marriage places on them. Women who take one of few choices available and work for populist causes, find the work does not live up to the romantic ideal and react to this; Masha in *My Life* comes to despise the peasants, Lida in *The House with the Mezzanine* becomes obsessively self-righteous, Yelena in *Uncle Vanya* rejects outright the possibility of fulfilment through such work.

Parallels between the situation of women and that of the serfs were widely discussed after 1861. Various writers treated the situation of women, including Chernyshevsky in *What is to be done?* In the absence of democratic structures, a women's emancipation movement could not proceed along European lines and so securing the right for women to education was seen as the best way forward by progressive thinkers. The authorities found this a threat: the higher educational courses for women that had begun in the 1870s were closed in the repression of the 1880s, until the late 1890s.

Education in itself was only a partial answer: the sisters have had a private education, but do not know what to do with it. Masha states: 'In this town knowing three languages is a superfluous luxury' – a point that is contested by Vershinin – and Irina tearfully says she cannot remember the Italian word for 'window', or 'ceiling': the education her father gave her has no practical purpose (Chekhov 2005: 259, 288). Shevtsova notes that the Prozorov family as a whole

> represent the Enlightenment values of critical reason, productive knowledge, social justice and personal ethics, as well as the Renaissance ones of individual liberty, honour and dignity.
>
> (2006b: 96)

Their values are not respected by those representing the new social forces in the town.

As well as questioning what educated and socially privileged women can do with their lives, Chekhov questions the traditional view of women finding fulfilment through romantic love. The women are thwarted and their lives constrained: Masha feels obliged to accompany Kulygin to an evening at his headmaster's and Kulygin thinks his headmaster would think it improper for Masha to play in a concert for the relief of the fire victims (Chekhov 2005: 261, 284). Peace analyses the lines from Pushkin that Masha repeats in the play (Chekhov 2005: 253, 303), which subconsciously express her state of mind.

> Near the curved seashore is a green oak tree.
> On this oak is a golden chain.
> And day and night a learned tomcat
> Keeps going round and round on the chain.

He asserts that the oak tree, a symbol of strength (Masha), is in a 'provincial backwater in direct symbolic contrast to Moscow, moreover it is attached by a golden bond (marriage) to a "learned tomcat" (the pompous schoolmaster Kulygin) who with his prattle and fussing around her constantly hems her in' (1983: 79).

At the beginning of the play, the sisters believe that their lives are incomplete without romantic relationships. The idealized longing for Moscow has parallels in Olga and Irina's idealization of married life. Masha, disappointed in hers, seeks fulfilment in an affair. Critics often view her liaison with Vershinin romantically; Kramer comments that she 'temporarily' finds 'real love' (1981: 62; see also Magarshack 1980: 247, 257). The text can be read as indicating that Masha may be one in a string of the 'lovesick major's affairs' (Chekhov 2005: 256); his adultery perhaps provoking his wife's suicide attempts. The attempt to find happiness through romance fails. The reality of her situation at the end is that she is left with her sisters, and her husband, who says he forgives her affair. Also, Irina sees that her dream of Moscow, where she would meet her true love, is foolishness (Chekhov 2005: 289).

Recent feminist analyses of Chekhov consider how he enables his audience to take a critical perspective on the values his society ascribed to gender. Tait questions readings of the sisters' predicament as 'tragic', in her analysis of how the emotional responses of male and female characters are culturally designated. She asks whether Chekhov's texts can be 'perceived to resist as they replicate the social paradigms of literary and theatrical representations of love' (2002: 55). Marsh discusses how Chekhov challenges theatrical convention, particularly the stereotypical representation of women in the melodrama of his day, using the stage representation of women not only to make a social point but to change the form of the plays, questioning gender and identity (Marsh 2000; see also Schafer 2001). That Chekhov works against conventional representations of femininity, seeing his women characters as acting in ways which are socially conditioned, is borne out by linguistic analyses. Borker and Garnica identify some characters with certain speech patterns; Masha Kulygina's speech style is 'rich in areas associated with masculine assertiveness', similarly to that of Masha Shamrayeva in *The Seagull*, whose speech behaviour would be 'traditionally labelled as unwomanly or negative for a female according to the prevailing social code', whereas Natasha's speech displays 'feminine' wiles (1980: 14, 16).

Natasha uses the role of housewife and mother to gain power. She is a woman 'who is willing to exploit her sexuality to achieve her mostly material aims' (Marsh 2000: 221–22). She has been viewed by a number of critics as the villain of the piece: Magarshack describes her as 'satanic … devilish' (1972: 140, 181). Hahn sees Natasha as a caricature (1977: 289). She can be compared with malevolent women in Chekhov's stories such as Aksinya in *In the Ravine*. Natasha's history is not known, but like Aksinya, she may have had an oppressive and brutal upbringing. Andrey describes her as an animal (Chekhov 2005: 297); she is stunted in some way. She is unable to see others except in terms of their utility to her (Hahn 1977: 304). Her marriage brings her social status. In an early draft, in Act 4, Andrey delivered a monologue about the petty bourgeois philistinism (*meshchanstvo*) of many Russian women: preserving 'poetry and femininity' until they marry, then letting themselves go, wearing a dressing gown and slippers at home and tasteless, expensive outfits outside. Chekhov sent an instruction to the MAT that this monologue was to be replaced simply by 'A wife is a wife!' (Stanislavski 2008b: 207). Masha too calls Natasha *meshchanka* (Chekhov 2005: 277).

The sisters, to some extent, provoke Natasha's behaviour. They have an elevated status in the provincial town. They despise and humiliate her; in Act 1, Olga criticizes the belt she is wearing, reducing her almost to tears (Chekhov 2005: 263). They apply double standards; Natasha's treatment of Anfisa in Act 3 may appal Olga but Masha too has ordered the old lady about and shouted at her (Chekhov 2005: 282, 274). The bond between the sisters gives them power: Andrey is afraid of them (Chekhov 2005: 267). Natasha's attitude to them and her gradual manipulation of the situation indicate her desire for revenge and also her aspiration to be like them. The sisters, fluent in other languages, do not utter any foreign words in the play, whereas Natasha attempts to emulate the sisters' cultivation by speaking (badly) in French for which she is derided (Chekhov 2005: 275, 301). She is heard playing the piano, imitating Masha's accomplishment, and also attempts to demonstrate that she has gained superiority in Act 4, when she criticizes Irina's belt publicly (Chekhov 2005: 304).

Chekhov's men

Chekhov questions masculinity; Andrey cannot live up to the ideal of his father as a strong man who observes his duty to his country and family. This is in fact a false ideal, as it is suggested that rather than presiding over a well-regulated happy family,

General Prozorov's authority was undermined: his wife was loved by Chebutykin and it is possible that, like Masha, she was unfaithful to her husband. Andrey's life was planned for him by his father:

IRINA: Papa was a military man but his son chose an academic career.
MASHA: As Papa wished.

(Chekhov 2005: 257)

He cannot take responsibility for the sisters, as they think he should, and gain the professorship that will transport them to Moscow. Masha compares Andrey to a bell, hoisted up by thousands of people, which falls to the ground and smashes (Chekhov 2005: 296). This suggests that he breaks under the weight of expectations placed upon him by his father and sisters, then his relationship with Natasha, eating and gambling compulsively as ways to escape pressure.

Other male characters also fail to live up to the masculine ideal of the noble, educated army officer. Dr Chebutykin is seemingly a father figure, on affectionate terms with the sisters. He sits in a chair with the newspaper, reading out useless pieces of information, as Chekhov's own father did (McVay 1995: 15), and is a burden on the household. Vershinin is twenty years older than Masha, and is perhaps, like Kulygin, a father figure. He appears initially as a glamorous stranger from Moscow. Pitcher notes that Vershinin's name suggests 'peak' or 'summit' and regards his utopian visions of the future as Chekhov's (1985: 144; see also Valency 1966: 243). But as McVay notes, Vershinin is ambiguous as a lover and visionary (McVay 1995: 14). As a husband and father, he appears neglectful. He leaves his wife and terrified children in Olga's care for an assignation with Masha on the night of the fire; his talk of the future is just talk.

Overall, the provincial community is hostile to change. Andrey says the influence of *poshlost'*, of gossip, vodka, cards, crooked deals and secret affairs, has a bad effect on the children, who repeat the patterns of their parents' lives, including gendered behaviour. 'They become the same miserable, identical dead things as their fathers and mothers … ' (Chekhov 2005: 300).

Philosophizing: work and the future

Characters in Chekhov's plays 'philosophize'. Peace notes that both Tusenbach and Vershinin prefer 'philosophizing to taking action' (Jackson 1993: 143). Vershinin's wife, according to Tusenbach, 'only talks about highfalutin stuff, philosophy' (Chekhov 2005: 251). There are no great thinkers in Chekhov's plays, simply ordinary people trying to make sense of their lives, often discussing half-digested ideas. While remaining sceptical about philosophy for its own sake, writing on one occasion 'To hell with the philosophy of the great men of this world!' (Chekhov 1973: 203), Chekhov asks philosophical questions in the plays by the way in which the debates relate to the events of the play.

In *Three Sisters*, one discussion is on the topic of 'progress'. Teleological ideas about progress had begun to shift from the mid-nineteenth century when existing values were challenged by positivism and Schopenhauerian nihilism. In Russia, the nihilism of the 1860s was future oriented:

> the 'annihilation' – figurative and literal – of the *past* and *present*, i.e. of realized social and cultural values and of such values in the process of realization, in the name of the *future* i.e. for the sake of social and cultural values yet to be realized.
>
> (Kline 2001: 805)

This was widely articulated by Bakunin, Pisarev and others.

Vershinin and Tusenbach espouse opposed points of view on the future and life's purpose. Vershinin says those alive at present are creating the future; he idealizes progress, envisaging a beautiful and happy future when life as it is at present will seem strange (Chekhov 2005: 259, 271). Tusenbach denies that life will change essentially in the future; it will remain full of impenetrable mysteries and it will be possible to be happy, as he is now (Chekhov 2005: 272). Like Trofimov in *The Cherry Orchard*, he foresees political revolution.

> The time has come, there's a thundercloud looming over us, there's a bracing, mighty tempest lying in wait, close at hand and soon it will blow away all the indolence, apathy, prejudice against hard work, putrid boredom out of our society.
>
> (Chekhov 2005: 252)

He wants to participate in life through work; as an aristocrat, this represents a rejection of his upbringing. The ideology of work was a strand in intellectual thought from the 1860s and the ideal of the 1880s–1890s Russian democratic intelligentsia that labour is ennobling (working towards a Russia where there would be equality of opportunity) was followed by the glorification of *trud* or labour by the Marxists. The sincerity of the characters is questionable; Kramer notes that 'Vershinin's philosophical ramblings are primarily a way of wooing' Masha (1981: 66) and Tusenbach's 'happiness' may be a delusion; at that point in the play he loves Irina and lives in hope that she may come to love him. His decision to leave the army and run a brick factory may also be an idealization; he dies before he begins the work.

For women, the question of work is even more vexed, as the choices are fewer. In Act 1, Irina sees manual labour bringing happiness; she cries about their situation: 'life has choked us, like weeds' (Chekhov 2005: 252, 262). The thought of work cheers her up. The question is what kind of work may be rewarding. Despite oppressive policies towards women's education, as the Russian economy changed in the second half of the nineteenth century, more jobs in more fields were available for women but there were still great limitations. It is only during Irina's lifetime that women have been allowed to work at a post office (Saunders 1992: 314), so the job may appear to her to have a novelty and glamour that is far from actuality.

Teaching, one of the few possible careers for women, is shown to have both limitations and possibilities. Olga finds her job stressful and unwillingly takes promotion. Apparently, a headmistress could earn a very large salary, as statistics published in 1903 and 1904 show (Schuler 1996: 20), so with that and her allowance, she is guaranteed financial independence even after the loss of the house. Irina chooses at the end of the play to become a teacher too. Chekhov often satirized teachers; *Man in a Case*, the study of *futlyarnost'*, was based on a teacher he himself had, and Kulygin also is seen as limited and dominated by his headmaster. Despite this, Chekhov valued education highly; he had three schools built and was governor of a girls' school in Yalta. His brother Ivan and sister Masha were both teachers.

Chekhov's own view of work and the future is indicated by the fact that he worked for change and the relief of suffering throughout his own life. A young doctor, M. A. Chlenov, was involved through Chekhov's recommendation in a scheme to build a hospital in Odessa. He wrote that he would never experience 'personal happiness', and so would work instead 'on behalf of science and general ideas'. Chekhov replied: 'To work on behalf of science and general ideas – that's what personal happiness is' (Chekhov 1981b 10: 54).

Philosophizing: nihilism / creating meaning in life

The play also depicts the consequences of the adoption of pessimistic attitudes when life does not meet up to expectations by those who give up on the pursuit of happiness. All the characters have to cope with disappointment; none have any certainty about life's purpose. (Only Anfisa, whose needs are small, says she is happy, in Act 4.) Tusenbach, despite his contention that he is happy in the first part of the play, has to face the fact that Irina does not love him and appears to go willingly to his death. Chebutykin's pessimism and Solyony's romanticized nihilist pose are shown to have destructive consequences in the death of Tusenbach.

In Act 3, the alcoholic doctor has got drunk, after two years' abstinence. He talks to himself, revealing that in the previous week a woman he was treating died and this was his fault; there is a parallel here with Astrov in *Uncle Vanya*. He says:

> Maybe I'm not even a human being, but just seem to have arms and legs ... and a head; maybe I don't even exist at all, but it just seems to me I walk, eat, sleep ... Oh if only I didn't exist!
> (Chekhov 2005: 283)

Ischuk-Fadeeva notes that Chebutykin's statement denotes 'purely philosophical subjective idealism', linking this with Schopenhauer's 'joyful will to death' as opposed to Chekhov's will to live, as expressed in the comedy of the plays and his own life (1997: 106). Peace draws a connection between Chebutykin and Russian nihilist writer Saltykov-Shchedrin's hero in *The Adventures of Kramolnikov*, who wakes up one morning and realizes that he does not exist (1983: 14). Chebutykin's depression and dismissal of his own life extends to a negation of the importance of life at all with terrible consequences.

He says of Tusenbach before the duel: 'One baron more or less – does it really matter?' (Chekhov 2005: 297).

He deliberately smashes the clock that belonged to the sisters' mother in Act 3, after Irina has been talking about going to Moscow. This is

> a commentary on the theme of Moscow; but at the same time it is also a commentary on Chebutykin's attitude to Irina: the clock was her mother's. The loss of Irina would mean the shattering of something extremely valuable and fragile – link through time with her mother.
>
> (Peace 1983: 89)

The gesture has also been construed as 'trying to destroy time itself, which separates him from his love, but he is also deliberately destroying a material object that belonged to her; it may also be a gesture of denial that his love ever existed' (Kramer 1981: 64), and that 'action depicts time itself as going to pieces', or the Prozorovs' family dream of Moscow as falling apart, or the very house in which they live as no longer belonging to them (Bristow 1981: 85). The destructive gesture can also be seen as a commentary on nihilist ways of thinking which deny the present, the importance of life here and now.

Solyony's romantic pessimist pose is based on the idea of the 'superfluous man'. He is also the most extreme example of self-dramatizing in a character in Chekhov, modelling himself on the poet Lermontov. Chekhov wrote:

> Indeed, Solyony thinks he is like Lermontov; but of course he isn't – it's funny to even think it … he should be made up to look like Lermontov. His resemblance to Lermontov is enormous but this is only Solyony's opinion.
>
> (Chekhov 1980b 9: 181)

He is constantly picking arguments: presenting himself as a combative person who will not brook a rival for Irina. He habitually puts scent on his hands (which he claims smell like a corpse) as part of his pose. Solyony quotes Lermontov's *The Sail* and Pushkin's *The Gypsies*, the hero of which, Aleko, kills his wife and her lover.

Chebutykin and Solyony's fatalistic pessimism influences others. In Act 4, Andrey turns to Chebutykin as to a father in his despair but the only advice Chebutykin gives him is to run away; this would not save Andrey. Initially, the sisters adopt attitudes that are fatalistic to some degree; Masha says of her affair, 'I love – which means it's my fate' (Chekhov 2005: 289). The sisters rely on God, fate or chance to determine the likelihood of their return to Moscow. Irina plays a game of patience in Act 2 that does not work out and this means, she says, that she will not go to Moscow. In Act 4, she states, 'So I came to my decision: if it's not my fate to live in Moscow, so be it. After all, it must be fate. Nothing to be done about it ... Everything is God's will, true enough' (Chekhov 2005: 295). They and Andrey willingly submit to 'fate' and let events in which they could intervene happen around them. They do not go to Moscow, stop Natasha, prevent the duel. In Act 2, Masha says 'indifferently' about Andrey losing money: 'What can you do now!' (Chekhov 2005: 270).

The play discusses fatalism and simultaneously shows how lives are shaped by time and the importance of acting in time. 'No play has ever conveyed more subtly the sense of the transitory nature of human life ... ' (Valency 1966: 219). It is set over a longer time span than the other plays and there are constant markers of time: anniversaries, births of the two children, changing foliage (see McVay 1995: 48–51). Photographs and the spinning top also act as metaphors of time (Allen 2000: 182–86). In Act 4, Olga says, 'Time will pass, and we'll be gone forever, people will forget us, they'll forget our faces, voices and how many of us there were' (Chekhov 2005: 305).

Masha believes that life should not be wasted. She responds to Vershinin and Tusenbach's argument about the future:

> It seems to me, a person ought to believe in something or to look for something to believe in, otherwise his life is empty, empty ... To live and not know why cranes fly, why children are born, why stars are in the sky ... Either you know why you live or else it's all senseless, gobbledygook.
>
> (Chekhov 2005: 272)

When the sisters give up the idea of going to Moscow, they find some measure of maturity and begin to work out their destiny in the world they really inhabit. Olga states in Act 4, 'Nothing works out the way we'd like it to. I didn't want to be a headmistress, but even so I am one. Which means, not being in Moscow' (Chekhov 2005: 302). At the end of the play Tusenbach's death shocks them into a further realization of the importance of living in the present as opposed to in memories or dreams of the future. The end is the only time all three are grouped together since the beginning of the play. Masha avows the need to go on living, Irina says she will work and devote her life to others and Olga affirms that though they as individuals will be forgotten, their suffering will bring happiness for others. Their life is not over yet. She adds, 'it looks like just a little while longer and we shall know why we're alive, why we suffer ... If only we knew, if only we knew!' (Chekhov 2005: 305). Kramer contends that 'we see a number of positive elements in the finale that invert the hopeless and desperate attitudes of the opening ... the play moves from both naïve faith and despair to a heightened awareness of possibilities in life and a more solidly rooted ability to endure' (1981: 70). The play ends with Chebutykin continuing to mutter 'doesn't matter', as Olga continues to say 'if only we knew!' The denial of the importance of life heightens the insight Olga expresses that being alive, even if one does not know why, is what matters most.

Key productions

Early productions of Three Sisters

Chekhov first introduced the play at MAT in 1900, where again the company were perplexed by it, so he spent time in rehearsals for several months, clarifying and rewriting. He was very particular about customs of military life, and a colonel was appointed to attend rehearsals to verify details of military conduct. Stanislavsky describes tormenting rehearsals where he struggled to find a way to bring the play to life. At one point, the cast were sitting apathetically in semi-darkness, and someone scratching on a chair reminded Stanislavsky of his childhood. This produced the insight, by some subconscious connection, that 'Chekhov's people ... do not wallow in their misery. No, they look for happiness, well-being. They want to live, not vegetate' (Stanislavski 2008b: 206). Stanislavsky's production of *Three Sisters* emphasized the disparity between *byt* and 'the dream of distant Moscow, between the poetry and prose in the existence of Chekhov's heroes' (Stroeva 1973: 75). The 'dangerous force' of *poshlost'* was shown in Natasha's take-over of the house; the stage and its furniture, in Act 2, was strewn with children's clothes, toys and blankets (Stroeva 1967: 123). This was the MAT's 'best presentation both for the perfection of the ensemble and Stanislavski's direction' (Stroeva 1973: 77–8), and Gorky wrote to Chekhov that the production was 'better than *Uncle Vanya* ... music, not acting' (Benedetti 1995: 103).

F. F. Komissarzhevsky's 1926 production of *Three Sisters* was a landmark in British productions of Chekhov. Radical alterations were made to make the play more accessible to a British audience: the relationships were romanticized and more dramatic action introduced on stage (see Emeljanow 1981b, Allen 2000). This influenced the history of productions in Britain for a time. Allen discusses Jonathan Miller's 1986 production as a blow against the romantic tradition of Stanislavsky and Komissarzhevsky (2000: 173). Meanwhile, in Russia, Nemirovich-Danchenko's 1940 production was a polemic with Stanislavsky and the idea of a 'Chekhovian mood' (Kirillov 2001), in which he chose to emphasize the courage of the intelligentsia and 'longing for a better life'.

Three Sisters *at the Taganka Theatre*

In 1981, Yury Lyubimov's seminal production, a development of work on the play by Yury Pogrebniczko, took place at the Taganka theatre in Moscow. The set, designed by Yury Kononenko, was abstract, with a wooden stage and a mix of domestic and army barrack furniture. All characters wore or donned army overcoats at times. 'The dominating grey overcoat colour of the costumes and set was clearly associated with contemporary militarism' (Kirillov 2001). The presence of the army was enhanced by the use of military music by composer E. Denisov, distorting and interrupting the action and speeches. A panel in the Taganka theatre wall was opened to enable the audience to see historic Moscow: an ironically fairy-tale view of Sadovaya Circle. 'The image of Moscow is merely a metaphor for the impossibility of their hope for another, more

Figure 6.1 Three Sisters at the Taganka theatre. Photograph by A. Sternin

free and active life, unlike anytime soon in the real Russia' (Gershkovich 1989: 101). The production used non-naturalistic techniques
to comment on Soviet Russia in Brezhnev's time: the characters
spoke as though they did not hear each other, emphasizing a loss of
individuality and isolation under the regime. Attention was drawn
to the fact that in the play no one attempts to prevent the duel
despite presentiments of disaster. Chebutykin several times threw
down a glove before Tusenbach and Solyony and led them into a
duelling posture in the course of the action. Natasha stops the
Maslenitsa masquerade from visiting the house and this was linked
in this production with the suggestion that the characters were
puppets of the regime, as the characters frequently put on festival

masks. 'The themes of automatism and blind submission to power are suggested' (Mal'tseva 1999: 81–83). The characters delivered their speeches, sometimes directly to the audience, spreading their hands in a gesture of helplessness, a gesture repeated throughout. Chebutykin has the habit of communicating by knocking with the Prozorovs and this was also repeated; the knocking becoming frightening.

The themes of work and the future were played down so the production focused on the present and 'the spectators were challenged, almost reproached for the situation and thereby reminded of their power to produce change ... ' (Beumers 1997: 183–84). Alla Demidova's Masha reinforced this with her delivery of the speech 'I think a human being ought to believe in something ... Either you know what you are living for or it's all nonsense, drivel' (Senelick 1997a: 227).

Cheek by Jowl's Three Sisters

Cheek by Jowl's 2006 production, directed by Declan Donnellan with Russian actors, was performed in Moscow and touring in Europe alongside his production of Shakespeare's *Cymbeline*. Donnellan saw the themes of death and the possibility of redemption linking the two productions. In contrast to Lyubimov's production, the struggle of his three sisters is more within themselves than with external forces; their need to survive and their commitment to work for social improvement as the most positive step they can take were emphasized.

Donnellan respected the specific historicity of the play, rejecting the need to mediate the work for a contemporary audience, staging the production in a Russian 1901 setting. 'To take Chekhov out of that context would be quite wrong ... Every aspect ... is imbued in the culture.'[3] He stated that if Chekhov had lived longer ' ... his plays would have become more epic. He dovetailed with Stanislavsky, with naturalism, but there is the feeling it is going to break apart.'[4] The symbolic aspects of the play were heightened: Nick Ormerod's minimalist staging used a dolls' house, which for one reviewer represented 'the sisters' secure childhood and expectant youth'.[5] The drama of the house was represented as the model was placed at centre stage at the beginning, then pushed to one side,

Figure 6.2 *Three Sisters* by Cheek by Jowl, Chekhov International Theatre
Festival, Moscow, Russia. Nelli Uvarova as Irina. Photograph by
Igor Zakharkin

knocked over and finally packed away. For Donnellan 'the house put on stage is an infantilized world, like a fairytale', which is set aside as the sisters mature.[6] A gramophone was used instead of a piano and the rest of the set consisted mainly of chairs and tables; in Act 2, Vershinin and Tusenbach use the tables as a debating platform. The backdrop, in a classical style but with tilting walls and windows, suggested the world of tradition gone awry. Photographs of trees were used in Act 4.

> We designed the entire house and the actors built a model of it. The way the actors move on stage is an equal part of the design. Even when the stage is empty, it still has to be carefully designed – the spaces between them – where they enter and where they leave. The stage is not just a literal space; it's a psychic space, as well.[7]

For Donnellan, Chekhov's symbolism eludes exact definition:

> In Chekhov it is more than a code. Irina and the locked piano, the fork that Natasha finds – it is all resonant. The artist produces something – you don't know what it means – a constellation, a crystallization. The task of the director is to explore and invest in it so everyone knows what the object looks like – you feel it, you don't interpret it.[8]

Donnellan opposes the tradition of British Chekhov, stating:

> It's in the stories where you sense Chekhov's position – there is no autumnal glow, there is savage irony. There is no reason why those women living together in that house would live in an autumnal glow – it's a patronising view of women. They must have been driving each other mad.[9]

The opening image combined intensity and humour. The sisters and Andrey stand grouped as if for a portrait or photograph, 'civilised, harmonious and in a pose that, while it would have gratified their father, the General, is simply unsustainable since his death, which has left them stranded as over-educated, self-doubting misfits in this remote, crashingly dull provincial town'.[10] The pose asserts this image and subverts it; Masha whistles throughout. The idea of themselves as cultivated, superior beings is emphasized, and this places pressure on Andrey to live up to their expectations and fulfil their collective dreams. When he enters in Act 1, the sisters circle around him adoringly and insistently. It is important for Donnellan that the sisters do not go to Moscow, where they would be seen as provincial. Perhaps unconsciously, they have chosen to be important in their town rather than risk invisibility in the metropolis.

The extent to which the sisters' attitudes shape Natasha's behaviour is evident. Ekaterina Sibiryakova's performance as Natasha in Act 1 is 'pretentious and ambitious, yet touchingly gauche'.[11] The sisters despise her utterly: Masha sits waiting for her to slip up when they are at table and does not disguise her revulsion. In Act 3, after Natasha walks through the house with a candle, Masha mimics her and the three sit on the floor, laughing hysterically, mocking her broad face and how she speaks. Donnellan saw her as a prototype *kulak,* literally 'fist', a term given to rich peasants with independent farms. Natasha comes into a chaotic household where there is a power vacuum. Her gaucherie is transformed; at the end of Act 2 she presents a formidable figure, dressed in black, leaving to go out with Protopopov. In this production Solyony has just attacked Irina, as she resists him trying to kiss her: Natasha sees this and passes it off indifferently.

Donnellan challenged the view of Chebutykin as a kindly old doctor, mildly destructive, comparing him to doctor Ragin in *Ward No. 6,* 'a reckless monster', and viewed all the characters as responsible for Tusenbach's death. Like Lyubimov, Donnellan used a motif to foretell the death of Tusenbach; in Act 1, the characters stage a mock funeral around Tusenbach, who is drunk, lying prone on the floor.

The production reflected on fatherhood:

> I think a lot about the little children who are destroyed. In Ireland Bobik would be the designated delicate child, the 'sick' child used by the mother to gain her own ends and also abused. Then there is Sophie and her two fathers, and the other children, Vershinin's children – what kind of a daddy is he? In one way I hope that the children grow up to become revolutionaries.[12]

Alexander Feklistov's Vershinin addresses his philosophizing straight to the audience and also his line 'life is difficult', exposing, with the cliché, the character's insincerity. Donnellan points out the age difference between Masha and Vershinin: 'Vershinin comes on the prowl – a man in a house of women.' In contrast, there is a more sympathetic view of Kulygin; he has a vitality that perhaps explains Masha's initial attraction to him. He adores Masha and cannot keep his hands off her; in one scene he sits at her feet burying his head on a cushion she holds on her stomach 'as if yearning for the children and happy home she might give him'.[13]

Reviewers noted ' ... a strong sense of people striving to rouse themselves from depression';[14] ' ... there is a vigour and urgency about the sound of the language that instantly banishes the wan, droopy quality of second-rate English productions of Chekhov'.[15] Donnellan noted:

> Chekhov's objectivity is unsentimental, full of love, stern and forgiving. His greatness is to do with his objectivity but because it leaves an empty space in the plays it is terribly easy for them to be appropriated. I wanted to get away from the nauseating preconceptions that the plays are portraits of people who are noble and suffered ... in the time before tinned food was invented. Chekhov shows that none of us is here as a private individual: you have to purify what you do.[16]

7 Modernization and change
The Cherry Orchard

The Cherry Orchard offers a perspective on the changing social, economic and political order in Russia at the end of the twentieth century and political and personal responses to this. The older generations represent the old feudal order, whereas the younger characters have grown up since serfdom was abolished. The play was begun in 1902 and premiered at the Moscow Art Theatre in 1904, six months before Chekhov's death. The 1890s had seen the problems in many rural economies worsening, with heavy taxation, depression in peasant farming, cholera and typhus epidemics. Criticism of the regime for its failure to find long-term solutions for the peasants' situation had become increasingly open. Crop failures in 1901 were followed by a number of violent peasant protests in provinces of Russia and other parts of the empire, and increased political tensions and unruly public behaviour had come with peasant migration to towns (Hosking 2001: 364). Also, by 1903, almost one-half of all private land in Russia (excluding peasant land) was mortgaged, forcing the landed gentry to sell their estates and join the professional or commercial classes (Chekhov 2005: 335 n). By 1905, this had declined to 22 per cent, of which one-third was rented to the peasantry, much of the rest being run by incompetent managers (Braun 2000: 112). *The Cherry Orchard* deals with the sale of such an estate and one of its former owners, Gayev, takes a job in a bank to survive. The play as a whole demonstrates shifts in class identities and social relationships (Lopakhin is the first main character from the merchant class in Chekhov's plays) and the increasing redundancy of a social order where the upper classes do not work and are served by a vast, impoverished peasantry.

The estate and its cherry orchard are near a large town and the play makes reference to the growth of industry, the expansion of towns and the development of the railways, expedited by de Witte from 1893. Between 1898 and 1913 railway traffic increased 2.5 times, reaching 128 million people by 1904 (Golub 1994: 28). The impact of industrialism on the natural environment develops the theme of deforestation raised in *Uncle Vanya*. Parts of the country-side also saw the construction of *dachi*, which had been country homes in the eighteenth century for the social elite. As the urban populations grew, Russians of a variety of backgrounds began to construct holiday homes of all kinds away from the cities (Bartlett 2004: 97). Chekhov himself had houses constructed at Autka and Gurzuf in Yalta.

The industrialization process offered new possibilities for Russia but the question of whether the country could or should take the path of adopting western style capitalism was far from clear, and the oppositional voice of socialist groups began to be heard after 1900, despite continued censorship. Trofimov, a student, represents radical views. *The Cherry Orchard* debates topical politics more overtly than Chekhov's other plays, while relating that discussion to wider questions and indicating Chekhov's practical view of social progress.

THE CHERRY ORCHARD – A COMEDY

The play was conceived while Chekhov was staying on Sta-nislavsky's Lyubimovka estate, where there was a cherry orchard. Chekhov had planted his own cherry orchard at Melikhovo and, later, was horrified to learn that the person to whom he had sold the estate had cut it down. He had also observed the decline of the estate belonging to his friends the Kiselyov family (Braun 2000: 113). Connections have been drawn with the Chekhovs' own loss of a house in Taganrog in Chekhov's youth. Rayfield notes that other aspects of the setting for the play are redolent of Chekhov's birth-place, 'the countryside around Taganrog, the Donets hills, the unseen mine-shafts that honeycomb the countryside, the sheep and the pan-pipes, the filthy kitchens and servants quarters … ' (1975: 64). Geographies of reference are wider than in previous plays: the city of Kharkov is nearby, Yaroslavl and Moscow are mentioned and Lyubov arrives from and returns to Paris. She had to sell a villa in Mentone, a town on the Mediterranean in France. Her impoverished situation is like that of the aristocratic émigré Russians Chekhov had encountered on his trips to Europe.

The play spans spring to autumn, from May to October. The journey from birth to death is suggested, as the first and last setting is the nursery of the house on Lyubov Andreevna Ranevskaya's country estate, and in the final scene, Firs, an aged valet, who has not long to live, is accidentally left alone in the closed-up house. An atmosphere of expectant waiting is established. It is almost two o'clock on a May dawn and the cherry trees on the estate are in bloom, despite a frost. Dunyasha, a maid, and Yermolai Alexeyevich Lopakhin, a local merchant and millionaire, are waiting to welcome Lyubov home. Her daughter Anya and the governess Charlotta Ivanovna have brought Lyubov back from Paris. Leonid Andreevich Gayev, Lyubov's brother, lives on the estate with Varya, the housekeeper, Lyubov's adopted daughter. Characters from a variety of class backgrounds and three generations are presented: the middle-aged Lyubov and Gayev and the elderly Boris Borisovich Simeonov-Pishchik, another impecunious local landowner, are the gentry. Firs, at 87, represents the generation of former serfs who are dying out. All the other major characters were born after emancipation: Lopakhin's father, like Chekhov's, was born a serf and became a shopkeeper; Trofimov, the student son of a chemist, is 26 or 27; Yepikhodov, the estate clerk, Dunyasha and Yasha are all young; Anya is 17, Varya 24. Charlotta Ivanovna, 'brought up by a German lady', does not know how old she is.

The central strand of the plot concerns the sale of the house and estate with its cherry orchard, famed throughout the region, to cover the family's debts. Money is again a central concern. Despite her problems, Lyubov still lives expensively. The opposite to *The Seagull's* Arkadina, she literally lets money run through her fingers; throughout the play she drops, gives away or lends what cash she has. Lopakhin proposes a solution to the problem: if the land were cleared and divided into lots for building it could be leased out for building *dachi* and could generate an income of 25,000 roubles per year (a huge sum). Lyubov and Gayev cannot countenance the thought of pulling down the house and chopping down the cherry orchard in view of what they represent; their aristocratic heritage, family home and name. Lyubov dismisses *dachi* and their owners as 'so vulgar' in Act 2. Gayev hopes that their aunt, a countess in Yaroslavl, might help, though she disapproves of the family, as Lyubov married a barrister, not a nobleman, and is, in Gayev's words, a 'depraved' woman (Chekhov 2005: 337). However, the family pin their hopes on ancestral family loyalties. Lopakhin continues to put forward his proposal in Act 2, stating that another local merchant, Deriganov, intends to buy the estate at the auction on 22 August. Gayev announces that he has been offered a position at the bank for 6,000 roubles a year. Lyubov is scandalized at the thought of her brother going into commerce. Gayev's other plan is to visit a general who may lend some money. Both Lopakhin and Lyubov know this is a false hope. Entwined with the theme of the cherry orchard and the house is Lyubov's personal history: her memories of her mother, her first husband, who died of alcoholism six years previously, and her seven-year-old son Grisha, who drowned in the river on the estate only months afterwards.

The secondary plot line is the unrealized romances between Varya and Lopakhin, Anya and Trofimov and the comic love triangle between Yepikhodov, Dunyasha and Yasha. Dunyasha reveals to Anya in Act 1 that Yepikhodov has proposed to her but Yepikhodov, with his squeaking boots, his clumsiness, his nickname of 'twenty-two misfortunes', pales in comparison with Yasha and his Parisian airs. Varya and Lopakhin are purported to be engaged but no proposal ever takes place. Lyubov gives Trofimov permission to marry Anya if they so wish, but he protests that they are above such things. Waiting continues to be the keynote for the play: all await the fate of the estate and the orchard, Varya waits for Lopakhin to propose, Trofimov is waiting for change in Russia.

In Act 3, the estate is up for auction and a ball is held at the house, with the music of a Jewish orchestra and dancing as backdrop for arguments and tensions. The stationmaster and the post-office clerk are the only guests mustered. The first part of the act is driven by Lyubov's anxiety about where Gayev is and what has happened. The great-aunt in Yaroslavl has sent authority to buy the estate in her name with 50,000 roubles, which will not cover the interest. The servants know before the masters that the cherry orchard has been sold: Anya announces that someone in the kitchen has said this. Eventually, Lopakhin and Gayev return, revealing that Lopakhin has outbid Deriganov, purchasing the estate for 90,000 roubles over the mortgage. Varya throws the house keys at Lopakhin's feet and leaves the room as he rejoices drunkenly: 'beaten, barely literate Yermolai, who used to run around barefoot in wintertime ... bought the estate, the most beautiful thing in the world'. He picks up the keys and calls for music:

> See how Yermolai Lopakhin will swing an axe in the cherry orchard ... We'll build cottages and our grandchildren and great-grandchildren will see a new life here ...
>
> (Chekhov 2005: 361)

He appreciates the orchard's beauty, but has no problem sacrificing it to a vision of a more egalitarian world where many can enjoy the countryside. Lyubov is very distressed; Anya tries to comfort her, promising that they will plant a new orchard.

In Act 4, it is a sunny day, as preparations to leave the house take place. There is 'a feeling of emptiness' (Chekhov 2005: 362). The nursery is almost bare and luggage is piled up in a corner. Anya asks Lopakhin to stop the chopping of the trees until her mother has left. Lyubov enquires whether Firs has been taken to the hospital and Yasha is offended that she does not trust him to have done so. Goodbyes are bid to the house. Lyubov is going to Paris to live on the money sent by the Yaroslavl aunt, though she knows it will not last long. Anya is happy, as her new life is beginning – she is going to pass her high school exams and intends then to work to help her mother. She envisages a future where her mother returns to Russia and they will read books together. Lyubov promises to return.

Pishchik dashes in, revealing that his fortunes have changed, as some Englishmen have found white clay on a plot on his land, and he has leased it to them. He repays some of his debts to Lyubov and Lopakhin. Lyubov urges Lopakhin to propose to Varya. He seeks her out but finds himself unable to ask the question. The bustle of departure covers the emotional tensions. Briefly alone, Gayev and Lyubov sob in each other's arms and Lyubov says, 'Oh, my darling, my sweet, beautiful orchard! ... My life, my youth, my happiness, goodbye!' (Chekhov 2005: 371). In counterpoint, Anya and Trofimov's voices are heard shouting happy farewells. The party leave and the doors are locked. In the quietness, the sound of the axe is heard and Firs appears. He is ill. He finds he is locked in but is more concerned about whether Gayev is wearing a warm coat. He mutters, calling himself a 'half-baked bungler', and lies immobile. The play ends with the sound of a breaking string, first heard in Act 2, and the sound of the axe at the trees.

A comedy in four acts

Chekhov wrote to Olga Knipper when the play was in genesis: 'My next play will certainly be funny, very funny. At least, that's the way I see it' (Benedetti 1998: 115), later stating in 1903, 'My play hasn't turned out to be a drama but as a comedy, at times almost a farce' (Chekhov 1982b 11: 248). Chekhov synthesizes elements of farce and physical comedy typical of his vaudevilles in *The Cherry Orchard* to a greater extent than in his other plays. For example, in Act 1, Lopakhin puts his head round the door and bleats, mocking Anya and Varya's laments about the forthcoming sale of the estate. In Act 3, Varya picks up a stick to threaten Yepikhodov and nearly hits Lopakhin. Yepikhodov bumps into the furniture and galoshes are thrown about in Act 4. There are metatheatrical moments when Charlotta entertains, performing magic tricks, ventriloquism, making jokes, and the performance of Alexei Tolstoy's poem 'A Sinful Woman' by the stationmaster in Act 3 is an ironic allusion to perceptions of Lyubov's conduct.

The characters each have their own speech patterns, often comical: Yepikhodov's malapropisms, Gayev's recounting of imaginary billiard games, Charlotta's caustic comments. For example, in Act 2, she says of Yasha and Yepikhodov, 'Horrible the way these people sing ... Phooey! A pack of hyenas' (Chekhov 2005: 340; see Senelick 1985: 132–34 and Anderson 1991). Yepikhodov, who could be compared with Lomov from *The Proposal*, and Simeonov-Pishchik are the closest to pure vaudeville characters (see Chapter 3). True to the description Stanislavsky gives of vaudeville characters, Pishchik is often 'astounded' and has 'one idea': he cannot think of anything but money. His actions are often comic routines – he loses his money and finds it again, he falls asleep, snores and wakes himself up in doing so.

As in *Swan Song* and *The Harmfulness of Tobacco*, the vaudeville elements are combined with pathos. Chekhov wrote to Nemirovich-Danchenko, 'Pishchik is a true Russian, an old man afflicted by the gout, old age and too much to eat' (1973: 463). In the play of class difference and identity, the comedy cuts down pretension; Pishchik represents his family's ancient lineage as descended from Roman Emperor Caligula's horse. Potentially dramatic moments are transformed into comedy. The revolutionary Trofimov declares melodramatically after his row with Lyubov, 'All is over between us', then falls downstairs in an undignified way (Chekhov 2005: 351–52, 356–57). As Stanislavsky put it, objects 'have their own language', functioning often to move poignancy to humour; in Act 1, Pishchik swallows all Lyubov's pills, the symbol of her unhappiness and anxiety; Charlotta ends her monologue in Act 2, speaking of her searing loneliness, by munching on a pickled gherkin she has pulled from her pocket. Gayev arrives at the ball with a gift of anchovies and smoked herring intended for a celebration, crying because of the loss of the orchard, then hears the sound of a billiard cue striking a ball and stops crying immediately. The interplay of objects between masters and servants reveals how status is changing; Yasha handles and receives money from his impecunious mistress; Lyubov gives him a gold coin when Varya has nothing to feed people on in the house and he drinks the champagne intended for his masters in Act 4.

Conversely, comedy is also undercut by the poignancy of the human dilemmas. The scene between Lopakhin and Varya, where he intends to propose but cannot bring himself to do so, is emotionally fraught. Though they part on a note of slapstick, where Varya pulls a parasol out of a bundle and he pretends to be scared (Chekhov 2005: 370), underlying this is heartbreak, for Varya and Lopakhin's future life promises nothing but work. Gayev pronounces ridiculous monologues, after which an embarrassed silence falls: his speech to the bookcase 'nurturing in us ideals of decency and social consciousness', the purple prose of his speech about nature (Chekhov 2005: 333, 348). Gayev desires to create an impression, to enter into discussion with Trofimov and Lopakhin. Lyubov's emotive speeches command attention and draw people to her, whereas he is laughable.

The play eludes definition as to what kind of 'comedy' it is: it has been related to new or Roman comedy (Senelick 1985: 123); Pitcher discusses the aspects of farce and Yermilov calls the play a 'parody of tragedy' (Pitcher 1985: 166–67, 175). In some ways, Chekhov is deconstructing and parodying his own work: for example, guns appear in this play – possessed by Charlotta and Yepikhodov – but are not fired as part of the dramatic action, even offstage as they have been in previous plays, in his continued innovation of theatre writing. The comic aspects of this last work of Chekhov's accentuate the seriousness of the situation in Russia, to which he draws attention.

Self-determination and dependence

Development has been defined as 'the process by which society gains control over the environment, achieves increasing control over its own political fate, offers its members increasing control over themselves' (Epskamp 2006: 24). The play demonstrates Russia's 'underdevelopment' (see Berman 1983: 174–75), the effect of the slow pace of modernization in comparison with Europe's industrialization, and the effect of living in an autocratic society on those of all classes. For all the characters, with the exception perhaps of Anya, living in such an unequal society has stunted growth and maturation. All the characters possess childlike qualities or are emotionally undeveloped; in Firs' idiosyncratic word, they are '*niedotyopy*', 'half-baked bunglers'. Gayev eats sweets and enacts his imaginary billiard games like a small boy. Charlotta feels she is 'oh so young'. There is childish teasing: Trofimov taunts Varya, calling her 'Mrs Lopakhin' and, in revenge, Varya calls him a 'perpetual student' (Chekhov 2005: 340, 354).

The aristocrats

While characters such as Lopakhin struggle to 'wring the slave' out of themselves, as times change, the upper class characters prove to be incapable of looking after themselves and of fulfilling the responsibilities traditionally associated with their rank. They depend on family ties: the aunt in Yaroslavl is the only hope of saving the orchard. Pishchik depends on loans from others, Gayev on Firs to dress him. Gayev and Lyubov are incapable of running the estate and leave it to the youthful and inexperienced Varya.

Lyubov lacks control over her romantic life and money and is ineffectual in caring for those who have been her dependants; Firs is left in the house, she cannot arrange Varya's marriage successfully. She paints a tragic picture of herself, talking about her 'sins': squandering money, marrying a drunkard who produced only debts. (The aunt in Yaroslavl does not approve of the family because Lyubov has broken the rules of behaviour of her class.) She then fell in love with another man but received her first 'punishment', when Grisha drowned. She went abroad, pursued by her lover, who robbed her and had an affair. She tried to poison herself (the theme of suicide occurs in this way in the play). For her, the orchard is a symbol of her youth and innocence. However, despite the grief and sense of guilt that she expresses at different points in the play, her mood can switch, in a childlike way, in an instant. In Act 2, she pleads 'Lord, Lord, be merciful, forgive me my sins! Don't punish me any more!' (Chekhov 2005: 344). She takes out a telegram from her lover, which she rips up, signifying determination to do without him, to 'sin' no more, then hears music and plans to hire the Jewish orchestra and throw a party. Chekhov suggests and subverts the theme of suffering in Russian literature, particularly Dostoevsky and Tolstoy's belief that salvation comes through suffering. Lyubov is not a tragic heroine. He wrote to Knipper, 'The only thing that can chasten a woman like that is death' (Chekhov 2005: 450). Lyubov means 'love'; the other characters adore her, she is charming and witty. Her relationship with her lover is self-destructive: she does not seek independence, but defines herself through her love of him. There is nothing inevitable about her fate: she ultimately chooses to go back to her lover, as she chooses not to consider Lopakhin's money-making plans, and to let the cherry orchard go.

Gayev is unable to control his tongue or exert any authority. He swears on his honour to the young women that he will not permit the estate to go to auction, a promise he knows he will be unable to fulfil, signalled by the fact that he immediately puts a sweet in his mouth, to cover his embarrassment. At the end of the play, Gayev says of himself and Lyubov that everyone is 'dropping them' and they have become 'superfluous'. This references the idea of the 'superfluous man', but is an empty pose (see Chapter 4). He takes a fatalistic attitude as a way to avoid moral responsibility. He attempts to counter Trofimov's impassioned speech-making, saying 'all the

same, you'll die' (Chekhov 2005: 367, 347), the sort of cynical pro-
nouncement favoured by Chekhov's 'Moscow Hamlet'.

New social identities

Trofimov, Lopakhin and to an extent Anya are the only characters
seeking self-determination, though the difficulties of doing so in
their social situation, and their lack of personal development, are
indicated. Chekhov said that Anya's role was 'not particularly
important' (Chekhov 1973: 462), but she has the possibilities of
education, like Nadezhda in Chekhov's last story *The Marriageable
Girl*. The future, unknown but with possibilities, is hers. Trofimov,
as Lyubov points out, is emotionally undeveloped: his sexual
immaturity is suggested by the fact that his beard has not grown.
His energies are directed to the revolutionary cause. Chekhov wrote
to Olga Knipper expressing concern about a 'certain sketchy quality
in the role of Trofimov ... After all, he is constantly being sent into
exile, he is constantly being expelled from the university. How can
you put all those things across?' (Chekhov 1973: 456). He is the
'perpetual student' because students with political convictions like
his were prevented from taking examinations and completing their
courses. Some of Trofimov's lines protesting about serfdom were
cut by the censor and restored only after the 1917 Revolution.

Lopakhin represents the end to the old life, as now some of those
born into serfdom have the possibility of becoming entrepreneurs.
However, despite his success, he continues to think of himself as
inferior, saying of himself in his expensive clothes, that he is 'like a
pig's snout on a tray of pastry'. He says, self-deprecatingly, that like
his father (who was drunken and violent) 'deep down I'm the same
kind of blockhead and imbecile. I never studied anything, my
handwriting is disgusting: I write, I'm ashamed to show it to
people, like a pig' (Chekhov 2005: 324, 345). Lyubov, whom he
adores, represents for him a refinement and elegance he believes he
cannot attain. Styan suggests that Lopakhin cannot bring himself to
marry Varya because it would be a blow against social convention
as she is, though adopted, still a daughter of the house where his
father was a serf (1968: 98). Rayfield notes also that marrying Varya
would oblige him, as a son-in-law, to bail out the cherry orchard
(1999: 249). His social position embodies the conflicts of the

changing society. Chekhov noted to Stanislavsky: 'Dunya and Yepikhodov stand in Lopakhin's presence, they do not sit. Lopakhin, after all, deports himself freely, like a lord' (Chekhov 2005: 454). In the reversal at the end of the play, Lopakhin becomes master of the estate and begins to assume responsibility for others, promising to help Charlotta find a new position.

Confusion over social identities in Russian society at this time has been documented (Fitzpatrick 1982: 16). Charlotta epitomizes this; she has no identity papers, does not know how old she is, and knows little about her parents, who were travelling performers. Her sexuality is also ambivalent: as Marsh points out, she adopts a seductive approach to Simeonov-Pishchik in Act 1, then spurns him. She appears in masculine clothing (hunting gear, with a gun) in Act 2, performing in male evening dress in Act 3, parodies motherhood in a ventriloquist act with an imaginary baby, which she drops in Act 4 (2000: 220). The ambiguity of her gender indicates a wider existential problem: she does not know who she is and she has no one (Chekhov 2005: 340).

Varya, too, has an ambivalent social status; she is possibly the illegitimate child of Lyubov's dead husband, or Gayev and a peasant girl. Such children were often adopted into the upper-class family. Now, the only way she can be spared a life as a housekeeper is through marriage, but as she says, she cannot propose herself (Chekhov 2005: 354), in view of the restrictive gender roles of the time. In Act 1, she says her purported marriage to Lopakhin is like a dream and the motif of dreaming, as self-dramatization and escape, is linked to Varya and other characters in this play, as a symptom of immaturity, an inability to face the realities of life. She dreams of Anya marrying a rich man, so she can then become a pilgrim or enter a convent (as she says, romanticizing the religious life) (Chekhov 2005: 328–29, 354). Others dream; the naïve Anya dreams of a new wonderful world, in which she and her mother will be engaged in study. The servant Dunyasha has romantic dreams (Chekhov 2005: 366, 359), like the upper-class young women have had in previous plays. Lopakhin is the only person in Chekhov's plays who makes his dream come true. His is not an idealistic or romantic dream: he has bought the cherry orchard after years of hard work.

The servants in this schizoid society aim for self-determination by adopting the behaviour of their masters. Dunyasha is a parody of

Lyubov in her attempts to be 'ladylike': her view of a lady is to have soft hands, to powder her face, to be delicate, noble, but also fearful. Comically, the vaudeville motif of fainting in this play is mostly associated with her, though no one takes any notice when she says she is about to faint. Again, this parodies Lyubov, who nearly faints when she learns the estate has been sold in Act 3. Yepikhodov, a parody of the superfluous man, one of Gayev's poses, cannot work out whether he wants to live or die and carries a revolver, hinting he will use it because of Dunyasha's involvement with Yasha (Chekhov 2005: 341). Dunyasha thinks he may commit suicide, and Rayfield notes that his song in Act 2 is that of a man who has killed his lover (1999: 252). Yepikhodov's hints and threats remain just that; he is also a comic version of the malevolent Solyony of *Three Sisters*. Firs remains locked in the past, seeing the turmoil in social identities brought by emancipation as 'the troubles'. He regrets the loss of the certainties of the past when everyone knew their place. He has had no life beyond his situation as valet: Lyubov asks him what he will do if the estate is sold and he answers 'Wherever you order, there I'll go' (Chekhov 2005: 348, 346, 358).

Another symptom of insecurity in social identity is in the way the characters attempt to assert higher status by insulting each other: Gayev calls Lopakhin an 'oaf, a money grubbing peasant' (Chekhov 2005: 331); Gayev and Lyubov assert their refinement by complaining about smells and sounds, usually associated with the servants, patchouli, herring, Yasha's revolting cigars; the restaurant in town has tablecloths that smell of soap. Lyubov says the restaurant also has revolting music and she and Gayev claim to hear the Jewish orchestra in the distance whereas Lopakhin cannot hear anything. Unlike the educated three sisters of the previous play, theirs is an empty refinement; their major claim to status is that their cherry orchard is mentioned in 'the Encyclopaedia' (Chekhov 2005: 332). In the last act, Lyubov and Gayev ignore Lopakhin as he beseeches them to take a farewell drink. Yasha repeats this behaviour; he cannot be bothered to say goodbye to his mother, and dismisses Dunyasha's tears, saying soon he will be away in France, implying that they, and Russia in general, are beneath him. He has no respect for age or class, saying to Firs, 'You bore me, granddad. How about dropping dead?' and to Gayev, 'I can't hear your voice without laughing' (Chekhov 2005: 343). Though of peasant stock himself he distances himself, stating ' ... they're decent enough people, but not very bright' (Chekhov 2005: 362). There are varied reactions to the peasants; Gayev's pose as a populist who understands the peasants is also empty. He thanks the peasants who come to say goodbye warmly, having claimed earlier that the peasants love him, but rebukes Lyubov who has been unable to stop herself giving them her purse. Trofimov is their champion but offers no practical solutions to their plight.

The lower classes, who have been kept in their place by force for so long, are now encroaching on what was formerly the province of the gentry. Varya describes an 'uprising'. The old servants, Yefi-mushka, Polya, Yevstignei and Karp, have been letting vagrants stay in the servants quarters (Chekhov 2005: 339). The servants complain about what they are given to eat whereas Lyubov drinks coffee and eats in restaurants. In Act 2, after the suggestive sound of the breaking string, a drunken vagrant (also 'passer by' in Russian) appears. He declaims excerpts from poems evoking the suffering of the peasants in the past. He represents a new, disturbing phenomenon: unruly behaviour, which has no respect for the upper classes and the former conventions of estate life, a force in society which will have to be reckoned with in the future. Golub writes, 'The presence of the Passerby alerts, stimulates and terrorizes the present with static images of the past and the future, while also suggesting, along with his name, that time passes by' (1994: 23).

Chekhov focuses on class in this play but, with his balanced view, his treatment of the aristocracy is as sympathetic as that of the self-made millionaire and the political radical. The class most satirized in the play is that of the servants: a change from previous plays and a typically Chekhovian reversal.

Philosophizing and politics

The philosophizing of Chekhov's characters reflects current ideological thought, though, as in previous plays, the popular ideas sometimes distort or over-simplify the philosophies from which they are drawn and Chekhov often subverts the discussions with comic touches. The debates about love, work and politics, between Lyubov, Gayev, Lopakhin and Trofimov, reveal differing moral and political codes.

Love and truth

Lyubov and Trofimov argue about love and truth, adopting different positions, the personal and the political, as the ideal of romantic love is opposed to revolutionary ideals. In Act 3, Trofimov complains about Varya following Anya and himself, to prevent them falling in love; he is 'so removed from banality'. Lyubov's riposte is that she must be 'beneath love'. Insensitively, in view of the fact that she is very upset about the sale of the estate, Trofimov urges her to look the truth straight in the eye for once and see that the estate way of life has long been over. She replies:

> What truth? I can't see anything. You boldly resolve all the major problems – but life is still hidden from your young eyes. Spare me, this is where I was born ... after all, this is where my father and my mother lived, my grandfather, I love this house, without the cherry orchard I couldn't make sense of my life.
>
> (Chekhov 2005: 355)

Trofimov lacks compassion for Lyubov's plight and she lacks understanding of him. The figure of Rakhmetov in Chernyshevsky's *What is to be done?* had great influence on the revolutionaries in his self-sacrifice and advocation of study, moderation and sexual abstention; Trofimov adopts these ideas. In *The Story of an Anonymous Man*, Chekhov portrays a terrorist, who also rejects human love, but changes when the care of a motherless child falls to him. Trofimov maintains his ascetic pose, explaining to Anya, 'we're above love. Avoiding the petty and specious – that keeps us from being free and happy, that's the goal and meaning of our life' (Chekhov 2005: 349–50). Lyubov thinks that the goal of life for everyone must be romantic love. She says Trofimov may marry Anya but he must finish his degree, make his beard grow and stop being tossed about by fate. Trofimov wants her to see the truth about her love affair, that her scoundrel of a lover has robbed her. Lyubov gets angry and calls Trofimov a 'schoolboy, a puritan, a freak, a half-baked bungler' as he does not have a lover at his age (Chekhov 2005: 356). The juxtaposition of the two points of view questions the idealization of romantic love and the abstention from it in order to further the cause of revolution.

The future

Discussing the way forward for Russia, Trofimov challenges Gayev's romantic views: referencing Gorky's *The Lower Depths*, a revolutionary play, Gayev appears to be the defender, like Luka, a character in the play, of pride in humanity, a romantic notion of the greatness of human beings. Trofimov argues that this is mysticism:

> what's the point of human pride … if man is poorly constructed physiologically, if the vast majority is crude, unthinking, profoundly wretched. We should stop admiring ourselves. We should just work.
>
> (Chekhov 2005: 346)

Actually, Trofimov is proud in an inverted way. In Act 3, he takes pride in being called a 'scruffy gent' by a woman on the train, in Act 4, of being a 'free man' and his role 'in the front ranks' as 'humanity is moving towards the most sublime truth, to the most sublime happiness possible on earth' (Chekhov 2005: 364).

Lopakhin's vision for the future contrasts with that of Trofimov, capitalism in counterpoint to revolution. He foresees the estate full of *dachi* owned by the grandchildren and great-grandchildren of his generation who 'will see a new life'. His vision is balanced with practicality; he says, ' … Lord, you gave us vast forests, boundless fields, the widest horizons, and living here, we really and truly ought to be giants … ', but his experience is that there are so 'few decent, honest people' in this corrupt society with whom he can work. Trofimov thinks Lopakhin's ventures are ultimately pointless but says that as a future millionaire, Lopakhin is essential, as 'an essential component in the conversion of matter is the wild beast that devours whatever crosses its path' (Chekhov 2005: 361, 364, 346), referencing, obliquely, the Marxist view of capitalism as an essential stage on the way to the establishment of socialism. Trofimov's inspirational speeches in Act 2 graphically describe the situation of the peasants and condemn the intelligentsia. His rhetoric about the future, as Senelick points out, is 'patched together from Pushkin, Pleshcheyev and the Decembrists' (1985: 133). His philosophizing is comically undercut: 'Happiness is coming – it's getting nearer and nearer' when actually at that moment it is Varya who is getting nearer and nearer, in anxious pursuit of Anya (Chekhov 2005: 351).

Both see work as the way forward: Trofimov thinks unremitting work should atone for the idleness of the intelligentsia but does not give any practical programme of what should be done, and it is unclear how exactly he occupies himself. Lopakhin works from dawn until dusk, which appears to him to give some meaning to his life. He leaves for Kharkov at the end of the play for the winter, stating that hanging around on the estate with nothing to do has worn him out. Lopakhin works for money, aiming in this way for self-determination. Trofimov rejects the need for money, claiming that in doing so, he is 'free … And everything that you all value so highly and fondly, rich men and beggars alike hasn't the slightest effect on me; it's like fluff floating in the air' (Chekhov 2005: 347, 363–64). Lopakhin offers him money, which Trofimov turns down, saying he has received some money for a translation.

Chekhov considered it important that Lopakhin was not perceived as mercenary. He wrote to Stanislavsky that Lopakhin's was the central role, adding, 'Varya loves Lopakhin and she is a serious, religious young girl, she wouldn't be in love with some little moneygrubber'. He emphasized the sympathetic aspects of Lopakhin, adding lines to the first version of the play where Trofimov says, 'Anyhow, I can't help liking you. You've got delicate, gentle fingers, like an artist, you've got a delicate, gentle heart' (Chekhov 2005: 451, 364). Chekhov gives a similarly sympathetic portrait of the millionaire Laptev in *Three Years*, who inherits a factory from his father, who, like Lopakhin's father, is a former serf and also a brutal despot. Laptev's marriage is unhappy and he says, 'I simply can't adjust to life and master it … I explain all this … by my being a slave – the grandson of a serf. Before we dregs work our way onto the right road, many of us will leave our bones behind!' (Chekhov 2003: 137). He sees that the money he inherits could ruin his life and enslave him in another way. He chooses to begin to redress some of the exploitative ways the factory is run and to open himself to new possibilities in the future.

Parodies of philosophy

The more comic characters parody the philosophizing; Pishchik relates that his daughter Dashenka says that Nietszche says it is all right to counterfeit money. Later, he says he has been talking to someone on the train who says a great philosopher recommends jumping off the roof and that will solve the whole problem (Chekhov 2005: 352, 367). Yepikhodov enquires whether Dunyasha and Yasha have read Thomas Henry Buckle, whose materialist *History of Civilisation in England* (translated into Russian in 1861) was well-known though outdated by the end of the century (Chekhov 2005: 341). Yephikhodov, in this aspect, is a parody of Gayev, who clings to outdated ideas in an attempt to appear to have informed views. Gayev styles himself a 'man of the eighties' and says:

> people don't put much stock on that period but all the same I can say I've suffered for my convictions to no small degree in my time. There's a good reason peasants love me. You've got to study peasants!
>
> (Chekhov 2005: 339)

Gayev's claims to be a populist are little but empty posturing as this was a period of inertia and disillusionment under the autocratic Alexander III, and there is no evidence either for his suffering or of the peasants' love for him.

Modernization and development: the breaking string and the cherry orchard

Images of industrialism encroach upon nature in the settings for the play, suggesting that Russia as a whole is on the brink of change. The beginning of Act 2 is in June, near sunset, as life on the estate draws near to its end. The setting is a field bordering the cherry orchard. An abandoned chapel and slabs that were once tombstones indicate changing values – shared worship is no longer part of estate life. There is a road to the estate and a large town in the distance and telegraph poles that bring messages from Paris to Lyubov. The railway has wrought changes – Gayev says that now there is a railway 'you ride to town and have lunch'. The vagrant in Act 2 is on his way to the station. Lopakhin and Varya will be borne away to different destinations on the train. In Act 4, Yasha says, 'In six days I'll be in Paris again. Tomorrow. We'll board an express train and dash away, we'll be gone in a flash' (Chekhov 2005: 342, 365).

He will be abroad, away from a Russia he considers 'uncivilised'. Pishchik's English entrepreneurs have discovered clay on his land, to be used in ceramic factories. The almost magical transformation of Pishchik's situation comes from 'abroad', an idealized topography in the play, as Moscow is in *Three Sisters*. Dunyasha envies Yasha spending time abroad. The malaprop Yepikhodov, in his way, summarizes the characters' attitude: 'Abroad everything long ago attained its complete complexification'. Trofimov states that Russia is at least 200 years behind the times (Chekhov 2005: 341, 350).

'Abroad' holds one set of meanings for the characters and the cherry orchard another. Anya's image of the orchard has changed from beauty to an image of slavery under Trofimov's influence, whereas for Gayev and Lyubov it is the past, their heritage, their happy youth. Critics similarly invest the symbol with meaning; for Styan, the orchard symbolizes the aristocratic past (1971: 241), for others the cherry orchard is an imaginary landscape, somehow unreal. 'A cherry orchard that could glut the world with cherries and yet cannot make its authors a living symbolises a decrepit Russia for which ordered destruction is the only alternative to disordered ruination' (Rayfield 1999: 248–49). Peace also discusses the orchard as a symbol for nineteenth century Russian society, comparing Chekhov's orchard with an allegory of the forest in an essay by Dobrolyubov, in which the Russian intelligentsia attempt to lead the ordinary people through a dangerous forest but themselves climb trees to avoid the danger and there find fruit. They ignore the people below and the latter, in desperation, begin to hack down the trees, which represent the institution of serfdom (1983: 136–37).

Lyubov and Gayev may cling to the past but Lopakhin is both a constant reminder of time passing and a catalyst. His first words are to ask what time it is, his last look to the future, 'Til we meet again!', though the group may never do so (Chekhov 2005: 324, 370). He repeatedly looks at his watch, and tells Gayev and Lyubov that time will not stand still. When Lyubov cries after the estate has been sold, he tells her, reproachfully, 'you can't undo it now', adding the wish 'if only our ungainly, unhappy life could be changed quickly' (Chekhov 2005: 342, 361). Other characters point out to each other how they waste time: Trofimov says to Simeonov-Pishchik, 'if the energy you've wasted in the course of a lifetime tracking down money to pay off interest had been harnessed to something else, you probably ultimately could have turned the world upside down' (Chekhov 2005: 352). Lyubov criticizes Lopakhin, who refers to a play he has seen at the theatre, and others for the way they spend time, 'You have no business watching plays, you should look at yourselves more. You all lead such gray lives, you talk such nonsense' (Chekhov 2005: 345). Lopakhin says to Trofimov in Act 4:

> We turn up our noses at one another, while life keeps slipping by. When I work a long time nonstop then my thoughts are clearer, and I even seem to know why I exist. But pal, how many people there are in Russia who don't know why they exist.
>
> (Chekhov 2005: 364–65)

As Act 4 draws to a close, 'ending' acts as a refrain; Lopakhin pronounces 'So ends life in this house', Anya and Trofimov chorus 'Good bye, old life! … Hello, new life', giving the end of this play a finality that differs from the end of the previous plays. Firs, in his final speech, says, 'This life's gone by like I ain't lived' (Chekhov 2005: 369–71). The final stage directions are the sound of the breaking string, Chekhov's most arcane symbol, then, after a silence, there is the sound of an axe on a tree, both audible only to the audience. When the sound of the breaking string first occurs in Act 2, Lopakhin explains it as a bucket falling in a mineshaft, a motif that also occurs in Chekhov's story *Fortune* of 1887. The other characters choose to interpret the sound variously, and ominously. Bartlett sees the sound as Chekhov's homage to the beauty and austerity of the steppe, the landscape, which inspired him (2004: 53). Rayfield finds a reference to an image in Tolstoy's *War and Peace* of imminent political crisis as a 'string about to break', and for Chekhov associated with 'the death of nature, industrialisation, the crippling of human beings … threat from an underground world to the gentry' (1999: 255).

Once the drama of the sale of the estate is over, life goes on. Pishchik notes that 'everything in this world comes to an end' and as Gayev says, ' … once the matter was settled finally, irrevocably, everyone calmed down, even cheered up … '. Cutting down the orchard and letting the estate go to auction means the characters can let go of the past and move on. Lyubov says 'Now we can go' (Chekhov 2005: 366, 368). She is to return to Paris with Yasha, Anya's new beginning is to take her high school exams and go on to higher education, Gayev has taken up a position in a bank, earning his own money for the first time in his life. Varya and Charlotta will have new jobs with other families. Lopakhin, in cutting down the orchard, possibly frees himself of his brutalized peasant background, and Trofimov hopes that Russia can put an end to the past. Chekhov wrote that 'the last act will be cheerful' (Chekhov 1982b 11: 253). The play proposes a Voltairean solution to the family's problems: when they let go of their false ideals, of fighting the inevitability of change, stop desiring life to be different to what it is and get on with the practicalities of what must be done, they create possibilities for themselves in the future. Firs' final words, that he has not lived, indicate that life is too precious to waste. In 1900, Suvorin was writing a play that was to end with a melodramatic scene involving nihilists. Chekhov advised him not to do so, writing 'what your play needs is a quiet, lyrical, touching ending. If your heroine grows old without getting anywhere or coming to terms with herself ... and that she has let life pass her by – isn't that more frightening than the nihilists?' (Chekhov 1973: 378). Chekhov chose such an ending for his final play.

Key productions

The first performance of *The Cherry Orchard* was at the Moscow Art Theatre on 17 January 1904, celebrating the twenty-fifth anniversary of Chekhov's writing career. Chekhov, now seriously ill, expressed dissatisfaction with aspects of the production. Stanislavsky argued that the play was a tragedy not a comedy (1995: 505), and the view has persisted that Stanislavsky made of the play a farewell to the traditions of the Russian upper classes in the nineteenth century, creating an atmosphere of 'Chekhovian melancholy' (Gottlieb 2005: 3, ixxviii). This has been challenged; Worrall indicates how Stanislavsky emphasized the childlike, emotionally immature aspects of all the characters and concludes that the score manifests a light-heartedness suggesting that Stanislavsky did understand that Chekhov had written 'a comedy, at places even a farce' (1999: 539; see also Hristic 1995 and Allen 2000: 29–35). Chekhov initially wanted Stanislavsky to play Lopakhin, but he chose the part of Gayev, saying of him that he was 'something of an aristocrat, but a bit stupid' (Benedetti 1995: 174), evidently not seeing him as a tragic figure. There were some staging problems; Meyerhold noted that Stanislavsky's production was too naturalistic and Nemirovich-Danchenko wrote that the theatre had struggled with the fact that Chekhov had 'refined his realism to the symbol', and the need to find a way to express heightened, poetic realism conflicted with Stanislavsky's directorial methods at that time (Stroeva 1973: 121–22).

Griffiths and politicized Cherry Orchards

Whatever Stanislavsky's production had been, émigrés who had left Russia after the Revolution 'identified so closely with Ranevskaya and Gayev that they disseminated a nostalgic view of the gentry's plight throughout the west' (Senelick 1985: 120; see also Senelick 1997a: chapter 8). A key issue in more recent productions is the reading of the political imperatives of the play. Trevor Griffiths' 1977 version, directed by Richard Eyre at the Nottingham Playhouse, resisted possibilities for audience identification with the plight of the upper classes, an interpretation that had persisted for fifty years. He wrote:

> For half a century now, in England as elsewhere, translation followed translation, *that* idiom became 'our' idiom, that class 'our class', until the play's specific historicity and precise sociological imagination had been bleached of all meanings beyond those required to convey the necessary 'natural' sense that the fine will always be undermined by the crude and that the 'human condition' can for all essential purposes be equated with 'the plight' of the middle classes.
>
> (2007: 266)

Griffiths reduced Lyubov's role, particularly the emotionalism of her speeches, which captivates the other characters and potentially also audiences. He saw Lopakhin and Trofimov as each representing the only two possibilities for the future 'bourgeoisification and commoditization, or revolutionary change' (Allen 1993: 157) and therefore boosted their roles. He made textual alterations, for example, Trofimov's speech in Act 2 was changed:

> Mankind is advancing, perfecting its powers. Everything that's unattainable for us now will someday come within our grasp and understanding, only we've got to work, to help the truth-seekers with all our might. So far, here in Russia, very few people do any work ... There's only dirt, vulgarity, Asiatic inertia ...
>
> (Chekhov 2005: 347)

In Griffiths' version this reads:

> Man can make progress, struggle for perfection. There is a discernible future in which we'll find solutions to the problems that confront us now; but we'll achieve it only through unremitting struggle, by working with all our strength to help those who are even now seeking the answers. Here now in Russia, very few are embarked on that course ... What we have achieved is widespread misery, bourgeois vulgarity and moral barbarism.
>
> (Griffiths 2007: 294)

This gives a politicized reading: the Marxist term 'struggle' is used instead of 'work', the ideal of the democratic Russian intelligentsia. 'Bourgeois vulgarity' is substituted for the Russian concept of *aziatchina*, the inertia that Chekhov saw as a widespread problem in Russian culture rather than a class-based one.

Griffiths makes some statements more overt: Trofimov says that if the authorities have their way he will never graduate (Griffiths 2007: 282), a statement which Chekhov could not have made because of censorship. Firs' speech, 'The peasants stood by the masters, the masters stood by the peasants, but now it's every which way, you can't figure it out' (Chekhov 2005: 346), becomes in Griffiths' version, 'The serfs belonged to their masters and the masters owned the serfs. Now it is all so messy and you can't make sense of any of it' (2007: 292). Arguably, this obscures the fact that Firs, unlike Lopakhin, does not remember his life of serfdom as a life of brutal floggings, but of having security, a place in a family whom he loved. Chekhov abhorred serfdom, but indicates reasons for Firs' attitudes, raising questions about the society that has replaced serfdom.

Griffiths' version may be seen as a teleological reading of the play, reading its events as leading up to 1917. Gottlieb argues against this, noting that 'where a production or version of a Chekhov play has overtly brought out political significance', such as Trevor Griffiths' 1977 version of *The Cherry Orchard*, then this has been seen a forced or unnatural 'grafting purely for the sake of left-wing ideology' (1993: 147). She points to an anomaly; following the MAT productions, Chekhov's plays are generally staged within a period setting,

> but with very few exceptions the period and social content of the plays has been ignored. We are presented with 'the period' visually but almost never in substance. The characters wear late nineteenth century dress, but the plays do not 'voice' the economic, social, philosophical and political conflicts and issues of Chekhov's Russia.
>
> (1993: 151)

One exception was Janet Suzman's adaptation, *The Free State* (2000), set in the eastern free state in South Africa, which explored both racial tension and class conflict. Conciously choosing to read Chekhov's play through 'the prism of politics' Suzman transforms Lopakhin into Leko, a rich black entrepreneur, who debates with Pitso (based on Trofimov), a radical and idealistic student, making reference to Bram Fisher, the Afrikaans dissident who led the defence of Nelson Mandela in 1964 and later died in imprisonment.

Chekhov at the Royal Shakespeare Company

Adrian Noble's production in 1995 with Penelope Wilton as Lyubov, David Troughton as Lopakhin and Alec McCowen as Gayev aimed to foreground class and history in a way that was faithful to the text. The minimal set was filled with servants carrying luggage in the first act and out in the last acts, the bustle emphasizing the arrival and departure and, more widely, a sense of people in transit: in particular, the class that still has quantities of possessions and has to be waited on is going away now, perhaps forever. Lopakhin's constant reiteration of his peasant origins and sense of inferiority was emphasized in David Troughton's performance, as for example when he enacts abasement: hitting himself and falling at Lyubov's feet at the end of his speech about buying the estate in Act 4. Lyubov and Gayev similarly enact superiority, adopting a supercilious attitude and reciting the facts about the cherry orchard as they have done many times before, a family ritual in Act 1.

Despite these emphases, Tulloch, Burvill and Hood argue that the end result was to 'occlude class' (1997: 318). They note that the family house was central to the production. Noble staged the play in what was his 'house', the Swan Theatre, as he was then the artistic director of the Royal Shakespeare Company in Stratford-upon-Avon. This and his use of the actors' emotional memories about the homes of their childhood in rehearsal positioned class and history in an essentialist way, reducing the political aspects of the play to a sense of the mere inevitability of modernization and change (Tulloch, Burvill and Hood 1997: 327).

Figure 7.1 The Cherry Orchard at the Swan Theatre, Stratford-upon-Avon, Malcolm Davies Collection. Copyright Shakespeare Birthplace Trust

Other commentators said that the production challenged received opinions on Chekhov. One reviewer, acknowledging that the production was sited 'firmly in its historical context', deplored the absence of 'notes of elegiac regret' in this production, finding that the gentry were played in a way that meant they were 'not candidates for sympathy' and that Troughton's performance was 'vulgarly emphatic'.[1] Most other reviewers applauded the production: 'the finest RSC production of anything for several seasons' in which, beneath the 'luminous' details, 'history itself can be felt in flux'.[2] Mark Lockyer as the unpleasant Yasha was described as 'sobbing into a stolen glass of champagne in tipsy terror at the prospect of spending the rest of his life in the kitchen ... To lose your foothold in these shifting social sands is catastrophic.'[3] Ranevskaya and Gayev were viewed as 'charming but indifferent to the seismic shifts taking place in society. The class theme is most clearly articulated in David Troughton's ebullient but insecure Lopakhin ... the new merchant class still weighed down with the burdens of the past.'[4]

Afterword

Chekhov's plays can be discussed in terms of gender, social class, economic and cultural factors and offer a critical perspective on the norms held by his society. One of the main questions asked by the plays is about the extent to which the individual can take responsibility for his or her life in a repressive social environment; how those from serf backgrounds, women and also privileged and socially conscious men can 'wring the slave' out of themselves in a society where structures to support progressive thinking are lacking or inadequate. The plays achieve a philosophical dimension by asking such questions, which have relevance beyond the world in which the plays are situated. The consideration of a multiplicity of responses to life's challenges, whether to accept a superficial life, to involve oneself in artistic activity, education or to work for social change, to do some kind of work, extends this relevance. The four major plays in a way represent a movement through life: in *The Seagull*, young people facing difficulties in life choose between endurance and giving way to despair; Vanya survives his mid-life crisis and picks up his pen to work; the three sisters live through destruction brought about by others and find a way to carry on; *The Cherry Orchard*, the most humorous of the major plays, written when Chekhov knew he would not live much longer, affirms letting go of the past and moving on. Chekhov's mastery of the tragicomic, his humour, the innovatory nature of his approach to theatrical representation, the profundity of his philosophy mean that the plays continue to offer challenges for actors, directors and audiences.

Notes

Chapter 1

1 'Beautiful Soul' was the term used by German Romantic writer Friedrich von Schiller to define the morality of a person who was so pure that in ethical decisions they could be guided by emotion rather than will.
2 *Zemstvo* is singular, *zemstva* plural.

Chapter 2

1 Cited by Alfred Appel, Jr. (1970) *The Annotated Lolita*, New York: McGraw-Hill: xlix–1.
2 The term comes from Chekhov's story *Man in a Case* (1898).

Chapter 3

1 See Senelick, 'Offenbach and Chekhov; or La Belle Helena', in Jackson (1993) for Chekhov's interest in Offenbach's comic opera.
2 Interview with Meyerhold about *33 Swoons*, 20 March 1935, RGALI 998 1 665.
3 *Ibid*.
4 A tape recording of a fragment of *33 Swoons*, with famous actor Igor Ilinsky in the role of Lomov, is in the Bakhrushin Museum in Moscow.
5 *Pravda*, 3 September 1935.
6 *Literaturnyi Leningrad*, 4 January 1935.
7 Interview by the author with Terence Mann, 21 January 2008.
8 *The Times*, 28 September 1988.
9 Programme note for *The Sneeze*, 1988: 9.
10 *The Sunday Times*, 2 October 1988.

Chapter 4

1 *The Guardian*, 20 February 1997.
2 Senelick points out that this was a common formula in police reports (Chekhov 2005: 161).

3 Treplyov originally explained that he had been expelled from university because of his political activities but, to get past the censor, Chekhov had to signal this to the audience without being explicit (Chekhov 2005: 140).

4 Despite this, Schuler describes 'the Nina Zarechnaia epidemic', where aspiring actresses flocked to theatres throughout Russia after the play was produced. For some Russian woman of the epoch, this 'potentially subversive transgression of class barriers, gave them access to public space and a voice in public affairs' (1996: 19, 21).

5 Golovachyova analyses Chekhov's own intertextuality, with references to *The Unnecessary Victory*, *Three Years*, *My Life* (2001: 19–34).

6 Bird imagery features in other plays, particularly *The Wood Demon*, *Uncle Vanya* and *Three Sisters* (McVay 1995: 40–41).

7 Turgenev's friend Herzen, seeing its effect on Turgenev, condemned it as a 'nihilism of exhaustion and despair' (Kelly 1998: 91).

8 Chekhov was preparing to write a parody of B. E. Markevich's *The Fumes of Life* in 1884 as he wrote to Leykin on January 30th.

9 Senelick translates *bred*, delirium as 'gibberish'.

10 Ben Whishaw, *The Sunday Times*, 25 June 2006.

11 *The Guardian*, 17 June 2006.

12 Interview by the author with Katie Mitchell, 30 November 2006 at the National Theatre.

13 Interview with Katie Mitchell.

14 Natasha Tripney, www.musicOMH.com.

15 *The Guardian*, 1 July 2006.

16 *New Statesman*, 17 July 2006.

17 *Sunday Times*, 2 July 2006.

18 Interview by the author with Ian Rickson, 26 July 2006.

19 Michael Coveney, www.whatsonstage.com.

20 Interview with Ian Rickson.

21 Interview with Ian Rickson.

22 *The Stage*, 31 January 2007.

23 *Time Out*, 30 January 2007.

24 *The London Lite*, 26 January 2007.

Chapter 5

1 See Durkin (1981) for a consideration of references to Dostoevsky in *Ward No. 6*.

2 Valency points out that Helen of Troy returned to a husband she despised.

3 The situation of Chekhov's women is often expressed by images of the piano; Yelena is like Masha in *Three Sisters*, who is forbidden by her husband Kulygin to play the piano in public, and Irina in the same play says her heart is like a piano to which the key has been lost (Chekhov 2005: 299).

4 *New York Times*, 16 October 1994.
5 *Moskovskie Novosti*, 13 September 2005–19.05.
6 Dodin's Maly Drama Theatre website: http://www.mdt-dodin.ru/about/
  plays/uncle_vania/index.html. Accessed on 29 April 2010.
7 I dozhd' smyvaet vsye sledy *Chas Pik*, 29 June 2003.
8 *Russkii Zhurnal*, 6 May 2003.
9 *Niezavisimaya Gazeta* No. 110 (2943), 4 June 2003.

Chapter 6

1 The theme of suicide occurs offstage in this play. Notes for the play
  show that Masha was originally to attempt suicide in Act 3 (McVay
  1995: 25).
2 Chekhov's women have been discussed by Lafitte (1973), Llewellyn
  Smith (1973), De Maegd-Soëp (1987), Moravcevich (1981), Hahn (1977),
  as well as Marsh and Tait. Earlier analyses attribute a certain level of
  misogyny to Chekhov, challenged by the more recent analyses that discuss Chekhov's interrogation of gender and theatrical norms.
3 *Metrolife*, 8 May 2007.
4 Interview by the author with Declan Donnellan, 26 October 2007.
5 *The Financial Times*, 19 May 2007.
6 Interview with Declan Donnellan.
7 *Metrolife*, 8 May 2007.
8 Interview with Declan Donnellan.
9 Interview with Declan Donnellan.
10 *The Independent*, 4 May 2007.
11 *The Times*, 30 April 2007.
12 Interview with Declan Donnellan.
13 *The Times*, 30 May 2007.
14 *The Independent*, 4 May 2007.
15 *The Daily Telegraph*, 17 May 2007.
16 Interview with Declan Donnellan.

Chapter 7

1 *Evening Standard*, 5 July 1995.
2 *The Financial Times*, 5 July 1995.
3 *The Times*, 6 July 1995.
4 *The Guardian*, 6 July 1995.

Bibliography

Note: The second edition of Chekhov's *Complete Works* (*Polnoe Sobranie*) was published in 30 volumes between 1974 and 1983. There are 18 volumes of Chekhov's works and 12 volumes of letters. References to the works are indicated by 'a', references to the letters by 'b' 1–12 and the date of publication of the volume is also given.

Allen, D. (1993) '*The Cherry Orchard*, a new English version by Trevor Griffiths', in P. Miles (ed) *Chekhov on the British Stage,* Cambridge: Cambridge University Press.

——(2000) *Performing Chekhov*, London: Routledge.

Anderson, G. (1991) 'The Music of *The Cherry Orchard*: Repetitions in the Russian Text', *Modern Drama*, 34: 340–50.

Andrew, J. (1980) *Writers and Society During the Rise of Russian Realism,* London: Macmillan.

——(2007) *Narrative, Space and Gender in Russian Fiction 1846–1903,* Amsterdam, New York: Rodopi.

Barricelli, J-P. (ed) (1981) *Chekhov's Great Plays*, New York: New York University Press.

Bartlett, R. (2004) *Chekhov, Scenes from a Life*, London: The Free Press.

Bel'chikov, N. (ed) (1930) *Chekhov i ego sreda*, Leningrad: Akademia.

Benedetti, J. (ed and trans) (1995) *The Moscow Art Theatre Letters,* London: Methuen.

——(ed) (1998) *Dear Writer … Dear Actress … The Love Letters of Anton Chekov and Olga Knipper*, London: Methuen.

——(ed) (1999) *Stanislavski, His Life and Art*, London: Methuen.

Berman, M. (1983) *All That Is Solid Melts into Air, the Experience of Modernity*, New York: Simon & Schuster.

Beumers, B. (1997) *Yury Lyubimov at the Taganka Theatre 1964–1994,* Amsterdam: Overseas Publishers Association.

Bjørnager, K. (2005) 'The Masculine Triangle in *Uncle Vanya*', *Essays in Poetics*, 30: 45–52.

Borker, D. and Garnica, O. (1980) 'Male and Female Speech in Dramatic Dialogue: A Stylistic Analysis of Chekhovian Character Speech', *Language and Style*, 13, 4: 3–28.

Brahms, C. (1976) *Reflections in a Lake: A study of Chekhov's four greatest plays*, London: Weidenfeld & Nicolson.

Braun, E. (1982) *The Director and the Stage; from Naturalism to Grotowski*, London: Methuen.

——(1998) *Meyerhold: A Revolution in Theatre*, London: Methuen.

——(2000) 'The Cherry Orchard', in V. Gottlieb and P. Allain (eds) *The Cambridge Companion to Chekhov*, Cambridge: Cambridge University Press.

Briggs, A. (1994) 'Two Months in the Country: Chekhov's Unacknowledged Debt to Turgenev', *New Zealand Slavonic Journal*, 17–32.

Bristow, E. (1981) 'Circles, Triads and Parity in *The Three Sisters*', in J-P. Barricelli (ed) *Chekhov's Great Plays*, New York: New York University Press.

Brodskaya, G. (2000) *Alekseev-Stanislavskii, Chekhov i drugie. Vishnevosadskaya epopeia*, 2 vols, Moskva: Agraf.

Chamberlain, L. (2004) *Motherland – a Philosophical History of Russia*, London: Atlantic Books.

Chances, E. (1978) *Conformity's Children: An approach to the superfluous man in Russian literature*, Columbus, OH: Slavica.

——(2001) 'The superfluous man in Russian literature', in N. Cornwell (ed) *The Routledge Companion to Russian Literature*, London: Routledge.

Chekhov, A. (1961) *Chekhov i teatr – pis'ma, fel'etony, sovremenniki o Chekhove, dramaturge*, E. Surkov (ed), Moscow: Iskusstvo.

——(1967) *The Notebooks of Anton Tchekhov together with Reminiscences of Tchekhov by Maxim Gorky*, S.S. Koteliansky and Leonard Woolf (trans), London: The Hogarth Press.

——(1973) *Anton Chekhov's Life and Thought; Selected Letters and Commentary*, M. Heim (trans), in collaboration with S. Karlinsky (ed) and Introduction by S. Karlinsky, Evanston, IL: Northwestern University Press.

——(1974–83) *Polnoe Sobranie Sochinenii i Pisem v tridsati tomakh*, 1–18a (works) 1–12b (letters), Moskva: Nauka.

——(1974) *Letters of Anton Chekhov*, A. Yarmolinsky (ed), London: Jonathan Cape.

——(1997) *Ivanov*, adapted by David Hare, London: Methuen.

——(2003) *Seven Short Novels*, B. Makanowitzky (trans), New York: W. W. Norton.

——(2004a) *Perepiska A.P. Chekhova i O.L. Knipper*: v dvukh tomakh, Moskva: Iskusstvo.

——(2004b) *Anton Chekhov: A Life in Letters*, R. Bartlett (ed and trans), London: Penguin.

——(2005) *Selected Plays*, L. Senelick (ed and trans), London: W. W. Norton & Company.

——(2006a) *The Complete Plays*, L. Senelick (ed and trans) London: W. W. Norton & Company.

——(2006b) *The Seagull*, adapted by M. Crimp, London: Faber & Faber.

——(2007) *The Seagull*, adapted by C. Hampton, London: Faber & Faber.

Chekhov, M. (1981) *Vokrug Chekhova*, Moskva: Khudozhestvennaya Literatura.

Chepurov, A. (2006) *A. P. Chekhov i Aleksandrinskii Teatr na rubezhe XIX i XX vekov*, Sankt-Peterburg: Baltiiskie sezony.

Chudakov, A. (2000) 'Dr Chekhov: a biographical essay (29 January 1860– 15 July 1904)', in V. Gottlieb and P. Allain (eds) *The Cambridge Companion to Chekhov*: Cambridge: Cambridge University Press.

——(1983) *Chekhov's Poetics*, E. Cruise and D. Dragt (trans), Ann Arbor, MI: Ardis.

Clayton, J. (ed) (1997), *Chekhov Then and Now: The Reception of Chekhov in World Culture*, New York: Peter Lang.

Clyman, T. (1974) 'Čexov's Victimised Women', *Russian Language Journal*, 28: 100: 26–31.

——(1985) *A Chekhov Companion*, Westport, CT: Greenwood Press.

Coope, J. (1997) *Doctor Chekhov: A study in literature and medicine*, Chale: Cross.

Deak, F. (1993) *Symbolist Theatre: The formation of an avant-garde*, Baltimore, MD and London: Johns Hopkins University Press.

De Maegd-Soëp, C. (1987) *Chekhov and Women: Women in the Life and Work of Chekhov*, Columbus, OH: Slavica.

Dolzhenkov, P. (1998) *Chekhov i Positivizm*, Moskva: Dialog-MGU.

Dorra, H. (1994) *Symbolist Art Theories: A Critical Anthology*, Berkeley, CA: University of California Press.

Durkin, A. (1981) 'Chekhov's Response to Dostoevskii: The Case of "Ward Six"', *Slavic Review*, 40, 1: 49–59.

Eekman, T. (ed) (1960) *Anton Čechov, 1860–1960. Some essays*, Leiden: E. J. Brill.

Emeljanow, V. (ed) (1981a) *Anton Chekhov, the Critical Heritage*, London: Routledge.

——(1981b) 'Komisarjevsky's *Three Sisters*: The Prompt Book', *Theatre Notebook*, 44, 2: 56–66.

Epskamp, C. (2006) *Theatre for Development: An introduction to context, applications, and training*, London: Zed.

Esslin, M. (1982) 'The stage: reality, symbol, metaphor', in J. Redmond (ed) *Drama and Symbolism,* Cambridge: Cambridge University Press.

Finke, M. (1994) 'The Hero's Descent to the Underworld in Chekhov', *The Russian Review*, 53: 67–80.

——(2005) *Seeing Chekhov, Life and Art*, Ithaca, NY: Cornell University Press.

Fitzpatrick, S. (1982) *The Russian Revolution*, Oxford: Oxford University Press.

Flath, Carol A. (1999) 'The Seagull: The Stage Mother, the Missing Father, and the Origins of Art', *Modern Drama*, 42, 4: 491–510.

French, Philip (2000) 'Chekhov on Screen', in V. Gottlieb and P. Allain (eds) *The Cambridge Companion to Chekhov*, Cambridge: Cambridge University Press.

Gershkovich, A. (1989) *The Theater of Yuri Lyubimov*, Michael Yurieff (trans), New York: Paragon House.

Gillès, D. (1968) *Chekhov: Observer without Illusion*, C. Markmann (trans), New York: Funk and Wagnalls.

Gilman, R. (1995) *Chekhov's Plays: An opening into eternity*, New Haven, CT and London: Yale University Press.

Golomb, H. (1986) '*Hamlet* in Chekhov's Major Plays: Some Perspectives of Literary Allusion and Literary Translation', *New Comparison*, 2: 69–88.

——(2000) 'Referential Reflections: Reciprocal Art/Life Embeddings in Chekhov's *The Seagull*', *Poetics Today*, 21, 4: 681–709.

Golovachyova, A. (2001) '*Syuzhet dlya nebol'shogo rasskaza*', in V. V. Gul'chenko (ed) *Chekhoviana. Polet 'Chaiki'*, Moscow: Nauka.

Golub, S. (1994) *The Recurrence of Fate: Theatre and memory in twentieth century Russia*, Iowa City, IA: University of Iowa Press.

Gorchakov, N. (1960) *The Vakhtangov School of Stage Art*, G. Ivanov-Mumjiev (trans), Moscow: Foreign Languages Publishing House.

——(1973) *Stanislavsky Directs*, Miriam Goldina (trans), Westport, CT: Greenwood Press.

Gorky, M., Bunin, I. and Kuprin, A. (2004) *Reminiscences of Chekhov*, Whitefish, MT: Kessinger Publishing Company.

Gottlieb, A. (2000) *The Dream of Reason: A History of Philosophy from the Greeks to the Renaissance*, London: Penguin.

Gottlieb, V. (1982) *Chekhov and the Vaudeville: A study of Chekhov's one-act plays*, Cambridge: Cambridge University Press.

——(1993) 'The dwindling scale: the politics of British Chekhov', in P. Miles (ed and trans) *Chekhov on the British Stage,* Cambridge: Cambridge University Press.

——(ed)(2005) *Anton Chekhov at the Moscow Art Theatre*, London: Routledge.

Gottlieb, V. and Allain, P. (eds) (2000) *The Cambridge Companion to Chekhov*, Cambridge: Cambridge University Press.

Green, M. (1986) *The Russian Symbolist Theatre*, Ann Arbor, MI: Ardis.

Griffiths, T. (2007) *Theatre Plays I*, Nottingham: Spokesman.

Hahn, B. (1977) *Chekhov: A study of the major stories and plays*, Cambridge: Cambridge University Press.

Hingley, R. (1976) *A Life of Anton Chekhov*, Oxford: Oxford University Press.

Hollosi, C. (1983) 'Chekhov's Reactions to Two Interpretations of Nina', *Theatre Survey,* 24, 1, 2: 117–25.

Hoover, M. (1974) *Meyerhold: The Art of Conscious Theatre*, Amherst, MA: University of Massachusetts Press.

Hosking, G. (2001) *Russia and the Russians*, London: Penguin.

Hristic, J. (1985) 'Time in Chekhov: The Inexorable and the Ironic', *New Theatre Quarterly,* 3, 1: 271–82.

——(1995) 'Stanislavsky's Notebooks and the Chekhov Productions', *New Theatre Quarterly,* 9, 42: 175–83.

Huneker, J. (1905) *Iconoclasts: A book of dramatists*, New York: Charles Scribner's Sons.

Innes, C. (ed) (2000) *A Sourcebook on Naturalist Theatre*, London: Routledge.

Ischuk-Fadeeva, N. (1997) 'Filosofskie Aspekty v Poetike Chekhovskoi Dramy (A. P. Chekhov i A. Schopengauer)', in *Khudozhestvennaya Literatura c Sotskul'turnom Kontekste'*, Moskva Dialog-MGU.

Jackson, R. (ed) (1967) *Chekhov: A Collection of Critical Essays*, Upper Saddle River, NJ: Prentice Hall.

——(1981) 'Chekhov's Seagull: The Empty Well, the Dry Lake and the Cold Cave', in J-P. Barricelli (ed) (1981) *Chekhov's Great Plays*, New York: New York University Press.

——(1993) *Reading Chekhov's Text*, Evanston, IL: Northwestern University Press.

Karlinsky, S. (1985) *Russian Drama from Its Beginnings to the Age of Pushkin*, Berkeley, CA: University of California Press.

Kataev, V. (2002) *If Only We Could Know! An interpretation of Chekhov*, H. Pitcher (trans and ed), Chicago, IL: Ivan R. Dee.

Kelly, A. (1998) *Toward Another Shore: Russian thinkers between necessity and chance*, New Haven, CT and London: Yale University Press.

——(1999) *Views from the Other Shore, Essays on Herzen, Chekhov and Bakhtin*, New Haven, CT and London: Yale University Press.

Kilroy, T. (2000) 'The Seagull – an Adaptation', in V. Gottlieb and P. Allain (eds) *The Cambridge Companion to Chekhov*, Cambridge: Cambridge University Press.

Kirillov, A. (2001) 'Tri Sestry Pyati Rezhisserov', *Kommersant'* 23, 9.2.

——(2004) 'Vishnevyi Sad' A. P. Chekhova: V poiskakh utrachennogo vremeni', *Toronto Slavic Quarterly*, 10.

Kline, G. (2001) 'Russian Nihilism', in *The Cambridge Dictionary of Philosophy*, R. Audi (ed), Cambridge: Cambridge University Press.

Konrad, L. (1982) 'Symbolic Action in Modern Drama: Maurice Maeterlinck', in J. Redmond (ed) *Drama and Symbolism,* Cambridge: Cambridge University Press.

Kramer, K. (1970) *The Chameleon and the Dream: The Image of Reality in Čechov's Stories*, The Hague: Mouton.

——(1981) '*Three Sisters* or Taking a Chance on Love', in J-P. Barricelli (ed) *Chekhov's Great Plays*, New York: New York University Press.

——(1999) '"A Subject Worthy of Ayvazovsky's Brush": Vanya's Misdirected Fury', *Modern Drama*, 42, 4: 511–18.

Krasner, D. (1994) 'The Symbolic Function of Sleeping and Awakening in Chekhov's *Uncle Vanya*', *Theatre Studies,* 39: 5–18.

Kuzicheva, A. (2004) *Chekhovy. Biografiya Sem'i*, Moskva: Artist. Rezhisser. Teatr.

Lafitte, S. (1973) *Chekhov 1860–1904*, M. Budberg and G. Latta (trans), New York: Scribner.

Le Fleming, S. (2006) *Gospoda Kritiki i Gospodin Chekhov*, Sankt-Peterburg: Letnii Sad.

Listengarten, J. (2000) *Russian Tragifarce: Its cultural and political roots*, London: Associated University Presses.

Litvinenko, N. (1981) *Tvorcheskoe Nasledie: stat'i i vospominaniya o R.N. Simonove*, Moscow: Vserossiiskoe Teatral'noe Obshchestvo.

Llewellyn Smith, V. (1973) *Anton Chekhov and the Lady with the Dog*, London: Oxford University Press.

Magarshack, D. (1970) *Chekhov: A Life*, Westport, CT: Greenwood Press.

——(1972) *The Real Chekhov: An introduction to Chekhov's last plays*, London: Allen and Unwin.

——(1980) *Chekhov the Dramatist*, London: Methuen.

Mal'tseva, O. (1999) *Poeticheskii Teatr Iuriya Liubimova: Spektakli Moskovskovo Teatra i Komedii na Taganke, 1964–1998*, Sankt-Peterburg: Rossiskii institut istorii iskusstv.

Marsh, C. (1999) 'Realism in the Russian Theatre 1850–1882', in R. Leach and V. Borovsky (eds) *A History of Russian Theatre*, Cambridge: Cambridge University Press.

——(2000) 'The Stage Representation of Chekhov's Women', in V. Gottlieb and P. Allain (eds) *The Cambridge Companion to Chekhov*, Cambridge: Cambridge University Press.

Matura, M. (2006) *Three Sisters, after Chekhov*, London: Oberon.

McVay, G. (1995) *Chekhov's Three Sisters*, London: Bristol Classical Press.

——(2002) 'Anton Chekhov: The Unbelieving Believer', *Slavonic and East European Review*, 80, 1: 63–104.

Merlin, B. (1999) 'Which Came First, the System or the Seagull?', *New Theatre Quarterly*, 59: 218–27.

Miles, P. (ed) (1993) *Chekhov on the British Stage*, Cambridge: Cambridge University Press.

——(2008) *Brief Lives: Anton Chekhov*, London: Hesperus.

Moi, T. (2006) *Henrik Ibsen and the Birth of Modernism: Art, theater, philosophy*, Oxford: Oxford University Press.

Moravcevich, N. (1981) 'Women in Chekhov's Plays', in J-P. Barricelli (ed) *Chekhov's Great Plays*, New York: New York University Press.

Morson, G. (1993) 'Uncle Vanya as Prosaic Metadrama', in R. Jackson (ed) *Reading Chekhov's Text*, Evanston, IL: Northwestern University Press.

Moser, C. (1964) *Antinihilism in the Russian Novel of the 1860s*, The Hague: Mouton.

Nagel, T. (1971) 'The Absurd', *The Journal of Philosophy*, 68, 20: 716–27.

Nicholls, M. (1999) 'The Influences of Eastern Thought on Schopenhauer's Doctrine of the Thing-in-itself', in C. Janaway (ed), *The Cambridge Companion to Schopenhauer*, Cambridge: Cambridge University Press.

Obraztsova, A. (1993) 'Bernard Shaw's Dialogue with Chekhov', in P. Miles (ed) *Chekhov on the British Stage,* Cambridge: Cambridge University Press.

O'Connor, K. (1987) 'Chekhov on Chekhov: His Epistolary Self-Criticism', in A. Crone and C. Chvany (eds) *New Studies in Russian Language and Literature,* Colombus, OH: Slavica Publishers.

Odesskaya, M. (ed) (2007) *Ibsen, Strindberg, Chekhov*, Moscow: RGGU.

Offord, D. (2001) 'Nineteenth-century Russian thought and literature', in N. Cornwell (ed) *The Routledge Companion to Russian Literature,* London: Routledge.

Ogibina, A. (2004) 'Zapis' repetitsii spektaklya «Dyadya Vanya»', *Baltiiskie Sezony*, 9: 41–65.

Papernyi, Z. (1982) *'Vopreki Vsem Pravilam ... ' P'esy i Vodevili Chekhova*, Moscow: Iskusstvo.

——(2007) 'Spor s Ibsenem', in M. Odesskaya (ed) *Ibsen, Strindberg, Chekhov*, Moskva: RGGU.

Pavis, P. (2000) '*Ivanov*: the invention of a negative dramaturgy', in V. Gottlieb and P. Allain (eds) *The Cambridge Companion to Chekhov*, Cambridge: Cambridge University Press.

Peace, R. (1983) *Chekhov, a study of the four major plays*, New Haven, CT and London: Yale University Press.

——(1993) '"In Exile" and Russian Fatalism', in R. Jackson (ed), *Reading Chekhov's Text*, Evanston, IL: Northwestern University Press.

Pine, R. (2006) 'Friel's Irish Russia', in A. Roche (ed) *The Cambridge Companion to Brian Friel*, Cambridge: Cambridge University Press.

Pitcher, H. (1979) *Chekhov's Leading Lady*, London: J. Murray.

——(1985) *The Chekhov Play: A new interpretation*, Berkeley, CA: University of California Press.

Popkin, C. (1993) *The Pragmatics of Insignificance: Chekhov, Zoshchenko, Gogol*, Stanford, CA: Stanford University Press.

Porter, R. (1981) 'Hamlet and the Seagull', *Journal of Russian Studies,* 41, 1: 23–32.

Rayfield, D. (1975) *Chekhov: The Evolution of his Art*, London: Elek.

——(1985) 'Chekhov and the Literary Tradition', in T. Clyman (ed) *A Chekhov Companion,* Westport, CT: Greenwood Press.

——(1995) *Chekhov's Uncle Vania and The Wood Demon*, London: Bristol Classical Press.

——(1998) *Anton Chekhov: A Life*, London: Flamingo.

——(1999) *Understanding Chekhov: A critical study of Chekhov's prose and drama*, Madison, WI: University of Wisconsin Press.

Redmond, J. (ed) (1982) *Drama and Symbolism*, Cambridge: Cambridge University Press.

Reid, J. (1998) 'Matter and Spirit in *The Seagull*', *Modern Drama,* 41, 4: 607–22.

Rogger, H. (1983) *Russia in the Age of Modernization and Revolution 1881–1917*, London: Longman.

Saunders, D. (1992) *Russian in the Age of Reaction and Reform, 1801–1881*, London: Longman.

Schafer, C. (2001) 'Chekhov's Three Sisters, Exploring the Woman Question', *Journal of Dramatic Theory and Criticism,* 16, 1: 39–58.

Schopenhauer, A. (1969) *The World as Will and Representation*, Vols 1 and 2, New York: Dover.

Schuler, C. (1996) *Women in Russian Theatre: The Actress in the Silver Age*, London: Routledge.

Senderovich, S. and Sendich, M. (eds) (1987) *Anton Chekhov Rediscovered: A Collection of New Studies with a Comprehensive Bibliography*, East Lansing, MI: Russian Language Journal.

Senelick, L. (1982) 'Chekhov and the Irresistible Symbol: A Response to Peter Holland', in J. Redmond (ed) *Drama and Symbolism,* Cambridge: Cambridge University Press.

——(1985) *Anton Chekhov*, London: Macmillan.

——(1987) 'Stuffed Seagulls', *Poetics Today*, 8, 2: 285–98.

——(1997a) *The Chekhov Theatre – a century of the plays in performance*, Cambridge: Cambridge University Press.

——(1997b) *Russian Comedy of the Nikolaian Era*, Amsterdam: Overseas Publishers Association.

——(2004) 'Stanislavsky's Second Thoughts on the Seagull', *New Theatre Quarterly*, 20, 2: 127–37.

Seymour, A. (2001) '*Rabotaya s sovremmenoi metaforoi "Chaiki"*', in V. V. Gul'chenko (ed) *Chekhoviana. Polet 'Chaiki'*, Moscow: Nauka.

Shakh-Azizova, T. (1966) *Chekhov i Zapadno-Evropeiskaya Drama ego Vremeni*, Moskva: Nauka.

——(2000) 'Chekhov on the Russian Stage' in V. Gottlieb and P. Allain (eds.) *The Cambridge Companion to Chekhov*, Cambridge: Cambridge University Press.

de Sherbinin, J. (1997) *Chekhov and Russian Religious Culture: The poetics of the Marian paradigm*, Evanston, IL: Northwestern University Press.

Shevtsova, M. (2004) *Dodin and the Maly Drama Theatre; process to performance*, London: Routledge.

——(2006a) 'Lev Dodin and the Maly Drama Theatre: *Uncle Vanya* to *King Lear*', *New Theatre Quarterly*, 22, 3: 249–56.

——(2006b) *Theatre and Cultural Interaction*, Sydney: Sydney Association for Studies in Society and Culture.

Simmons, E. (1963) [1970] *Chekhov*, London: Jonathan Cape.

Simonov, R. (1969) *Stanislavsky's Protégé: Eugene Vakhtangov*, M. Goldina (trans) New York: DBS Publications.

Sitkovetskaya, M. (ed) (1993) *Meyerkhol'd Repertiruet. Tom 2, Spektakli 30-kh godov*, Moskva: Artist. Rezhisser. Teatr.

Skaftymov, A. (1972) 'O povestyakh Chekhova "Palata No 6" i "Moya Zhizn"', in E. Pokusaev (ed) *Nravstvennie iskaniya russkikh pisatelei*, Moscow: Khudozhestvennaya Literatura.

Sobennikov, A. (1997) '*Mezhdu "est' Bog" i "net Boga" – ': o religiozno-filosofskikh traditsiyakh v tvorchestve A.P. Chekhova*, Irkutsk: Izdatel'stvo Irkutskogo universiteta.

Speirs, L. (1992) *Tolstoy and Chekhov*, Ann Arbor, MI: UMI.

Stanislavski, K. (2008a) *An Actor's Work*, J. Benedetti (ed and trans), London: Routledge.

——(2008b) *My Life in Art*, J. Benedetti (ed and trans), London: Routledge.

Stanislavskii, K. (1988–99) *Sobranie Sochinenii*, 1–9, Moscow: Iskusstvo.

Stanislavsky, K. (1952) *The Seagull Produced by Stanislavsky*, S. Balukhaty (ed), D. Magarshack (trans), London: Dennis Dobson.

Stelleman, J. (1992) *Aspects of Dramatic Communication: Action, non-action, interaction: A.P. Čechov, A. Blok, D. Charms*, Amsterdam: Rodopi.

Stenberg, D. (2002) 'Chekhov's Uncle Vanya Translated on 42nd St', *Literature Film Quarterly*, January.

Stepanov, A. D. (2005) *Problemy Kommunikatsii u Chekhova*, Moskva: Yazyki Slavyanskoi Kul'turi.

Stroeva, M. (1967) 'The Three Sisters in the Production of the Moscow Art Theatre', in R. Jackson (ed) *Chekhov: A Collection of Critical Essays,* Upper Saddle River, NJ: Prentice Hall.
——(1973) *Rezhisserskie Iskanie Stanislavskogo, 1898–1917,* Moskva: Nauka.
Stroud, T. (1958) 'Hamlet and The Seagull', *Shakespeare Quarterly,* 9, 3: 367–72.
Styan, J. (1968) *The Dark Comedy: The development of modern comic tragedy,* Cambridge: Cambridge University Press.
——(1971) *Chekhov in Performance,* London: Cambridge University Press.
Sukhikh, I. (ed) (2002) *Chekhov: Pro et Contra: tvorchestvo A.P. Chekhova v russkoi mysli kontsa XIX – nachala XX v. (1887–1914),* Sankt-Peterburg: Nauk.
Suzman, J. (2000) *The Free State. A South African Response to Chekhov's The Cherry Orchard,* London: Methuen.
Swift, M. (2004) *Biblical Subtexts and Religious Themes in Works of Anton Chekhov,* New York: Peter Lang.
Tait, P. (2002) *Performing Emotions: Gender, bodies, spaces in Chekhov's drama and Stanislavski's theatre,* Aldershot: Ashgate.
Toumanova, N. (1937) *Anton Chekhov: The voice of twilight Russia,* New York: Columbia University Press.
Troyat, H. (1987) *Chekhov,* M. Heim (trans), London: Macmillan.
Turkov, A. (ed) (1995) *Anton Chekhov and His Times,* C. Carlile and S. McKee (trans), Fayetteville, AR: University of Arkansas Press.
Tulloch, J. (1980) *Chekhov, a Structuralist Study,* London: Macmillan.
——(2005) *Shakespeare and Chekhov in Production and Reception; theatrical events and their audiences,* Iowa City, IA: University of Iowa Press.
Tulloch, J., Burvill, T. and Hood, A. (1997) 'Reinhabiting "The Cherry Orchard", Class and History in Performing Chekhov', *New Theatre Quarterly,* 52, 13: 318–28.
Turgenev, I. (1984) *The Diary of a Superfluous Man,* D. Patterson (trans), London: W. W. Norton.
Turkov, A. (ed) (1996) *Chekhoviana. Chekhov i ego okruzhenie,* Moskva: Nauka.
Turner, C. (1994) *Time and Temporal Structure in Chekhov,* Birmingham: Department of Russian Language and Literature, University of Birmingham.
Valency, M. (1966) *The Breaking String: The plays of Anton Chekhov,* London: Oxford University Press.
Vakhtangov, E. (1959) *Zapiski, Pis'ma, Stat'i,* Moscow: Iskusstvo.
Vitins, I. (1981) 'Uncle Vanya's Predicament', in J-P. Barricelli (ed) *Chekhov's Great Plays,* New York: New York University Press.

Volchkevich, M. (2007) *'Chaika' Komedia Zabluzhdenii*, Moskva: Probel-2000.

Voltaire (2005) *Candide or Optimism*, T. Cuffe (trans), London: Penguin.

Williames, L. (1989) *Anton Chekhov, the Iconoclast*, Scranton, PA: University of Scranton Press.

Winner, T. (1956) 'Chekhov's *Seagull* and Shakespeare's *Hamlet*, a Study of a Dramatic Device', *The American Slavic and East European Review*, 15, February: 103–11.

Woods, L. (1982) 'Chekhov and the evolving symbol: cues and cautions for the plays in performance', in J. Redmond (ed) *Drama and Symbolism*, Cambridge: Cambridge University Press.

Worrall, N. (1990) 'Stanislavsky's Production of Chekhov's *Three Sisters*', in R. Russell and A. Barratt (eds) *Russian Theatre in the Age of Modernism*, Basingstoke: Macmillan.

——(1999) 'Stanislavsky's Production Score for Chekhov's *The Cherry Orchard*', *Modern Drama*, 42, 4: 519–40.

Yermilov, V. (1957) *Anton Pavlovich Chekhov 1860–1904*, I. Litvinov (trans), Moscow: Foreign Languages Publishing House.

Zingerman, B. (2001) *Teatr Chekhova i ego Mirovoe Znachenie*, Moskva: RIK Rusanova.

Index